Recovering the Lost Tongue

Memoirs of a Romantic among the Bhils

RAHUL BANERJEE

2008

Published via CreateSpace

Cover Page images by Rahul Banerjee

Notes on the images (clockwise):

1. Picture of the great Bhil warrior Tantia Bhil riding a horse

2. A memorial to the ancestors who founded the village clan

3. The old man with spectacles is a highly revered bard who knew all the myths and many stories and songs. After his death his son sitting next to him is carrying on his tradition but he has not ben able to learn all that the father had known. His son is not interested in continuing with this.

Contents

A Tale of Two Worlds

In lieu of an Introduction

Bondarsingh was in dire straits. He had been sentenced by the High Court in Indore to either pay a fine of Rs.5,000, or failing to do so, serve six months in jail. The sentence was pronounced in May 2001. Bondar is an adivasi, alternatively known as tribals or indigenous people, who are usually short of hard cash at that time of the year. Since Bondar had already spent about two months in jail before getting out on bail, his lawyer suggested that he serve the remaining four-month jail sentence as well. However, for Bondar this would mean missing out on the kharif crop in the coming monsoon season. The past year had seen scanty rainfall, leaving him in a precarious situation, financially. He did not have the option to miss out on the approaching monsoon season. So the only alternative for Bondar was to borrow the fine amount from a sahukar or moneylender in the nearby weekly village market of Udainagar at an exorbitant rate of ten per cent per month.

Bondar is a Bhilala adivasi peasant of Hirapur village of Dewas district in the central Indian state of Madhya Pradesh in India. His parents, along with others in the village, had migrated from the Manawar tehsil of the nearby Dhar district about sixty years ago. They were brought and settled there by the Jagirdar or prince in Bagli in order to clear the forests and cultivate the land. However, almost immediately thereafter, India's independence in 1947 put a stop to this process of bringing forest land under plough, and following a settlement survey, the people of Hirapur and nearby villages were restricted to cultivating only some of the land they had been able to clear. The rest was taken over by the Forest Department. Over the years, as Bondar and his brothers were born and grew up, this land proved to be too little for providing a decent livelihood. Matters were made worse by the provisions of the Indian Forest Act, 1927, which prevented the adivasis from even collecting the wood and timber needed for basic functions such as cooking, housing, and farming. They were thus left at the mercy of the forest department staff.

About a decade ago, Bondar had gone to the forest one day to collect timber for fencing in his farm. When he was returning with the timber, he was accosted by a forest guard and his helper. As per a tacit understanding under the moral economy prevailing between the adivasis and the local forest department staff, in such circumstances, the forest guard simply takes a bribe and looks the other way. But this particular guard decided to sieze Bondar's cart. When Bondar protested, the forest guard hit him with a lathi. This violation of the moral economy angered Bondar, and he hit the forest guard on the head with a piece of wood, seriously wounding him.

Bondar was arrested by the police and sent to jail. He was released on bail after his brothers engaged a lawyer by borrowing money from a sahukar. Later, he was sentenced by the sessions court in Dewas to a jail term of three years. He borrowed money once again to appeal against this verdict in the High Court and managed to have it reduced to a fine of rupees five thousand, to pay which he had to yet again turn to the sahukar. Moreover, he had to rent out half his land to a fellow adivasi and send his son off to labour in the fields of a big landlord so as to pay off the sahukar's expensive debt.

The story of Bondarsingh is typical of Bhil adivasis living in the western Madhya Pradesh region. The adivasis are mostly landless labourers or marginal farmers with little or no irrigation facilities and with restricted access to the forests, which are central to their livelihoods. All this has forced most adivasis to rely on the sahukars to bail them, thus pushing them into debt bondage. Not only have post-independence development policies skirted the question of dismantling the feudal and colonial structures that oppress the adivasis, but ironically the very resources for modern development have been extracted from the remote forest areas in which they reside.

Bondar's tale of woe is in reality a tale of two opposing worlds. In the immediate context of Madhya Pradesh, it is the tale of the impoverished adivasis on the one hand and that of the non-adivasi sahukars and government officials who have prospered at their expense on the other. In the Indian context, it is the tale of the impoverished rural dryland areas that have borne the brunt of the cost of development of the urban industrial areas. In the global context, it is the tale of the world of the peripheral poor countries, which have paid with their underdevelopment for the wealth of the industrialised countries of the centre.

I, a city bred aficionado of rock music from the opposite world, met Bondar through a chain of events beginning with my first encounter—as a young student in college—with the darkness that had engulfed the world of the adivasis in this country. Along with Bondar and his tribe I and some more apostates from the world of modern development have been fighting over the last quarter of a century to break the barrier of exploitation that separates these two worlds. The tale that is about to unfold will tell the story of an environmental battle in the central Indian region— fought between the world of the adivasis who have traditionally lived in harmony with nature and the world that is greedy to extract as much as possible from nature to ensure personal gain. I am writing this story only because the Gayans or traditional Bhil bards, who are definitely more qualified to tell this story, do not care much for our "civilised" ways and are therefore disdainful of literacy. While this does not hamper their practice of oral recitation of their colourful myths, this lack of a culture of writing does put the Bhils at a disadvantage in negotiating the complexities of the other world into which they are forcibly integrated.

Thus, as one Bhil elder told me just a few days after I landed up in the Bhil homeland for the first time in 1985, they had become civilisation's discards in modern India because of their inability to put black on white—pen to paper. Twenty years later, as I recalled that conversation, I realized that activists like me, engaged in environmental movements, were figuratively in the same boat. That's because we have failed to convey to the world at large, our simple message of the need for humility and continence in our dealings with nature. On my part, I have remained faithful to the traditional romantic style of the Gayans while relating the saga of the modern day struggles of the Bhils.

A certain creation myth is sung in the villages near the river Narmada. The story narrates how God was suddenly beset with the idea of creating the universe, and he advised Relu Kabadi, a woodsman, to go into the jungle and fetch wood. Thus starts the tale of how gradually animals and plants are created, followed by the creation of the rivers Narmada and Tapti. These rivers eventually meet with the ocean Dudu Hamad in marriage, and over the course of their journey forward, villages, hills and valleys emerge.

The main story is interspersed with many smaller stories, all of which are sung through the night. This epic song, while being highly entertaining, also imbues the listeners with a sense of nature's vastness and the strength of natural processes. In doing so, it inculcates a respect for these phenomena, which is in direct contrast to the hubris of "modern" human beings, who have, over the past three centuries since the industrial revolution, only subordinated nature to their own ends, leading themselves to serious environmental problems.

The Bhils have achieved an admirable mix of veer or bravery, shringar or love and hasya or comedy in their story telling. This makes their tales enjoyable, while at the same time lending them an unobtrusive fable-like didactic character. The Bhil Gayans are not only great storytellers, but also first-class teachers of a pristine morality. The rationale for the ongoing movements of the Bhils is most succinctly brought out by yet another Bhil fable from which the name of this book has been derived.

There was once a woman, Jeevla Kuvar, who had disobeyed her husband and spoken against him. A panchayat meeting was called and it was deemed that she had spoken wrongly. As punishment, the elders ordered that her tongue be cut off and given to her husband to swallow. Although this was done, the tongue got stuck in the husband's throat forever. This quaint tale allegorically describes how women are oppressed in Bhil society or in any society for that matter.

However, the fact that the tongue wasn't swallowed completely left open the possibility of its being recovered. Indeed, not only women, but dalits, adivasis and other oppressed sections are all unable to speak out, and they all need to recover their lost tongues. This tale is about the joys and sorrows involved in an unfinished and simultaneously Herculean and Sisyphean task. That of a people, stifled for centuries by a deafening culture of silence, recovering their lost tongues.

An interesting yet puzzling aspect of the Bhils' myths and stories is the central and powerful roles played by women in them, which is in direct contrast to the reality of their society's patriarchal oppression. So to add a new gender-sensitive twist to the old tale of struggles against the exploitation of nature and adivasis, I have followed this commendable tradition in weaving the present story too. The stories of my wife and activist Subhadra's personal struggles as a dalit (those belonging to the previously untouchable outcastes of the majority Hindu society) and that of the Bhil women she has inspired, have been interspersed with many other narratives of the various mass movements of which we have together been a part. Since for militant women activists like Subhadra, personal as well as public struggles are both political ones, this story follows the Bhili tradition of having an undercurrent of morality in it. So it is not just a story of the garden variety, but also a fable.

Besides the Bhils, the other great set of indigenous people in central India is the Gond tribe. A section of the Gonds actually became feudal kings in the middle ages and ruled over a vast area, now known as Gondwana. The Gonds, put up a resistance even fiercer than the Bhils against both the Mughals and the British. To this day, they are fighting valiantly against the destructive development policies of the Indian state. For this reason, they too have entered this narrative in places. In a beautiful Hindi poem, a well-known modern poet, Bhavani Prasad Mishra, lyrically describes the nature-friendly ways of the Gonds. This stanza roughly translates as follows -

"Deep inside the Satpura hills in woods sleepy and unmindful,
Amidst their hens and pheasants all harmonious and peaceful,
In huts of mud and thatch live the Gonds dark and powerful.
When spring comes and the grass is swaying in song so lilting,
And mahua flowers mesmerising all with a scent so intoxicating,
Then dance the Gonds in gay abandon their drums a thumping."

Unfortunately, this idyllic lifestyle, not only of the Gonds, but also of indigenous peoples all over the world, has been torn asunder over the centuries in the greedy pursuit of pelf and power by non-adivasis. The present story is essentially about the attempts that are being made in central India to exorcise the evil spirits of destructive modern development that have caused this tragedy. My own involvement in these struggles is interspersed here and there in a stream of consciousness fashion.

When I completed writing this book, after a labour of love of three years, even though the composition seemed tuneful to my ears, it failed to make publishers and literary agents sing. I sent the manuscript to countless publishers and agents, only to be told it had no market value and was therefore not worth investing in. That's when I came across the idea of publishing the book on the World Wide Web. Here, there was no need to make a heavy upfront investment. I just had to upload the text on the Internet and then send the link to people all over the cyberspace and get it meta-tagged so that it turned up in search engines. If the material was good, people would automatically read it and word would spread. That was how this book first appeared—as an e-book on the Internet for free dissemination, quite in tune with the anarcho-environmentalism that is its core value.

A number of people who read the e-book liked it, and my long time school friend, Ramaswamy, mentioned it in his blog (cuckooscall.blogspot.com). Ramaswamy, who is a multifaceted personality engaged in activities as diverse as manufacture of industrial flow meters, running of schools for the urban underprivileged, planning of people friendly urban habitats and writing of poetry, in fact inspired me to set up my own blog (anar-kali.blogspot.com). Bhupinder Singh happened to read this post and he went on to read the book and write a detailed review, which he posted in various blogs including his own (readerswords.wordpress.com). This brought in more readers especially on blogbharati.com which is a platform that publishes selections from Indian blogs. Eventually a member of Blogbharati, Anandswarup Gadde, who is a retired professor of mathematics with an abiding interest in development and social issues (gaddeswarup.blogspot.com), expressed the desire to fund the book's print publication. This set off a new project, as the feedback that I had been receiving from many readers was that whereas the stories in the book were entertaining, the academic analysis that came with them was too arcane to grasp. So we decided that an edited version of the book would be prepared for print. Bhupinder, who too has a many splendoured profile being involved in the writing of software code, reviewing of books and dissection of political theory and who has by now become a fast friend, took on this onerous responsibility and reworked the entire book to make it approachable to more readers. Finally Bhaswati Ghosh, yet another accomplished blogger (athomewriting.blogspot.com) and a professional editor cum perceptive critic of literature, painstakingly improved the stylistic aspects of the book and added some class to it. This book is therefore, also a sign of the times in that it is a collaborative product of the social networking that has become possible as a result of the Internet. The actual printing of the book has been done by the venerable veteran of left publishing in India, P.P.C. Joshi. The original e-book, which has been written in a part narrative and part academic style, incorporating a fair amount of secondary research is available at my website: http://www.cgnet.in/Members/rahulb. Those who are interested in the detailed research that has gone into the writing of this book can read the e-book also.

1 Cry, The Beloved Country!

Ahot summer afternoon in April 2001 saw Motiabhai the Bhilala adivasi Patel of Katukia village in Bagli Tehsil of Dewas district in Madhya Pradesh sitting among the ruins of his house under the burning sun. He was angrily asking the then chairman of the National Scheduled Castes and Scheduled Tribes Commission, Shri Dilip Singh Bhuria, whether as a citizen of India he did not have the right to live with dignity under his own roof and could only live like the mice on his farm do, in their holes. Prior to this, in a secretly planned "Operation Clean," the government of Madhya Pradesh had carried out a sudden week-long campaign of mass destruction and loot of the houses of adivasis belonging to the mass organization Adivasi Morcha Sangathan without giving them any prior notice. Shri Bhuria was too dumbstruck by the scale of destruction to say anything other than some words in consolation.

Why is it that adivasis like Motia Patel are consistently denied full citizenship rights in India? Why is it that despite constitutional safeguards and other ameliorative legislation adivasis continue to face the iron hand of state repression whenever they demand their legally sanctioned rights in an organized manner? Why indeed does the demand for adivasi self-rule remain a cry in the wilderness even after six decades of independence, and why is this demand suppressed brutally by the state whenever it is voiced in a concerted manner? The history of the valiant but forlorn struggles of the adivasis over the past twenty-five years in the central Indian region provides some sad answers to these questions.

"Operation Clean" started in Kadoriya village on the morning of March 28th 2001, as hundreds of armed policemen and forest officials, accompanied by hired adivasis and led by the District Collector, Superintendent of Police and Divisional Forest Officer descended on the unsuspecting villagers. So that no one came to know of the operation beforehand, the state forces had got together in the district headquarters in Dewas even before daybreak to start the four-hour journey to Kadoriya village. They had taken the villagers by surprise just when the latter were letting their cattle out for grazing. Even though gripped by shock, the villagers put up a stiff resistance to this illegal raid. However, the might and numbers of the state forces soon overwhelmed them. The raiding team demolished a series of houses and seized the timber and other belongings of the adivasi villagers. Their grain and water were poisoned with pesticides. Thereafter, this team went to other villages, which were strongholds of the Sangathan, including the newly-enrolled Potla village where the women put up a brave front. The raiding team systematically destroyed houses, pillaged villagers' belongings and poisoned the grain and water. They then took their looting spree to the village of Katukiya on April 1, All Fools Day.

That night, the marauding team came back to Udainagar, the market village and administrative centre of the area and camped on the banks of the Luhar River. The team was preparing to cross the river and attack the core area of the Sangathan the next day. The members of the Sangathan had begun a peaceful sit-in on the road leading to their area, stopping all traffic to voice their demand that the administration stop its illegal campaign from the 30th of March. The administration, of course, did not pay any attention to their protests, bent as it was on wiping out the organization altogether. A confrontation appeared imminent as soon as the government forces crossed over the next day.

Mehendikhera village is situated picturesquely on the banks of the Luhar River on the other side of Udainagar. The river, like many others descending the escarpment of the Vindhyas from the Malwa plateau and flowing to the Narmada, goes dry in summer, but there are some deep pools in it near the village, which brim with water throughout summer and are full of fish. The area's children and youth enjoy swimming and catching fish in the summer months. This alone made this village a favoured meeting place of the Sangathan. But on April 2, 2001, the village had no people; everyone had gone to join the roadblock further down the road. At ten in the morning, when a long cavalcade of cars, jeeps and vans made its way into the village, it found no one there. Instead of going down the road to engage in a dialogue with the amassed people, the cavalcade swerved into the village and immediately set about with power driven saws and axes, cutting down the timber poles on which the houses had been constructed. Even as the poles were being brought down, these marauders went about catching the chicken and looting the grains and other possessions that lay in the houses. The District Collector, Superintendent of Police and Divisional Forest Officer all looked on as this illegal looting continued.

The people waiting down the road were angered by this callous attitude of the officials and rushed to the village to prevent this indiscriminate pillaging, only to be subjected to a hail of bullets as they came within range. Undaunted, they pressed on towards the marauders and faced more bullets. The conflict killed four of their comrades. Seeing the futility of pressing on against an inhuman dispensation, they withdrew with three of the dead bodies, while the fourth one was taken away by the marauders. The adivasis brought the dead to Indore in a tractor trolley for post mortem and to tell the world about the depths to which the country's administration had plumbed to stamp out the rising tide of protest against its unjust functioning. The press reporters who rushed to the hospital were confronted by the crying wizened old Jermabhai, a senior leader of the Sangathan, whose son Balram had been killed. Jermabhai asked the journalists, "What kind of a government is this that always wants to take away what little we adivasis have? Now they have taken away my son."

This confrontation was the culmination of a three-year-long struggle by the adivasi people for establishing the authority of the Gram Sabha or village council above the government administration with regard to running the village affairs. Taking this stance had immediately brought them into conflict with the Forest Department. The Department has traditionally claimed to be the sole controller of the reserved forests under the provisions of the Indian Forest Act (IFA), which had been enacted by the British, but had been perversely retained after independence. The indigenous people contested the Forest Department's monopoly, saying that the forests situated within their village boundary were to be managed and used by them. Sensing the inability of the local forest officials to withstand the mass strength of the Sangathan, the administration brought in forces from outside and teams of forest officials began touring the area. They arrested a number of unsuspecting people in the forest and beat them up, before sending them to jail on false charges of having contravened some section or other of the IFA.

Gaining in audacity by the day, the forest officials began raiding the villages by themselves early in the mornings to increase the chances of catching the people unaware and thus arresting them with ease. On September 23rd 1999, a team of forest officials raided the village of Katukya at 6 am and fired on and killed Roopsingh, who was returning after answering nature's call. The forest officials had ostensibly gone to arrest one Balu for allegedly cutting timber from the forest. The murder of Roopsingh evoked an immediate protest from the Sangathan members. They amassed in thousands in front of the police station in Udainagar with his dead body, demanding the immediate filing of a murder case and the arrest of the guilty officials. For a while now, tension had been building up among the people against the arbitrary and illegal manner in which the state was trying to suppress their legitimate aspirations. Consequently, there was a tremendous outpouring of anger. The administration, yielding to the adivasis' demands under public pressure, registered a murder case against the forest officials, who were arrested and sent to jail. Following this, the Sangathan became more powerful than ever at the local level, and the de facto rule of the Gram Sabhas was established.

However, since the forest officials had been acting at the behest of the administration, the police did not file a charge sheet in the case within the stipulated ninety days. This allowed the accused to get out on bail and have their suspensions revoked. Now, even after more than six years since the brutal killing, the charge sheet has still not been filed and the case has not been sent to the courts for trial yet. According to the provisions of the law, when an adivasi is murdered by a non-adivasi, the state has to provide monetary compensation to the heirs of the deceased. The Sangathan had pressed for this compensation to be paid to Roopsingh's widow, Sagarbai. Despite the completion of all the necessary formalities, the District Magistrate did not pay the compensation. He made the specious plea that since the forest guard who had fired on Roopsingh was an adivasi, the provisions of the Atrocities Act did not apply. The counter arguments by the Sangathan that all the members of the team--which included and was led by non-adivasis—had gone together and had illegally killed Roopsingh, were summarily brushed aside.

Next, in September 2000, the Sangathan moved the Indore High Court against this arbitrary decision of the District Magistrate. The petition was admitted and quickly came up for final disposal at the admission stage because the government prosecutor was not foolish enough to make the plea that since the murderer was a non-adivasi, the provisions of the Act did not apply in this case. However, on the day of the final hearing the honourable judge made an astounding pronouncement—that since the rules for Madhya Pradesh were framed in Hindi, he could not give a judgment, which had to be written in English. No amount of pleading that the rules in question had been published in the Madhya Pradesh gazette in Hindi only, could make the judge budge. In two hearings thereafter, the judge gave the same excuse for not giving his final judgment on the matter. Then, he moved the case from the fast-track admission stage to the motion hearing stage, where it had to wait its turn beneath the pile of cases already in place. Even though the case was finally decided in the Sangathan's favour and the government ordered to give compensation, the latter has now gone in appeal against the decision, thereby further delaying the payment. Such is the anti-adivasi perversity of the government, which, on paper, is supposed to affirmatively take care of them.

Since 1999, there had been insufficient rainfall in the entire western Madhya Pradesh region. Whereas some tehsils of Barwani and Jhabua districts had been officially declared drought hit, others in the region hadn't been. Even for the two districts that had been declared drought hit, paltry amounts between rupees three and four crores each had been sanctioned towards relief work. This was over and above the minimal amounts that are normally available through various central government schemes. The rest of the region did not even get these crumbs. All the adivasi mass organisations of the region, including the Adivasi Morcha Sangathan launched a massive campaign to put pressure on the government for taking adequate relief measures. Plans for soil and water conservation efforts were prepared by the people and sanctioned by the Gram Sabhas. These were forwarded to the administration for action. Subsequently, rallies, dharnas and blocking of roads were undertaken.

The government's failure to provide adequate relief resulted in more and more adivasis migrating to far off places for work. The entire western Indian region had been groaning under drought for nearly the past three years. So, even the places that normally offered work to the adivasis, like neighbouring towns and cities such as Indore and the intensively cultivated areas of the Malwa plateau and Gujarat had less work to offer. This combination of less available work and a rising number of migrant workers depressed wages to well below subsistence levels all over the region. As a result, the sahukars were having a field day. In the absence of any other support system, the adivasis were forced to go to these lending sharks and thus bear the burden of usurious interest rates that had shot up to 10% per month and more.

The adivasi mass organisations reviewing the situation found that the only way in which things could be improved was for the government to take action under the various laws at its disposal against the sahukars. Since this was unlikely, given the political power the sahukars wielded, plans were finalised for launching a mass action programme, pressing for punitive action against them. This campaign was to piggy-back on the other ongoing campaigns for access to and control over the natural resources of forests and water. Given the persistent drought conditions, the pressure on these resources had increased manifold. So had the confrontation with the state agencies regarding their proper utilisation. In the Udainagar area, the Gram Sabhas stopped the logging of timber by the Forest Department, saying if the government didn't have the resources to provide them relief to help them tide over their crisis, then it had no right to take resources out of the area to finance its other activities.

This was too much for the government to bear, and a high-level meeting, chaired by the Chief Secretary was held on February 17, 2001, in the state capital Bhopal. The meeting sought to work out the modalities of conducting what was ominously named "Operation Clean". It was admitted in this meeting that the lack of development and the corruption in government services had led to rising disaffection among the adivasis in the area, which was snowballing into organised protests of massive proportions. However, it was categorically stated that the might of the state apparatus and its rule over the area's people could not be allowed to weaken in the face of such protests, even if they were spurred by valid grievances. It was decided at the meeting that force would be applied to crush the organisation. The government pledged full support to the district administration and even brought police forces from outside to bring the operation to its logical conclusion—wiping out the Adivasi Morcha Sangathan and making the region "clean" for the state's dirty governance once again!

The administration was brazen in its efforts to cover up its lawlessness. It first tried to pass off the illegality of its actions with the claim that the adivasis had planned to wage a war against the state and had laid out mines to blow up the government force. When these accusations proved to be patently false it said the adivasis had been destroying the jungles and so the operation had to be carried out, when in reality the adivasis had blocked the logging of trees by the forest department. Despite independent commissions of inquiry indicting the administration for committing atrocities, no official judicial inquiry was instituted to investigate the incident. Instead, an administrative inquiry was conducted, which expectedly absolved the district administration of all blame, saying that since it had been given the order to "clean" the area, it had no choice but to adopt such draconian measures.

An organisation of adivasis, working within the limits set by the laws of the land, was first declared to be waging a war against the state without any legal procedure being followed to factually establish such a serious charge. This was followed by obliterating it through a sudden secret armed operation. The Sangathan was never given a chance to refute the charges brought against it. More alarmingly, the highest decision makers in the state sanctioned these illegal actions. The preamble to the Universal Declaration of Human Rights of which the Indian Government is a signatory says "... it is essential, if man is not to be compelled to have recourse, as a last resort, to rebellion against tyranny and oppression, that human rights should be protected by the rule of law." Yet politicians of all hues, civil service bureaucrats, the police and the local judiciary, all combined to facilitate a gross violation of the rule of law in Mehendikhera. No wonder then that adivasis in independent India continue to be in perpetual rebellion against various mining, dam and industrialisation projects that have been and are continuing to be implemented at a breakneck speed all over the country, regardless of the brute force they have faced in the many Mehendikheras.

There may not be de jure racism in India as there was in South Africa during the apartheid era. For the really poor adivasis, who have not received any advantage of the meagre affirmative provisions and enabling laws and policies that are in place, and have instead been forced to bear the huge environmental, economic and social costs of modern industrial development, however, the sad reality is that of a de facto racist rule by non-adivasis. What else can be said of a political dispensation in which even at the highest levels of decision-making there is no understanding or sympathy for the desperate circumstances in which the adivasis are surviving? When the adivasis' legitimate protests against their marginalisation are considered to be a serious threat that needs to be snuffed out through such a cynical "Operation Clean" then one can only echo Alan Paton and say, "Cry, the Beloved Country".

Mehendikhera derives its name from a field of Mehendi plants from which an organic colouring is extracted for decorating the palms of women on auspicious occasions. An assembly of big mango trees in one of its fields made this village the favourite spot for meetings and workshops during the Sangathan's initial days. On that fateful day in April 2001, however, it became the venue of a bloody and tragic climax of more than two decades of exhilarating mass mobilisation by the central Indian adivasis. I will now detail that struggle. But first, like Ishmael in Herman Melville's classic allegorical novel Moby Dick, I shall start by setting out my credentials as the storyteller. Whereas Ishmael survived to tell the story of how mother nature, in the form of the white whale Moby Dick, put paid to the rampant greed and vengeance of modern man personified by the cruel and sinister Captain Ahab, I have a much sadder tale to tell—of the legions of modern day Ahabs, armed with much more powerful technologies, putting paid to our valiant attempts to nail the coffin of unjust and destructive modern development. Nevertheless, the struggles go on as the deprived people in this country and all over the world fight the continual loss of their livelihoods and habitats.

2   A Mission Found

Asoothing cool breeze blew on a hot summer evening, as a friend and I chatted, lounging against the balcony wall in front of our second-floor hostel rooms in Kharagpur, West Bengal. We were cogitating over the publication of the next issue of an independent campus magazine, which my friend used to publish at the time. The year was 1983, and I was in my final year as a student of civil engineering in Indian Institute of Technology (IIT), Kharagpur.

At the time, the road from the rural interiors to Kharagpur town passed through the IIT campus, bifurcating it into two parts. On one side stood the administrative buildings and the academic departments, while and the hostels, recreation centres, markets and residences were on the other side. The hostel in which I used to stay was the first one on the side of this road and had a big open field in front of it. That evening, as we looked out onto this field, we saw a caravan of bullock carts laden with hay slowly winding its way into it.

In the past, too, I had seen these caravans come in on Thursday evenings to spend the night on the field and move out again the next morning. I felt a little curious and asked my friend if he was ready to come down with me to talk to these carters. He was reluctant at first, but when I pointed out to him that we might get a story for the magazine, he agreed.

By the time we reached them, the carters had already finished eating their frugal dinner and were preparing to stretch out for the night. They huddled together as we began talking to one of them. They were all adivasis living in villages on the banks of the River Subarnarekha, some twenty-five kilometres away. They were either landless or marginal farmers. In either case, they were short of cash all the time and undertook all kinds of odd jobs. One of these was to cart hay from the fields of big landowners to the weekly auction held every Friday in Kharagpur town. They were paid rupees two per day for their labours.

Our conversation warmed up and we asked the carters if they knew what the big buildings in front of their temporary camp were for. They said they didn't. My friend explained to them at length, patiently replying to their queries, the unique nature of the imposing buildings, before which they so regularly camped for the night.

On an impulse I asked them whether they thought that their children might some day study in these buildings. To this day, I cannot forget the wry smile on the emaciated face of an adivasi carter who asked me if I was joking.

Right from my fourth year at IIT, I had been troubled by the relevance of the education I was receiving with regard to the condition of the teeming poor of India. Some of us had formed a science education group and we used to go out to nearby villages and give free tuitions to school children in science and mathematics, the fearful bugbears. The plight in which they lived had made me wonder about ways in which their livelihoods could be improved so that they could have at least a level playing field rather than remaining stuck in the quagmire of poverty and lack of opportunity. For the life of me I could not see how the kind of engineering I was being taught could affect the lives of these people in a positive way.

For quite some time, I remained undecided about what to do with my future.

Towards my last years of schooling in Calcutta, too, I had had similar feelings. Jayaprakash Narayan's epoch-making Sampoorna Kranti Andolan (Total Revolution Movement) in 1975, which for the first time effectively questioned from within the constitutional framework the stunted and restricted nature of parliamentary democracy being practised in the country, the imposition of the draconian internal emergency by Prime Minister Indira Gandhi with its accompanying crackdown on civil liberties and mass incarceration of opposition politicians and activists, and the subsequent historic election victory of the Janata Party in 1977 had all stirred my teenage mind. I used to walk to school, and one day, for some unknown reason, the beggars on the road attracted my attention. I began thinking about the kind of insecure and useless life they led.

My thoughts also included the domestic servants who worked for us. They all hailed from nearby rural areas, but were forced to live in city slums. Their lives were totally insecure as well. I found it unjust that so many people had to live such demeaning existences without any hope of realising their potential as human beings. However, apart from doing some social work with the pastor of St. Paul's Church who used to come to our school to give us a sermon on Fridays, I did not pursue these thoughts in any practical way.

I had had no plan for the future at the end of my schooling either. Those were considerably easygoing times and we didn't have any career counsellor in our school. As for taking the IIT entrance examination, since all the better performing students in my class were appearing for the examinations, being one of them, I followed suit. In 1978, there were neither any coaching classes nor the kind of cutthroat competition visible now. I cleared the entrance test on the strength of my preparations for the school leaving examinations alone.

Thus, it was more due to inertia than because of any commitment to prepare myself for a career as a technologist or manager that I had joined IIT. Upon joining the institute, I forgot my niggling worries about the fate of the poor in the initial years. For the first time in my life I tasted the freedom of hostel life and the fun that came with it. There was no relative marking or cumulative grading system in those days. One could easily sail through the exams on the strength of the previous night's cramming sessions. Understandably, a whole bunch of IITians used to spend the better part of their time doing everything but studying.

But after three years and on the threshold of official adulthood (the voting age was twenty-one at that time), I had to finally decide what I wanted to do with my life. My old concerns about the poor and their insecure and demeaning livelihoods began troubling me again.

The adivasi carter's reply shook me to the core. What is the use of such high-quality institutions, I thought, if even after thirty-six years of independence the country's graduates had not been able to create an India in which the poorest of the poor could dare to dream big, which is the sine qua non of all advancement?

An arrogant saying amongst us deemed us IITians the cream of the nation.

As we came back to our hostel rooms, leaving the carters to their involuntary communion with nature, I joked to my friend that we might be the cream all right, but instead of producing butter we had gone rancid. That adivasi carter helped me find my life's mission. I decided then and there that I would devote the rest of my life to helping the adivasis better their lot.

At present, the entire IIT Kharagpur campus has become a high-tech island, walled within itself. The road from the rural heartland has been diverted, and it now innocuously skirts its periphery, as if to doubly ensure that such rural yokels do not accidentally find their way into the fast lane. Nor are there any possibilities for the hostel inmates to have informal encounters of the rural kind I had enjoyed. Instead, they spend their spare time surfing the Internet from the comfort of their hostel rooms, which are all wired. One inmate of the hostel I used to stay in recently hit the headlines for selling CDs of steamy video clips via the Internet and landing both himself and the CEO of the internet auction site BAZEE.COM in jail!

Embarking on my mission was easier said than done. I decided to read up for help in deciding on my precise course of action. The IIT Kharagpur library had an excellent humanities and social sciences section. In my third year, I had begun reading books on philosophy and social change as some good teachers of sociology, psychology, and economics triggered my interest in these subjects. I read voraciously—across the spectrum from left to right—to find answers to the questions my mind posed.

Hailing as I did from Bengal, which had remained a hot bed of communist activity since pre-independence days; I could not but be impressed by Marxism.

Right from the early 1970s, when I was in my teens and had become capable of cogent political thinking, I had been drawn to the idea of a revolutionary societal change. The idea of a revolution facilitated through an armed struggle by a congregation of the dispossessed masses to capture state power that forms the centre-piece of Marxist theory and practice.

This idea is especially appealing because it posits that revolution is inevitable. The history of the human race, Marx said, has been one of class struggles, in which with the rise in productivity due to improvements in the means of production, a stage invariably comes when further rise in productivity is impossible without a seizure of power by the newer classes that become conscious of their power. These newer classes then seize power at such times and bring about a new social order. This law of history, according to Marx, ordains that eventually the modern labouring class—the proletariat, too, will overthrow capitalism and bring about a new socialist order. All that one has to do is make the proletariat conscious of its power and the rest will follow as night follows day. The milieu in Bengal in the 1970s was very radical. Even though the heroic Naxalite uprising of the late 1960s under the aegis of the Maoist leaning Communist Party of India (Marxist Leninist) or CPI(ML) had been quelled, it had left a lasting impact and its reverberations could still be heard.

My maternal grandfather's youngest brother, who was just a little older than my father, had, in fact, joined the Naxalites and gone underground. He had subsequently been caught and tortured by the police, before being wondrously let off without any criminal case being instituted against him. During the peak of the Naxalite struggle, a young man hailing from the street where I lived in Kolkata had vanished. He resurfaced only after the Left Front Government came into being in West Bengal in 1978.

Unfortunately, by the time I passed out of school, heavy state repression had ensured that the Naxalite movement, though alive, had splintered into ineffective fragments. Moreover, the landslide victory of the electoral front of the parliamentary leftist parties led by the Communist Party of India (Marxist) or CPI(M) in West Bengal's legislative elections and the immensely successful "Operation Barga" launched by them to give permanent legal tenure to the shareholder tenant farmers of landlords had seemed to renew hope in the scope for radical action within a liberal democratic set up. Consequently, there wasn't any viable and practising revolutionary party I could turn to for firm guidance in the early 1980s, the period when all kinds of questions vexed me.

So I decided to try out the ideas of Mohandas Karamchand Gandhi regarding non-violent passive resistance and rural reconstruction through the formation of autonomous village republics as set out in his path breaking work "Hind Swaraj" or Indian Freedom. This was in part motivated by the fact that in my eclectic search for intellectual direction, I had also savoured the austere mystical wonders of Hindu Upanishadic philosophy, which form the bedrock of Gandhian thought and action.

Around this time I saw 'Aakrosh', Govind Nihalani's heart-wrenching film on the oppression of adivasis. The film had an idealistic young lawyer, who made a persistent effort to get a poor adivasi man, falsely accused of killing his wife, to tell the truth—that she had actually been raped and killed by an oppressor. An activist character clad in the traditional Gandhian dress of kurta and pajama chided this lawyer that he would not be able to understand the reality of the oppression of the poor that kept their lips sealed against injustice. At the same time, this activist tried his best to convince the adivasi man to speak up and in doing so, was killed by some goons.

The film made a deep impression on me and I came out of the cinema hall with the romantic notion of emulating the activist. Shortly after seeing this film, I laid my hands upon a copy of Ernest Hemingway's masterpiece, 'For Whom the Bell Tolls'.Reading it, my imagination was fired by the character of the American dynamiter Robert Jordan, who was engaged in a dangerous mission behind the fascist lines in the Spanish civil war of the late 1930s, which was doomed from the start.

What impressed me about this character was that he was ambivalent about ideology and the result of the war, but was still risking his life for a cause. By this time, my cumulative reading had matured my understanding enough for me to realise that the project of radical social change, whether of the Marxist or the Gandhian variety, would, in all probability, be a lost cause in the long run. Yet, I yearned to be a rebel with a cause. In the words of a famous ghazal or song sung in the Urdu language –

Ae meri jaan-e-ghazal (Oh my dear friend)
Chal mere saath hi chal (Come with me)
In samajon ke banaye hue bandhan se nikal (Break free of the shackles forged by society)
Kab badla hai jamana tu ye jamane ko badal (When has an era changed, change this one)

So while all my other classmates were busy trying to get jobs or seats in Indian Institute of Management and in American universities, I was floundering around in search of serendipitous utopias! My father, a no-nonsense, dyed in the wool technologist and manager, had by this time got an inkling of my predilections and had begun putting pressure on me to abandon what he considered to be nothing more than useless lotus eating. We have a saying in Bengali, which pejoratively depicts all voluntary social activism as a futile attempt to go out and chase wild bisons in the forest on the strength of frugal meals taken at home. My father would repeat this often and exhort me to leave this godforsaken country of ours and take wings to America.

The net result of my father's opposition to my lotus eating was that I decided to join the National Dairy Development Board (NDDB) as a trainee engineer. I was impressed by the literature I had read on the "white revolution" in the production of milk through cooperativ dairying brought about by the Kheda District Milk Marketing Federation in Gujarat, which had reportedly transformed the lives of poor farmers there.

It was a fine day in 1983 when I went to the NDDB office in Kolkata to report for work, dressed in the Gandhian dress of kurta, pajama and sandals. The first thing the officer there said on seeing me was that I wasn't properly dressed. This angered me, and I shot back that I was in our national dress and how could he be derogative about it. An altercation ensued, at the end of which I was unceremoniously shooed out of the officer's cubicle. Outside the cubicle, all the babus or clerks sat in front of their tables loaded with files in a big hall. I am a big fan of the British rock group Pink Floyd. That day, seeing the clerks and their files, a few lines from their great album "Wall" flitted through my mind involuntarily –

> We don't need no education
> We don't need no thought control
> No dark sarcasm in the classroom
> Teachers leave them kids alone
> Hey! Teachers! Leave them kids alone!
> All in all it's just another brick in the wall.
> All in all you're just another brick in the wall.

I came out of the office and dashed off a letter to my father saying I was leaving for the great unknown to fulfil my dreams. Then, I took off to the Santhal Pargana in Bihar, where some of my youth acquaintances, belonging to one of the many splinter groups of the CPI(ML), were working among the adivasis.

Soon, however, I felt uncomfortable there because of the dogma of my co-workers and a resistance on their part to question received wisdom. They would not budge from the position that the Indian state was semi-feudal and semi-colonial in character. This is how Mao Ze Dong had characterised the Chinese state in the late 1920s. Not only had such a blinkered approach of the CPI(ML) led to the dissipation of the Naxalite movement, but it wasn't helping us address the burning issues that faced the poor Santhals around us either. I felt that Marxism was a living ideology and had the capacity to be adapted to suit local conditions as a first step in order to build up a larger programme for challenging the state.

The challenge lay in formulating a praxis that was appropriate to the situation of the adivasis and their immediate problems, rather than chasing the romantic dream of a peasant revolution that depended on an archaic and downright naive characterisation of the Indian state for its success.

The more I studied, the more disenchanted I became. So much had been written on social change, but eventually little had been achieved that was lasting. One of the more inspiring predictions of Marx and Engels was that even though the modern state was a necessary evil that would continue in the interim after the proletarian revolution, albeit under the control of the proletarian party, it would later "wither away." As the productive forces of society grew sufficiently and the capitalist class had been uprooted completely, the state would wither away, since an ideal situation would come into existence. In such a scenario, the mode of production and distribution of the social product would be according to the principle of "from each according to their capacity and to each according to their need." A situation in which there would be no need for the disciplining force of the state, as people would generally be well disposed towards each other, bereft of selfish individualistic goals.

In reality, however, despite all practical efforts at change, the state had not withered. On the contrary, it had become stronger and stronger with the passage of time!

Both in capitalist and socialist dispensations, the basic credo of production and distribution of the social product was more or less the same—from each in inverse proportion to their power, to each in direct proportion to their power.. The difference between the two opposing dispensations was only in degree.

Nobel laureate author and educationist Rabindranath Tagore's Visva Bharati University in Santiniketan, where I was staying at the time, had itself drifted far away from his dreams of liberating humanity from self-made prisons. The university had been reduced to the performance of rituals, rather than posing a challenge to the rot in the education system.

I wanted to get down to work myself, but could not find any light. I felt there was no point in studying and writing any more, as almost everything possible had already been written. A lack of adequate good practice was the main problem of the various approaches to social change. There was a need for much more intensive field level work, especially in the rural areas, where the people were still unaware of their latent potential.

I also came round to the view that despite its limitations, the Indian Constitution, especially with its exemplary protective provisions for the adivasis, provided a legal space for dissent and mobilisation that had not been adequately utilised. In a direct reaction to the challenge of Marxism, capitalist liberal democracy had become much more mass oriented. This was reflected in some parts of the Indian Constitution, even though it largely retained the colonial oppressive character of governance inherited from the British times.

I was particularly disillusioned by the way in which the post-revolutionary states in the Soviet Union and China had been converted into anti-people apparatuses of domination, far removed from the democratic ideals espoused in Marxist texts. So I became increasingly inclined towards attempting to exhaust the liberal democratic methods, rather than launch into a premature armed struggle against the state.

The break came from an unexpected source altogether.

3   Comrades in Arms

One day, I went to a friend's place, only to find he had gone out somewhere. While waiting for him I began to flit through a back issue of Reader's Digest. In it, I came across an article on the work being done by the Social Work and Research Centre (SWRC) in Tilonia, Rajasthan.

This was the first time I had come across the mention of a secular social service outfit, a non-government organisation (NGO), working for rural development by adopting a mass participatory approach. Here was a chance to do something from a new angle. I wrote to SWRC, offering my services to the organisation. A positive response arrived soon and saw me heading for Tilonia.

When I reached Tilonia in the summer of 1985, Khemraj was the first person I met there.

He told me he hailed from a backward caste jat farmer family of Chittor district and was a first generation literate. While studying in college, he became involved in student politics and joined a radical students' union. A friend told him about Tilonia, hearing which he joined the SWRC. He felt that rural development work would remain limited, no matter how much one tried to make it participatory, as long as a direct attack wasn't launched on the opressive socio-economic structures that denied power to the poor.

I already knew this. But what interested me was that Khemraj had left Tilonia around two and a half years back and had gone to Jhabua district in Madhya Pradesh. There, he made an effort to organise Bhil adivasis to fight for their rights and made some actual ground-level progress. I asked Khemraj if I could come down and join him. He responded with a warm embrace, the memory of which still enthuses me after all these years.

I packed my bags and took off to work with Khemraj and the Bhil adivasis in Jhabua. At last, I had begun to realise my life's mission.

For almost a decade I lived in Jhabua among the Bhils. These have easily been the best years of my life.

It all began when I met the most colourful Bhil character I have known—my colleague and fast friend Khemla—in his small hut in Badi Vaigalgaon village.

The only one—out of five brothers—to have attended school, Khemla is a born rebel.

Traditionally, the Bhils make their children tend to cattle when they are young. Once they reach adolescence, they are married off and harnessed for farm operations. Not surprisingly, they are highly reproductive. This, combined with the continuous deprivation they face with regard to land, water sources, and forests, thanks to non-adivasis and the colonial and post-colonial states, reduces them to penury. By the time he grew to school-going age in the early 1970s, Khemla's family was living in such dire conditions. Seeing that there wasn't enough land to sustain all his sons, his father decided to send him to school.

The government had introduced a residential school system for adivasi children who cleared the primary level to counter the high dropout rate. Khemla went to study in class six at such a hostel school situated at the nearby weekly market village of Umrali. Unfortunately corruption, which has been, and continues to be the bane of Indian governance, meant that the children in the hostels were fed substandard food. Khemla protested against this. When the hostel supervisor beat him, Khemla hit him back and was rusticated for his pains. That was the end of schooling for Khemla.

Once he returned home, he naturally got married in accordance with the custom. But that did not douse his latent fire. He had taken training under a 'burwo', a traditional medicine man and was capable of going into a trance to commune with spirits. This made him highly revered to villagers far and near. He also delivered effective cures for sundry ailments.

About this time, the government decided to introduce a new scheme of barefoot doctors called the Jan Swasthya Rakshak Yojana or people's health protection scheme. Being educated as well as a burwo, Khemla was easily selected for this project. He was appointed after a short training. This increased his prestige even more within the community, as now he was a "sarkari" or government man.

What bothered Khemla the most was the tremendous repression and extortion his people suffered at the hands of local government officials and the ubiquitous sahukar. He found the behaviour of the police the most reprehensible. The Bhils had a traditional dispute resolution system, in which the aggrieved parties and the entire panchayat, which could be as big as the people of ten to twelve villages in the case of inter-village disputes, would sit together and sort out matters.

However, this obviously didn't bode well for the police as it reduced the scope of their earnings. So they systematically weaned the village patels or headmen off this system and encouraged people to report disputes to them. Over time, an excellent community system was destroyed and the misrule of the police established. Once this was done, custodial torture came into play in order to extort money from the illiterate adivasis.

Khemla began a single-handed crusade against this malpractice. Every time he heard of the police arbitrarily picking up some adivasi, Khemla would go to the police station and get him released. He even went to the tehsil town Alirajpur on a few occasions and submitted written complaints to the Sub-divisional Police Officer.

The news of his activism reached the local Member of the Madhya Pradesh Legislative Assembly (MLA) who was himself a patel and had been one of the first people to be lured by non-adivasis to break the traditional adivasi system.

He called Khemla to Alirajpur and told him to give up his foolhardy ways and join his political party instead. The MLA told Khemla he stood to gain a lot by cooperating with the police and other government staff and acting as their agent and informer. In his inimitable style, Khemla ticked off the MLA for being a traitor to his people and living off their blood and sweat. He returned more determined than ever to continue with his campaign.

No sooner had he dismounted off the bus at Umrali on his way home than he was arrested by the police and taken to the police station. There, he was stripped to his underwear and given the lambasting of his life by the assistant sub-inspector. He was also told to desist from his wayward ways. After spending the night in the lockup, he got a release the next day. Instead of going home, he took a bus back to Alirajpur and from there another one to Jhabua. He went straight to the District Collector, the head of the district administration, and handed him a written complaint as well as a vivid oral description of what the police had done to him. As a result the assistant sub-inspector was transferred and an inquiry instituted against him. These events added to the legend that Khemla was becoming and made him into a one-man army.

Khemla is a resourceful guy. He took constant advantage of the Integrated Rural Development Programme (IRDP) schemes of the government under which subsidised loans were given to poor people to start some income generation activity. On one occasion, he received ten goats and 2,000 rupees for tending to them as a loan.

He felt no money was required for tending to the goats, which just needed to be grazed in the forest. So he had immediately sold two of the goats for three hundred rupees apiece. Along with the 2,000 rupees of loan money, he had now collected the 2,500 rupees he had to pay back (there was a fifty percent subsidy). He deposited the amount in the bank and became debt free.

The remaining goats have gone on to provide some supplementary income. Since he paid back his loan promptly, he became eligible for another grant. This time, he received another 6,000 rupees for the construction of a hut under the Indira Awaas Yojana, a housing scheme and built his own home. At that time, this scheme was structured in a way that allowed for the grants to be given only to a group of people who were setting up a new colony. So Khemla roped in six other people from his village, did all the legwork, had a barren hillock sanctioned for the purpose, and got the money released for all of them together.

As per an arrangement, Khemla was to take me to Gendra village, where Khemraj stayed. On a hot summer in 1985, I got down from the bus at Umrali and found myself in the midst of barren hills dotting the landscape like red dragons. I had been advised to ask for directions at a paan or betel leaf selling kiosk. The owner of the kiosk raised a clenched fist in salute and greeted me "zindabad" - long live, when I introduced myself to him. He called a young boy and told him to take me to Khemla's hut.

On my way, I crossed the Angkhar River, a dry sandy bed and walked along a dirt track behind my young guide in between hedgerows of cactus boundaries of fields. Finally we reached the bottom of the hillock on which Khemla's hut stood. My young guide shouted out to him, and we climbed up the last few rocks to the hut. A dark short man with muscular limbs and a round face emerged and raised his fist in greeting saying as was customary –

"zindabad." I responded with the same refrain, even as a thrill gripped me within.

At last I had found my romantic revolutionary niche! Inside the hut was Thavli, Khemla's wife, a sharp-featured woman who was slim and taller than Khemla. As I would learn later, she was rather sharp tongued too! They had three daughters, one of them a toddler. All of them lived in a dark windowless hut, with shoulder high walls.

After spending a night in these surroundings, listening to Khemla's second daughter singing a lullaby while she swung her younger sister to sleep in an improvised cradle—made from a rope and a bed sheet—we set off for Gendra the next morning.

The dusty brown road from Umrali to Bakhatgarh was metalled but not macadamised. According to a local joke the road upto Mathwar that was further ahead was black only on paper as the money allocated for the road had been used to add colour to the lives of government staff, contractors and political leaders.

Khemla and I bumped along in a ramshackle bus for a while before getting off at a village called Palvi. From there, we trekked up to nine kilometers uphill and down dale to reach Gendra. Occasional shouts of "zindabad" greeted us as we wended our way to Gendra and the picturesque country-tiled primary school, a small room of which was to be my home. Khemraj came out and held me in a warm embrace. He said he was really happy to see me. At last he could boast, he said, that there was a man in the organisation who had actually read Marx in the original! He introduced me to Shankar, an adivasi boy who had just passed his higher secondary examinations. Shankar had heard of the activists' exploits and come to Gendra to meet them. He liked what they said and the work they were doing and decided to join them. Amit, another non-adivasi activist, had, at that time, gone home to Delhi for a change of air.

We immediately set off to swim and fish in a big tank in the nearby Kosaria village, some three kilometres away. Khemla dived into the water, and by some magic of his own caught six fish with bare hands. Upon returning, we cooked the fish over a slow wooden fire and polished them off with rotis made of maize flour—something I had never tasted before.

In the absence of electricity, we had a flickering lantern light dinner – all so romantic.

After dinner, Khemraj turned on a transistor and tuned it to the BBC Hindi Service station. A teacher who taught in the school and was staying in the other room joined us to listen to the news. Being a vegetarian, he hadn't shared the meal with us. Khemraj told me how, in the past, they considered even the radio to be an unnecessary luxury. But when Prime Minister Indira Gandhi was assassinated by her Sikh bodyguards in 1984, Khemla had not come to know of it until almost a week after the incident. That was when he decided to have at least one radio around to cut off the isolation.

Gendra is a lovely little village, perched on a series of hillocks. The Bhil adivasis living here build their houses on their farms. All the hillocks have houses on their crests with farms surrounding the houses. There are small gullies in between these hillocks, which flow down into the main stream Kara running through the village.

Just beyond this narrow stretch of private farmland hillocks rise the larger hills, which are separated by a demarcation line between the forest department and farms. Several trees dot the landscape, and unlike in Umrali, here one gets the feeling of being inside a forest. The kutcha road from Attha goes through Gendra to Mathwar and the school building is situated on the edge of a cliff by the side of this road.

The next morning, Khemla left, and Khemraj, Shankar and I went down to the stream to take a bath. Having missed bathing the previous day, I was itching for a bath. Khemraj said he bathed once a week. I made a face and said I was used to bathing every day. Khemraj smiled and said that soon I would sing a different tune. He had the last laugh of course, as the unavailability of water and the act of climbing up and down hillocks to reach a water source soon forced me to become, if not a weekly, at least a twice-a-week bather.

But such minor irritants could not bother me as I felt a deep sense of peace at having finally found myself among like minded comrades in a milieu appropriate to give shape to my mission in life. Before we launch into the main course of the modern day struggles against the marginalisation of the Bhils in which we have participated, we must have an entree to imbibe the true flavour of Bhil militancy with which this tale is liberally laced. This requires a brief perusal of their intriguing history, which finds little mention in standard history books.

4 Nature's Children Unarmed

The Bhil, Bhilala, Barela, Mankar, Naik and Patelia tribes together constitute the indigenous group of people known generally by the name of Bhils. They are the third most populous adivasi group in India, after the Gonds and the Santhals. The Bhils inhabit a large area spread over the states of Rajasthan, Gujarat, Madhya Pradesh, and Maharashtra. They find a mention in ancient Hindu texts of the third century AD. Originally, this indigenous group was concentrated in Sindh, Southern Rajasthan and Northwestern Madhya Pradesh. Traditionally, the Bhils lived by practising shifting cultivation, hunting and gathering in dense forests. Reduction in the fertility of their farms and occurrences of epidemics would cause them to move to new locations every few years.

Subsistence-level survival and extensive dependence on physical labour encouraged them to weave tightly knit communities marked by shared labour in most aspects of their material and cultural life. The egalitarianism of the Bhils was further ensured by customs that decreed that surpluses accumulated beyond a certain limit must be spent on communal merrymaking and feasting.

This also did away with the possibility of these surpluses being used to develop agricultural and artisanal production and for engaging in trade and further accumulation. Thus, these customs also served to protect the environment from over exploitation. Moroever, this aversion to trade meant that the Bhils eschewed the abstractions of literacy and arithmetic and remained firmly down to earth. They developed a rich oral animistic culture with nature at its centre.

Habitats being vital to their existence, the Bhils resolutely guarded them from encroachment by others. Historical evidence shows how the Bhils retained their independence by defying the might of the Gupta emperors with their superb archery skills. However, following the introduction of firearms into the subcontinent by the Muslims invading from the west, their freedom was circumscribed.

Initially, the Rajputs, who had been in ascendance over the northern and central parts of India, enlisted the Bhils in their fight against Muslim invaders. There is the famous example of the Rajput king of Mewar, Rana Pratap, securing the Bhils' help in his struggles. But later as the Muslims consolidated their rule over the region, the Rajputs had to move into the Bhils' territories.

Thus began the exodus of the Bhils. Over the centuries, this has led to their dispersal to the areas they now occupy. This process is described in stories that form their folklore. Even though the Rajputs ruled over them, apart from doing begaar or free labour and paying some nominal taxes, the Bhils remained largely free to pursue their nature-friendly subsistence lifestyle. They would frequently waylay trade caravans on the route from the north of India to the west, not so much for looting, but for preventing what they considered to be trespass into their territory.

The rise of the Marathas since the mid-17th century led to, for the first time, serious inroads into the Bhils' homelands in the western Madhya Pradesh region. In order to develop trade and settled agriculture so as to boost their revenue, sustained campaigns were carried out against the Bhils who resisted this incursion into their way of life. Peasants and traders from Gujarat and Maharashtra were encouraged to settle in the Bhil regions and forests were cleared to bring land under the plough. Thousands of Bhils were massacred when they rose in revolt against this policy. Thus, a process was started, which systematically dispossessed the adivasis of the fertile lands of the Malwa plateau and the Nimar plains flanking the Narmada River. They were subsequently pushed into the hills of the Vindhya and Satpura ranges.

In the early 19th century, the British came to power in the western and central Indian region after subordinating the squabbling Marathas. The imperial invaders carried forward the drive against the Bhils with even greater gusto. After decimating their own forests to fuel industrial development and international trade, the British began to exploit the forests of India.

This exploitation increased with the laying of railway lines, which began in western India in the 1850s. The extraction of timber required making deep inroads into the densely forested adivasi territory all over the country. This naturally meant encroaching upon the domain of the Bhils. The British also decided to fund this development and the accompanying administrative costs through enhanced land revenue collection and commercialisation of agriculture. All across India, the British embarked on a policy of displacing adivasis practising shifting agriculture, replacing them with more settled agricultural castes. The levels of land revenue were also hiked substantially.

In the western Madhya Pradesh region, the British followed the policy of the Marathas. They brought in Kanbi Patidar and Jat farmers from Gujarat and Rajasthan respectively and settled them on the Bhil lands in the plains. This was done with a view to increase the earnings from land revenue and commercial agriculture as well as to tame the militant Bhils. While some Bhils withdrew into the hills, most others were converted into serfs or bonded labourers of these non-adivasi farmers.

The British introduced a new land settlement regime, under which the earlier loose system of revenue calculation by the village heads was dispensed. A centralised system was put in place, with greatly enhanced levies on the farmers and the appointment of Malguzars or revenue collecting agents who had a free rein to extract as much commission as they could for themselves over and above the settlement.

Taxes in the central and western Indian regions increased to about 65% of the farmers' production from the 25% prevailing until then. Thus, the British systematically dismantled the older feudal system, which, especially in adivasi areas, had allowed the village councils a fair amount of independence. In its place, they put in a system that was feudal too, but with functionaries loyal to them, making the entire process considerably more exploitative.

All this seriously hampered the traditional livelihoods of adivasis living in the western Indian region. The rail line connected these regions with the rest of the country. Grain and minor forest produce began to be exported. The British appointed the trader bania castes as agents for collecting excise revenue on a commission basis. This led to the increasing infiltration of these traders into interior areas. They would often use dishonest practices to defraud the adivasis of their produce.

The surpluses the adivasis used to have to tide them over the occasional bad monsoon years were no longer available to them, and famines became the order of the day. The insistence of the British on payment of taxes, regardless of the harvest situation, resulted in the adivasis becoming perpetually indebted to trader-moneylender sahukars. Displacement from their lands and the decimation of their forests only added to the adivasis' misery. Sadly, this indebtedness, the foundations of which were laid by the British, continues to this day.

The Bhils have quaint stories about the way they have been dispossessed.

Once a bajariya, a non-adivasi man who lived in a bajar or market, came to their land and asked the king for some land on which to do business. He said he wanted only as much land as his buffalo's hide could cover. The unsuspecting king readily granted his wish. The bajariya promptly cut this hide into very thin strings of leather and tied them together to make a very long rope. He then used this rope to circumscribe the entire kingdom, thereby usurping all the Bhils' lands.

According to another story, the Bhil king, Motia, was invited to a banquet by some thakurs or Rajput princes who had come to visit his kingdom. The legend was that Motia could not be killed as long as he had his pugree or headdress on. So the thakurs dined and wined the king lavishly and slipped in a sleeping potion along with the food and drinks. When he fell asleep, they took down his pugree and cut off his head. Legend also said that even if Motia's head was cut off, it would find its body and get joined once again. So the thakurs cut his head, buried it immediately, took the body away across the River Narmada and threw it across the Satpura hill range. To this day, the place where Motia's head supposedly lies is known as Mathwar or the place of the head. The place where his body was buried is known as Dhargaon or village of the body.

The situation deteriorated even more after independence as the Indian state built its edifice upon the colonial structure of governance it had inherited from the British. The region's various Princely States were parcelled out arbitrarily between the four states of western India according to the whims and fancies of their rulers. This divided the Bhil homeland into pieces.

From 1949 onwards, a process of land settlement was started with the aim of stopping shifting cultivation. With the formation of Madhya Pradesh in 1956, the Indian Forest Act, 1927 was extended to the adivasi areas of the former princely states. The act's strict enforcement completely stopped shifting cultivation. The forests began to be worked for fuel and timber for the ongoing development of industrial and urban centres in western India. Timber contractors, in collusion with the corrupt

Forest Department staff began decimating the forests indiscriminately. This put the adivasis in a difficult position. They could not shift to newer locations any more, as the fertility of the soils decreased and simultaneously, the supplementary income and nourishment from minor forest produce also went down.

The aim of the government's social and economic development policies for the uplift of adivasis in Madhya Pradesh has been to integrate them into the modern market economy and culture. This has downgraded the Bhils' subsistence lifestyle. The syllabi and teaching methods of the education system are totally alien to their culture. For a long time, this dissuaded most Bhils to get educated. Those who did, mostly considered their own culture as primitive and sub-human in accordance with the prevailing modernist assumptions. These educated Bhils distanced themselves from their community. There were a few exceptions, of course. Like the firebrand Khemla.

However, the vast majority of Bhils remained unequipped to participate effectively in the modern economy into which state policies were relentlessly pushing them. This lack of modern education has meant that they had little knowledge of their rights and enabling laws. As a result, they have not only been unable to avail themselves of even the minimal services that have been provided to them, but have also failed to protest against the unjust development policies of the state and suffered the pre-capitalist and illegal exploitation of the sahukars.

Over the years, the whole region has become a chronic drought-prone area, and it's inhabitants have no option other than migrating, either seasonally or perennially, in search of employment as casual unskilled labourers and therefore living in perpetual debt bondage. Indeed, this labour circulation and the consequent proletarianisation of the Bhils to serve as grist to the mill of capitalist development in industry and agriculture around the metropolitan centres in western India is only the obverse side of the coin of modern development that has laid waste the subsistence economy of the adivasis.

Nothing is more evocative of this dehumanisation of the Bhils than the meaning that the illiterate among them give to the term adivasi. They pronounce it as "adhavasi" or half people and think of themselves as inferior and only half as human as the more well-heeled and educated "puravasi" or full people. The latter group pejoratively refers to them as "mama" or uncle said in a derisive tone. So widespread is the phenomenon of migration among the Bhils of Jhabua and Ratlam districts in Madhya Pradesh, that even during the busy monsoon kharif season there is always a rush of people travelling either way by the Vadodara-Kota passenger train that runs on the Delhi-Mumbai trunk rail route, passing through these districts. Consequently, this train has come to be called "mama gari"- the train of the mamas, by all and sundry!

This degeneration has come about because the adivasi's protests against this unjust process has been ruthlessly crushed. Throughout the 18th and 19th centuries the Marathas and the British had come up against stiff resistance from the Bhils—both spontaneous and organised in nature. Following the initial wars in the early part of the 19th century, the British embarked on a policy of pacification so as to tame the militancy of the Bhils with a carrot and stick policy. They set up a Bhil Corp for military operations with adivasi soldiers. Besides this, a separate Bhil force was set up to provide security to the arterial Agra-Mumbai road passing through the Sendhwa region on which the Bhils regularly raided trade convoys. However, taking advantage of the uncertainty created by the first war of independence in 1857, the Bhils, who were never very happy with the usurpation of their lands by the British, rose once again in revolt in what has come to be known as The Great Bhil Rebellion of 1857-60. Khajya Naik had been in the service of the British for twenty years—from 1831 to 1851 and was engaged in guarding the Palasner ghat in the Satpura hills on the Agra-Mumbai road. He was sentenced and sent to prison in 1851 for murdering a bandit after taking him into custody. But his previous track record led to his release in 1855. This incarceration angered Khajya; immediately after his release he began plotting against the British. He found eager accomplices among the Bhils in the hills who had been nursing ill will against the British for being displaced from their lands in the Nimar valley.

Khajya joined forces with Bheema and Mevashya Naik and provided help toTatya Tope in 1857. The British mobilised their forces, including the Bhil Corps, to not only defeat the rebellious Bhils in battles at Rajpur and later at Dhaba Baodi in Barwani district, but also used the services of informers to capture Khajya and Bheema. Khajya was pardoned in 1858, following which he acted as an informer for the British in their efforts to quell the uprising.

But in 1860, Khajya once again revolted, claiming that the British had not compensated him enough for his services. Immediately, the uprising gained momentum and under Khajya's leadership, the Bhils once again began waylaying the caravans on the Agra-Mumbai road in the Satpura Hills. Finally, the British summoned up forces from other areas in addition to the Bhil Corps. A fierce battle was fought at Ambapani near the Agra-Mumbai road. Even though the British emerged victorious in this battle, Khajya and Bheema Naik managed to escape. However, some traitors within the Bhil forces who were paid by the British, later killed them both. The British used a combination of force and treachery to subdue this rebellion.

Another such revolt was fought by the great Tantia Bhil. Tantia was born in the present day Khandwa district in 1842. Back then, this region fell under the direct rule of the East India Company. After the reorganisation consequent to the war of 1857, it was made a part of the Central Provinces. Like elsewhere, the British had introduced the zamindari system for collection of land revenue in this region too. Tantia's father was a small tenant farmer working for a landlord. He passed away in 1860, leaving Tantia to fend for himself. 1860s saw continuous monsoon failure for three years. The British refused to forego the collection of land revenue, putting the tenant farmers in a dire situation. Most farmers had to take loans from sahukars to pay their rent to the landlords. Tantia refused to do so and instead beat up the landlord and his men when they insisted that he pay the rent. This was deemed a a serious act of indiscipline, and the police immediately arrested Tantia. He was sentenced to a year's imprisonment. Even after his release, he was constantly harassed by landlords, sahukars and police, who kept bringing up false criminal cases against him.

Finally, fed up with this endless harassment, Tantia beat up the landlords once again and fled to the jungles. The year was 1872. In the forest, he slowly built a team of armed men and began looting landlords and attacking police stations. He and his men were caught on many occasions, but they managed to escape from jail. For a decade and a half, Tantia and his men defied the might of the British and their vassal landlords and sahukars. In fact, the adivasi leader and his brigade came close to establishing a parallel government. Tantia became famous for his Robin Hood style of functioning—looting rich landlords and distributing a big chunk of the loot among poor people. Bhil women regarded him as their saviour and brother and would tell their children of the exploits of their Tantia "Mama" or uncle. However, he was once again apprehended in 1888 through subterfuge and sentenced to death by hanging, following a summary trial in Jabalpur.

At about the same time, in the year 1881, the Bhils of Alirajpur in Jhabua district revolted under the leadership of Chhitu Kirar. It had been a bad year for farmers and famine was rampant. The patwaris or revenue officials had extorted as taxes, what little had been produced. Even at a time like this, the sahukars in the haat villages and towns possessed large stocks of hoarded cereals. Chhitu Kirar rounded up a force of men and attacked some of the haat villages. They pillaged the sahukars' grain stores and distributed the food among the people.

Subsequently, Chhitu aligned with a discontented military officer and his band of men belonging to the ruling princely family in Alirajpur. Together they threatened the seat of power itself. The British acted swiftly and brought in armed forces and cavalry to quell the rebellion. The battle fought in Sorwa village saw Chhitu and his men killing the British commander and routing his forces. This forced the British to send in more detachments, and in the next battle at Alirajpur, his forces were defeated and Chhitu had to flee to Gujarat. Later, with the help of informers he was apprehended and killed. Such was the prowess of Chhitu that even today he is considered a legendary figure, and the people say that there were as many people in Chhitu's force as flowers in a field of flowering gram plants.

In the 1930s, inspired by the legendary freedom fighter Baleshwar Dayal Dikshit, the adivasis of Banswara district in Rajasthan and Ratlam and Jhabua districts in Madhya Pradesh began organising against the feudal extortion of the princes and the sahukars. Despite severe repression, this movement was very successful in freeing the Bhils from the bondage of the feudal lords and sahukars in the areas of its influence. Dikshit quit the Indian National Congress after independence and along with Jayaprakash Narayan and others formed the Socialist party in 1950.

Thereafter the movement took on a pronounced leftist character with demands for land to the tiller, the abrogation of all debts to the sahukars, and strict regulation of their activities by the administration and access to forests. The members of this movement wore red caps to distinguish themselves; this lent the movement its name of the Lal Topi Andolan or red cap movement.

So pervasive was its influence that its candidates won the elections for the Lok Sabha, the lower house of the Indian Parliament and the Vidhan Sabha, the legislative assembly of the state, throughout the 1950s and the 1960s. Corruption of the administration and the activities of sahukars and feudal lords were curbed considerably at the local level. Unfortunately, elsewhere in Madhya Pradesh and India, the Socialist party failed miserably. Thus, the movement's radical demands could not be pursued at higher levels. Soon those adivasi leaders of the movement who had been elected Members of Parliament (MP) and MLAs fall prey to the sops offered by the local non-adivasi leaders of the Congress party.

By the early 1970s, these leaders, along with a major section of their followers, began to quit the movement and join Congress. What made this possible was the fact that there was a substantial increase in central government development funds flowing into adivasi areas about this time. The lure of these funds was used as a bribe to woo these leaders and their followers. Once the movement lost its unified face, severe repression was unleashed on those activists who refused to be bought. A plethora of false cases and severe custodial torture by the police made sure that these activists and their followers gave up their crusading work. The movement was totally crushed.

Khemla's father Chena was an active member of this movement. He once told me about the number of times he had been to jail and received police beatings. He said that the police began dominating the region only after the Lal Topi Andolan was smashed. He remembered with a wistful smile how in his childhood and early youth the whole region was peaceful and everyone had land to till and food to eat. The only problem he recalled was that of the begaar or free labour they had to put in on the king's fields.

Things took a turn for the worse as the people began fighting among themselves, looting and murdering each other. The police encouraged the spread of this internecine fighting so as to reap benefits from it with the help of dalals or agents. Chena had a colourful term for these dalals, "taplo chato" or dish lickers.

Whenever a policeman or forest guard came to a village, he would lodge himself at the dalal's house and ask him to prepare a meal of chicken and rotis. The dalal would go out into the village and extort a chicken from some poor adivasi and then cook it and serve it in a taplo or dish to his guests. At the end of the meal, the government staff would give the leftovers in the dish to the dalal, which the latter would eat, licking off the dish in the end. That is how they came to be called dish lickers!

Pushpendra, a journalist friend in Alirajpur, told me about a unique modus operandi adopted by the police for dealing with an offence as serious as murder. Whenever a murder took place, instead of preparing a FIR (First Information Report), the police would just record in the station's roz namcha or daily record that a dead body had been found. They would leave some blank space, to be filled up later. No post mortem report would be finalised by a doctor either. Time would be given to the opposing parties to reach an agreement, brokered by a dalal. If an agreement was reached and appropriate amounts of money changed hands between the parties the police as well as the petitioning party would register the case as a suicide in the Roz Namcha instead of as a murder. Accordingly, a post mortem report would be prepared. The papers would then be submitted to the Sub-divisional Magistrate for disposing of the case as one of suicide as per the provisions of the Criminal Procedure Code.

All the concerned officials would naturally have to be bribed to get such an elaborate charade through in a hush hush manner. We would later learn the hard way that the police regularly tampered with the Roz Namcha, which is supposed to be a check on the legality of the police's actions. Only if the aggrieved party did not agree to this would a proper FIR for murder be filed and the case proceeded with. Even then the conviction rate would be low because the murderer's kin would bribe the police to do a poor investigation and file a weak charge sheet. The accused would come out of jail and then someone from the aggrieved party would murder him one day and the vendetta would continue indefinitely, the police looking on in glee.

By the time Khemraj reached Alirajpur and met Khemla the once brave children of nature, the Bhils, had been totally cowed down and the dense forests of the region devastated through excessive logging by the state and its minions.

5   Nature's Children's Revival

Khemraj came to Alirajpur from Tilonia in 1982, searching for a canvas on which to paint his dreams. He put up in a hotel and began talking to the area's educated adivasis about the conditions in which the villagers were living. It soon became clear to him that the prevailing state of affairs was a sordid one.

Pushpendra, a local journalist, asked him to contact Khemla if he wanted to do any concrete work for the adivasis. Khemraj took a bus to Umrali and made his way to Khemla's hut in Badi Vaigalgaon.

And so began an odyssey that continues.

Khemraj told Khemla that there was a limit to what he could achieve with the kind of individual struggle he was waging, and that the adivasis had to be organised into a sangathan—a mass organisation—to make any lasting and sustainable impact. Khemla found himself in agreement with Khemraj, and the two began moving around villages to hold meetings in which they tried to convince villagers to come together to fight for their rights.

They were met with a quiet resistance.

The people were afraid of committing themselves, as they feared a backlash from the police. The village patels were also against the activists as they saw the formation of a sangathan as a threat to their power. Moreover, the memories of the administration's repression to crush the Lal Topi Andolan still lingered in the people's minds.

For quite a while, the duo made no headway. Yet another renegade from mainstream society, Amit, joined them in early 1983. Amit had quit his studies as a student of the School of Planning and Architecture in Delhi to come to Tilonia, where he met Khemraj. The now enhanced trio of activists began visiting villages on a regular basis to find issues around which to begin the organising process.

Soon, the proposed construction of a big earthen dam in Atthava village was announced. The village was upstream of Badi Vaigalgaon on the big stream that drained the watershed.

The irrigation department awarded the contract for the dam's construction to a non-adivasi sahukar contractor in Alirajpur. Posing as labourers, the activists infiltrated into the ranks of the construction workers and discovered that the contractor was paying the labourers a daily wage of three rupees, when the statutory minimum wage at that time was seven and a half rupees. The activists slowly began talking to the people about this deception and the need to do something about it. Their perseverance paid off; one day all the labourers, led by the trio, struck work, demanding payment of the minimum wage.

This created a sensation as this was the first time a strike had taken place in Jhabua. The then Subdivisional Magistrate (SDM) of Alirajpur was an Indian Administration Service (IAS) officer who was sympathetic to the problems of adivasis. He acted immediately and got the contractor to hike the wage rate to legal levels. The success of this action kicked off the sangathan process like nothing else could have.

The news of the action spread far and wide. Gulab, a resident of Badi Vaigalgaon, who had gone to live and farm in his wife's village in Attha in the nearby Mathwar Reserved Forest Range, came to know of the trio's deeds. He described to Khemla how the forest department staff was harassing the adivasis in the Mathwad Forest Range, beating them up and extorting cash and kind from them. He implored Khemla to come along with his two bajariya friends and help them counter the excesses of the forest department.

Khemraj and Amit set off with Gulab to his house in Attha for a preliminary survey of the conditions there, while Khemla remained in Umrali to continue with the organisational work. The other two members of the trio found the situation in the Mathwar Forest Range to be a classic case of adivasi deprivation amidst natural plenty. This had become the order of the day all over India due to faulty development policies adopted after independence.

Things could have been otherwise, however. The Constitution of India, in its Fifth Schedule, has provisions that for areas notified under it such as the district of Jhabua, the governor may, on the advice of the Tribal Advisory Council (TAC) composed of a selection of adivasi MLAs, have special laws enacted for these areas. The constitution further empowers the governor to direct that the laws enacted by Parliament or the state legislature for the state as a whole should not apply to them.

Similarly for the tribal areas of the north east too there is a special Sixth Schedule providing for self governance according to tribal customs. But like the British before them who first introduced similar measures in the Government of India Act of 1935, the rulers of independent India, too, thought nothing of disregarding grand provisions made on paper. Indeed, while introducing the first Government of India Act in 1858 after quelling the first war of independence, the British had guaranteed to the people of India inter alia that due regard would be paid to the ancient rights, usages and customs of India while framing new laws, and that these laws would be administered equally and impartially for the benefit of the people.

Almost immediately, however, these principles were breached. The Indian Penal Code (IPC) was enacted in 1860 and the Code of Criminal Procedure (CrPC) in 1861. These laws have been codified in such a manner as to provide the administration with a handy means of suppressing organised public dissent. A more harmful law from the point of view of the adivasis was the enactment of the Indian Forest Act (IFA) in 1864. Applying the principle of res nullius, which means that a particular property has no owner unless there is documentary evidence in support of its ownership, the British refused to recognise the customary community rights of the adivasis over the forests in which they resided. The forests were turned over to the Forest Department created for this purpose. It is evident how devastating this act has been from the point of view of the adivasis of Jhabua.

Yet another law that disinherited the adivasis from their main resource of land was the Land Acquisition Act (LAA) enacted in 1894, which, using the principle of eminent domain, empowered the government to dispossess the private owner of a piece of land for some public purpose in lieu of a paltry monetary compensation. These laws continue to be in force at present, albeit with minor modifications

After having to contend with organised and spontaneous adivasi militancy that was much fiercer than what they faced from the mainstream Indian society throughout their rule in India, the British had introduced some provisions that were to be later incorporated in the Fifth Schedule and the Sixth Schedule of the Indian constitution. These are applicable to some areas in the North East and aim to isolate the adivasis' areas and contain their militancy by providing some sops, thereby creating a wedge between them and mainstream Indian society.

Some well-meaning European anthropologists like V Elwin, C. V. F. Haimendorf, and W. V. Grigson encouraged the British in this regard. On the other hand, some nationalist freedom fighters, particularly the Indian anthropologist G. S. Ghuriye opposed this move. The British did some work in this respect because of the spin off they gained in terms of isolating the adivasi areas from the movement for independence during the crucial World War II years, when the pressure of the freedom movement was extremely high on them.

The presence of articulate adivasi leaders like Khan Abdul Ghaffar Khan and Jaipal Singh resulted in detailed debates in the Constituent Assembly regarding special provisions for the adivasis. These discussions reverberated with eulogies for the inherently democratic and non-exploitative nature of adivasi communities and with concerns about enabling them to negotiate the process of integration into the modern economy to their advantage. Nevertheless, there was strong opposition to the provisions of the Fifth and Sixth Schedules. The day was carried finally because these provisions received the backing of the first prime minister of India, Jawaharlal Nehru, and were incorporated in the constitution. These could easily have been used to prevent the application of the inimical laws such as IPC, CrPC, IFA and LAA in adivasi areas. This would have facilitated the seclusion of the adivasis from the onslaught of modern development and allowed them to gradually pick up the skills of negotiating a modern economy and polity, thus helping them become integrated on equal terms with the mainstream society.

Nehru's fascination with modern industrial development resulted in these provisions being ignored in actual practice. In Madhya Pradesh, the TAC was not constituted or remained only on paper for a considerable period of time. The state's governors never used their special powers to intervene on behalf of the adivasis. This led to massive land alienation due to development projects, deforestation and debt bondage. These provisions are not binding on the governor; they only state that he "may" utilise them. So if the government does not implement these provisions, it cannot be held responsible and taken to court for redressal. Consequently, the adivasis of Mathwar were in dire straits owing to the failure of affirmative governance in post-independence India.

Before independence, Mathwar was a small princely state. The Raja was still around and lived in opulence in his palace in Bakhatgarh, which also happened to be the range headquarters. When Khemraj and Amit went to meet him in the course of their preliminary travels through the area, he boasted in a perfect public school accent and a grand Selkirkian style that he was the "monarch of all that he surveyed." In reality, however, the forest and police department staff wielded the real power there. In leftist circles in India, a considerable amount of heat has been generated around the characterisation of the Indian state. The Maoists feel it is semi-feudal and semi-colonial in nature, whereas others argue that it has evolved into being a capitalist one. However, as far as the Bhil adivasis of Mathwar were concerned in the early 1980s, the state was both totally feudal and totally colonial. They had no conception at all about India being a sovereign democratic republic in which they not only had some basic inalienable rights, but also special affirmative provisions and laws to enable them to overcome centuries of isolation and domination by non-adivasis. At that time, very few adivasi people voted during the state assembly and parliamentary elections.

The provisions of the Indian Forest Act, 1927, are such that adivasis residing in a reserved forest area can be dubbed thieves as soon as they are born. The moment they step out of their fields, they become trespassers in the forest in which they have lived for generations. For even minor requirements such as wood for fuel or fodder for their livestock, they are at the forest guard's mercy. In the Mathwar range, the forest department staff had used this Act to unleash a reign of terror over the people. The adivasis had to regularly provide chicken, eggs, ghee, cereals and pulses to the forest guards and also pay bribes when they needed timber for making or repairing houses. The major problem, however, was about cultivating "newar" or encroached forestland. This was clearly against the law but was allowed by the forest department staff in exchange for huge bribes. Thus, the people had been cultivating forestland for years, of which there was no official record. Some of this land had initially been seized from them at the time of the settlement survey in 1949. Some of it was cultivated when the logging contractors had cleared the land of trees. Most of this cultivation dated back to the late 1970s. Given the tremendous pressure on land, the adivasis had no option but to cultivate this land. The forest department staff made hay by allowing them to do so unofficially and illegally. But after a point, the bribes and the beatings started becoming too much of a burden for the adivasis.

As in the Umrali area, the problem was complicated by the fact that the village patels were hand in glove with the forest department staff when it came to facilitating the process of extortion. They used the power they derived from their nexus with the forest department to keep the rest of the villagers in bondage and earn a commission from the bribes paid to their masters. Such was the power of the forest staff that the villagers had to bow down and wish them "Ram Ram" whenever they passed by. Failure to do so meant being subjected to thrashing. The adivasis were considered untouchables and special utensils were kept at the patel's house where food was cooked specially for the forest department staff. When they arrived, they sat in royal style on charpais or wooden cots with ropes intertwined in them, laid out with soft mattresses.

All this meant that organising the villagers to demand their rights was going to be a difficult proposition. Khemraj and Amit considered themselves lucky on the occasions when they found one or two villagers who were prepared to even talk to them. None of them, however, were prepared to participate in bigger meetings. Soon, word spread that two odd bajariyas who spoke the Bhili language, ate whatever the villagers themselves ate, and even sat cross-legged with them on the ground, were going from village to village. There were also rumours that these people were really evil spirits who were adept at removing the desi roof tiles of the adivasis huts and insinuating themselves into their houses at night to do all kinds of harm!

Since Attha was Gulab's village, it generated at least some response. Some people from the nearby villages of Chhoti Gendra and Mankhara also showed some interest. The patel of Chhoti Gendra proved to be an exception to the general run of patels. After some initial hesitation, he decided that the two activists meant well and warding off pressure from the forest department, invited Khemraj and Amit to stay in one of the two rooms of the government primary school. The school's teacher stayed in the other room. The children used to study sitting in the verandah. Even though the teacher had been there for some ten years, he had not been able to get even one student past the primary board examinations at the class five level. He had already heard of the kind of work the activists had done and so was apprehensive about staying alongside them, lest they created trouble. However, the sheer desire for Hindi speaking urban company in this back of beyond made him take in Khemraj and Amit under the school's shelter.

Weekly meetings began in the three villages, and a consensus was arrived at to raise the matter of cultivation of forestland with higher authorities. A delegation of three adivasis, along with the activists, decided to meet the Divisional Forest Officer (DFO) in Jhabua.

However, on the day the delegation was to set out, all three adivasis backed out and the programme fell through. Time was running out. The monsoons of 1984 were approaching and the forest guards had already sent out warnings that unless they were paid hefty bribes, no one would be allowed to cultivate their nevar land. Lalia of Attha, who had bled for three days from an internal haemorrhage the year before from the beatings he had received and had to borrow money at an exorbitant interest to pay both the forest guard and the doctor's fees, began crying in the meeting, imploring the others to do something. Seeing his desperate state, another delegation was put together. This one did manage to reach Jhabua and meet the DFO. The officer flatly refused to believe that there were so many encroachers on the forestland as the records revealed that Mathwar range had only two encroachers. He also refused to believe that his staff was behaving in an inhuman and illegal manner with the adivasis. Khemraj cautioned that if he did not come to Attha and judge for himself, they would be forced to begin a demonstration and approach higher authorities.

This was a bluff; the people were not organised or brave enough yet to embark on an agitation. But the organisation's reputation, resulting from the strike of the labourers in the Atthava dam earlier, had preceded Khemraj. The DFO came to Mathwar to investigate the situation first hand. This proved to be the turning point. The adivasis who had gone for the parley with the DFO came back and related how they had sat on chairs face to face with the DFO and that he had spoken very civilly with them and had even offered them tea and biscuits. They said that the officers higher up were much better, and it was only the staff in Mathwar who were beasts. Word spread that the DFO was coming to Bakhatgarh at the Range Headquarters for the express purpose of listening to the people's problems. Gulab went one step further and declared that the names of all those cultivating nevar would be recorded that day, and those who missed out on this meeting with the DFO would miss being registered for cultivation in the future.

On the appointed day, hundreds of people gathered at Bakhatgarh to press their claims regarding nevar and to complain about the repressive and extortionate behaviour of the local forest department staff. Some of the patels who were against this mobilisation had informed the local MLA, who soon arrived and immediately began berating the people for listening to the bajariya activists and not approaching him with their problems. The people retorted by asking him whether he had been sleeping all this while and whether it wasn't his responsibility to come and see if his electorate was doing all right or not. This altercation seemed to dismiss all hesitation and fear from the minds of the people. All the anger that had welled up through decades of suffering and humiliation burst forth in a mass catharsis as one after another adivasi rose to castigate the forest department staff and relate the sordid history of dispossession and repression of the past decades. The people were especially thrilled at the sight of the forest guards whom they had thought to be the lords of the forest, standing meekly with their hands folded behind their backs, unable to put a word in edgeways.

Nothing concrete came out of the meeting. The DFO announced he could not allow encroachments to continue as it was against the law. At the same time he admitted that the malpractices of the forest guards would be stopped, and no one would be beaten up or forced to pay a bribe. The people then pressurised the MLA to legitimise their nevars, as without them, they could not survive. The MLA gave a weak assurance that he would talk to the Minister of Forests about the problem.

The success of the meeting lay in the resounding departure from the culture of silence that had previously stifled the adivasis' powers of expression in the Mathwar area. This kick started a grassroots-level democratic process. Since people from several villages had come for the meeting, they too saw the power of organisation and realised that Khemraj and Amit were not talking through their hats. The two activists soon started receiving invitations for holding meetings in other villages.

All was not hunky dory however. As was to be expected, the forest department staff did not see these developments with a benevolent eye. They began visiting the villages, threatening people with dire consequences if they attended the meetings or thought of cultivating their nevars during the monsoon season. Regardless of these threats, people in villages such as Attha, Gendra, Mankhara and Mathwar did sow their newar lands when the monsoons arrived. They even formed teams to ensure the forest guards didn't intimidate them. Khemraj stayed on in Gendra, while Amit went to Mathwar to oversee the whole operation.

One day news came in from the village of Gondwani that a team of forest officials had arrested some people and brought them to the Range office in Attha. Khemraj and a few Attha villagers went to the range office to find out more.

No sooner had the unsuspecting Khemraj entered the office than the door was closed behind him and the forest officials began laying about Khemraj with lathis or batons. He was given a thorough lashing, interjected with cigarette burns and told to stop his "netagiri", a pejorative term for people who attempt to organise protests against the establishment. The treatment he had received was an appetiser, he was told. Finally, he was threatened that he would be bumped off if he did not leave the area immediately. They called the adivasis waiting outside who had fearfully heard the screams of Khemraj. The adivasis were told to take him away. Immediately, word was sent to Amit and Khemla.

Amit arrived in the evening, and the next morning, the team of people set out from Gendra with the injured Khemraj carried on an improvised stretcher. They were waylaid by forest officials at Attha. At this point, Khemla miraculously arrived from Umrali with a posse of his own men, armed with bows and arrows. They pushed the officials off the road and escorted the team on its way to Alirajpur. From there, things moved fast. A police complaint was registered against the offending forest officials and news of their attack on Khemraj hit the headlines. The SWRC support network both within and without the government became active. After almost a decade since the demise of the Lal Topi Andolan, a rally was taken out by adivasis in Alirajpur. The forest officials were suspended, and the government ordered an enquiry into the problems of the adivasis of the Mathwar range, to be conducted by the Conservator of Forests, Indore.

This incident and its fallout provided a crucial boost to the organisation process in two important ways. It extended the liberal democratic space and the operation of the rights framework guaranteed in the Indian Constitution to the Mathwar region, which had previously been kept outside its pale, thus putting an effective check on the arbitrariness of the forest and police officials. More importantly, it helped convince the adivasis that the activists were trustworthy and powerful people who could take on the might of the forest and police officials in the fight for their rights.

Once they felt that the leadership of the activists was credible and effective, the adivasis of Alirajpur again began organising to fight for their rights. The late sixties and the early seventies of the last century had seen the emergence of adivasi mass movements in western India, wherein the Bhils protested against their alienation from their resource base and their marginalisation in the modern economy. The Bhoomi Sena in Maharashtra's Thane district and the Shramik Sangathana in the Dhule district of the same state are notable in this respect. The base of the latter was just across the river Narmada from the Mathwar range. So Khemraj, Amit and Khemla, along with some other adivasis, decided to ford the river and climb the hills to meet the leaders of the Sangathana at their office in Shahada.

Upon reaching Shahada, they were lucky to meet the great adivasi leader and poet Vaharu Sonawane. He received them with warmth and greeted them with a raised clenched fist saying "Zindabad". "No more Ram Ram", a traditional greeting of the majority Hindu population invoking the name of their Lord Rama, he said to them, since that was the greeting of the bajariyas and exploiters. The clenched fist was to symbolise the organised power of the adivasis as opposed to the hand-folded in namaskar in which the fingers remained separate.

The greeting implied that the adivasis were going to fight for a respectable life. Recalling the great struggles they had fought against the landed non-adivasis who had not only seized their lands but also made them work as bonded labourers on them, Vaharu, in his inimitable style, danced and sang:

Nakedar ave kukri mange re (The forest guard comes asking for a chicken)

Vaghan vachhra aamu adivasi ra (We adivasis are the children of the tiger)

Hain juni apta ra, hain juni apta ra (Do not bend to the guard's demands anymore)

6 A Paradise Lost

The visit to Shahada proved an exhilarating trip for the activists, and they returned with renewed vigour to pursue their fight for justice in Alirajpur. The first thing they did upon returning was to call a mass meeting and announce that from now on they would greet each other with "Zindabad". Many years later I asked Vaharu why they chose just zindabad instead of the more popular "inquilab zindabad" - long live the revolution, which is what the communists use. Vaharu said that both the Bhoomi Sena and the Shramik Sangathana had begun as reactions to the mode of working of the Communist Party of India led peasant fronts, which did not respect the uniqueness of adivasi lifestyle and culture. These adivasi organisations were suspicious of the relevance of Marxist theory and practice with regard to their own situation, especially when it came to the idea of an armed revolution. As a result, the contentious inquilab or revolution was dropped from the greeting.

When I arrived in Gendra, there was still no formal organisation. Neither was there any hierarchy; just a loose gathering across villages with the activists as the leaders referred to as the "Sangath." The people would donate some amount of money, but there was no system in place for this. When the activists visited the villages and spent the night there to conduct meetings, the villagers fed them. The activists were affiliated to the SWRC, which brought in some meagre funds. Nobody took any salary. The expenses of local travel and food were taken care of, and the non-adivasis were advised to make their own arrangements for fare when going home and get their clothes by begging from somewhere! The adivasi activists, especially Khemla who had a family, were provided with a small stipend. The rule was that the activists should spend the maximum time touring the villages, as this served the dual purpose of reducing the expenses on food and also helped train people better because of increased contact. It was decided that I should live with an adivasi family in Attha to get a hang of the culture and to pick up the language fast. I would work with the family on its farm during the day. In the evening, I would conduct an adult education class for the members of the Sangath.

I went to stay with Avalsingh in Attha. He was a landless peasant, totally dependent on the piece of forestland he had encroached upon. He had a wife, Khetli, and two small children. On the evening I reached their home, they were preparing a gruel by boiling jowar or sorghum flour with the dried flowers of amari, a vegetable, which was called 'phulaan khaata'. The next day, for lunch we had fermented corn soup, which was called "rabri" but had no resemblance whatsoever to the rich non-adivasi sweet dish of the same name. Both khata and rabri saved on the amount of grains to be cooked in comparison to chapattis, or hand-baked bread, at the cost of nutrition. The adivasis had got used to eating this kind of food during the monsoon months, when they are short of cereals and cash and have to borrow from the sahukars and make do until the kharif harvest comes in.

For me, this was too much coming as it did at the end of a day's labour, weeding in the fields. *This is what 'declassing' is all about*, I consoled myself. What made things worse was the fact that Khetli would get up at four in the morning and start grinding the flour at the stone grinding wheel, which let off a monotonous wail right next to my ears, waking me up. Thereafter, I had to stay awake, smelling the stench of the dung and urine of the cattle and goats, which were also tethered inside the hut at night. To complete my rustic initiation, there were bedbugs in the charpai given to me for sleeping. My cup of sorrow was indeed full!

Life was hard for those at Gendra too. There was no electricity and hence no flour-milling machine in Attha. Wheat had to be bought, cleaned and milled in Umrali and brought by bus to Palvi and from there on foot to Gendra. Fifteen kilograms of flour had to be slung across the back in a sack improvised from a bed sheet. Sometimes the flour supply ran out. The only alternative in such situations was to grind maize or jowar flour on the adivasis' hand-operated grinding wheel. Although there were some small shops in Attha and Gendra, they did not stock good provisions, which too had to be brought on foot from the weekly market village at Chhaktala, some thirteen kilometres away. The food had to be cooked on a wooden fire. Lighting a wooden stove is a pain at any time, but during the monsoons when the wood is wet, it becomes an odyssey. Later, when my mother came to know that I could cook maize flour rotis on a wooden chulha and did it regularly, she said that for the first time she had found something for which to respect me!

The vegetable dish to go with these rotis had to be cooked in a round earthen pan called a tavla, which had a lacquered finish on the inside. Despite this, it would absorb some of the oil that was used to cook the dish. Water had to be brought up hill from a stream half a kilometre away in a round earthen vessel perched precariously on the top of one's head. Naturally, it was a precious commodity. So we rarely washed this tavla with water after a meal. Instead, we would wipe it clean with the last of the rotis to relish the concentrated taste of the spices and make it ready for cooking again, absorbed oil and all. The next time we put the tavla on the fire, the heat would make it release the oil it had absorbed earlier and we would singe the cut pieces of onion in this before putting in more oil for frying the rest of the spices, thus saving on oil use as well. After all, cooking oil too had to be lugged from Chhaktala. So unlike the well-heeled given to rolling their tongues around vintage wine, in Gendra we used to freak out on food prepared in vintage cooking oil!

A salvation of sorts came when Amit and I were arrested on the concocted charges of having "raided and ransacked" the forest department Dak Bungalow in Bakhatgarh. This put a halt to my stay in Aval Singh's house. The background story went like this: some forest guards had beaten up and arrested twenty-five villagers. This invariably happens with the onset of monsoons every year when nevar cultivation begins. We had gone to protest against this to the forest range office in Bakhatgarh. The forest officials abused us in the choicest language, and we lodged a complaint with the police regarding the beating up of the villagers and our own abuse. Instead of taking action on our complaint, the police registered a false complaint against us, made by the forest department staff.

Khemraj and Khemla got wind of our arrest and immediately organised a rally, followed by a dharna in Alirajpur. As chance would have it, Jhabua's District Collector knew us because of the episode involving the non payment of minimum wages back when he was the Sub-divisional magistrate in 1983. He got the arrested villagers released on personal bonds and promised not to dispossess those who were already cultivating encroached land.

Soon we took up other issues such as the extortion by the sahukars, the corruption of the rural development functionaries, the human rights violations by the police, and the struggle against the construction of the Sardar Sarovar dam being built on the river Narmada. We did not just engage in 'sangharsh' or struggle, but also in 'nirman' or constructive development. This saw us experimenting with joint forest management, watershed development, primary education in the Bhili language, primary health care through homoeopathy, formation of self help credit groups, running cooperative societies, and conservation of indigenous agricultural seeds and practices. Through a long and laborious process the Sangath was given a formal structure and registered as a trade union 'Khedut Mazdoor Chetna Sangath' (KMCS), Farmers and Labourers Consciousness Union, in 1991. As the fame of the 'Attha Group'(as we were known in activist circles after the village Attha where we were headquartered) spread, so did the number of non-adivasi activists working within it swell. At one time in 1993, eight of us were working in Alirajpur. Within a decade, leading up to 1993, the KMCS had made an impact with its work even at the national level.

I had a considerable amount of modernist hubris in me when I first came to Jhabua, not to speak of my revolutionary zeal to change society for the better. I had thought that my job would be initially to teach the adivasis how to pick up the skills of negotiating the modern economic and political systems. Later I would show them how these systems are tilted against them and the need to drastically change such systems. I had envisaged my ultimate aim to be to convince the adivasis to build up the power of their grassroots mass organisations vis-a-vis the state. Soon, however, the opposite happened, and the easy going worldview of the adivasis got the better of my critical tendencies. I lost my modernist impatience and became a much more casual person, content to let events unfold at their own pace, providing only an occasional push here and there. The years I spent in Jhabua were the best in my life.

Paradoxical as it may seem, the Bhils' worldview is a mix of both the opposing philosophies of stoicism and epicureanism. While in their merrymaking they are quintessential epicureans, in their work and in the fortitude with which they bear their travails, they are first-class stoics. Furthermore, given their propensity to live in small, comparatively egalitarian (except in matters relating to women) social units, closely knit together by customs of resource pooling, they are also the original anarchists.

There used to be a beautiful place in village Jalsindhi on the banks of the Narmada, which the Sardar Sarovar dam reservoir has submerged permanently. During winters, when the rocks on the banks became exposed, a patch would be revealed, in which the rocks were dented in the shape of giant footprints called "Dabaliya." Near these existed a deep, well like depression, and next to it stood a tall slim rock. The adivasis said that this was the place where the Gods once had a great celebration. They had prepared 'ghat', a pounded maize delicacy, by pounding the maize in the well like depression, which was the 'ukhal' or mortar, with the tall slim stone, which was the 'musal' or pestle. Then they had eaten and drunk mahua wine and danced; the dents in the rocks were their footprints. The Narmada used to become like a lake here because there was a deep depression in the riverbed also. So in winter and spring adivasis frequently visited this place to fish in this big lake. They would bring in their boats made from hollowed tree trunks. They also came here to propitiate the Gods. During my travels, I used to make it a point to spend a day in this place once a month, swimming in the lake. I would catch grasshoppers and earthworms to use as bait for the fish, then lay out the fishing lines in the river during the day and cook and eat the fish on wooden fires in the evening. The nights would be especially beautiful, as the adivasis would huddle around the bonfires to sing their lilting songs under the starlit sky to the accompaniment of the 'rantha' or horsehair violin and relate their myths and stories.

An incident related to the grasshopper baits remains indelibly imprinted on my mind - a resplendent picture of paradise captured off guard.

One of the monthly meetings of the central committee of the Sangath was held at this heavenly spot. After a day of swimming and fishing and a lovely dinner, we settled down to the serious business of the Sangath at night. The anti dam struggle was at its peak at the time, and we were having heated discussions on the future strategy. Khemla, excitable as always, rose up in the middle of the meeting and stated that if the government could not provide for the poor adivasis, then they would have no option but to blow up the dam. Before the rest of us could react to this bombastic announcement, Khemla was greeted by a chorus of croaks which refused to abate. When we looked around for the source of this cacophony, we found a bevy of frogs had overturned the bamboo basket in which all the fishing lines had been kept, ready for laying in the river in the morning. The frogs had happily swallowed our grasshopper baits. However, these baits got stuck in their throats, forcing them to issue resounding bugle calls in support of Khemla! The meeting had to be called off as all of us fell to laughing. The adivasis who find prolonged serious cogitations a pain at all times, broke into their traditional song and dance around the bonfires. A paradise that has been lost forever.

Another reason for these years being the best of my life was the happy-go-lucky nature of our group. We realised soon that there was little scope for us to effect any substantive change in the state policies. The most we could do was to facilitate the adivasis' access to the state system and reduce the transaction costs to an extent. As one of our mentors once told us in the initial stages of the anti-dam struggle, "You are two and a half people and yet trying to be so bold as to take on the Indian state and the World Bank at the same time"! Indeed, without the support of well meaning bureaucrats in the early phases, we would not have been able to put together the Sangath at all. For me, initially this was a painful process being steeped as I was in the belief that a radical overthrow of a black anti-people state was essential. However, the realities of working with a set of people who were still in a pre-capitalist mode of economic and cultural production, and the opportunities being offered for economic development and political organisation by the spaces provided by the liberal democratic and in some respects even socialistic and anarchistic Constitution of India, inevitably led me to reconcile myself to the idea of working within it.

In the decade up to the early 1990s, we mostly tasted success in our actions, given the fact that we were working among a people who had been severely deprived of the knowledge and fruits of the most basic economic and social rights, and we had just begun challenging the deeper injustices of state policy. One action I will always remember as one of the best I have ever instituted was a classical leftist "land to the tiller" operation. The former prince of the state of Mathwar who had initially boasted to us that he was the monarch of all he surveyed did in fact have that kind of aura among his tenant adivasi farmers. These poor landless adivasis were scared stiff of him and not only tilled his lands for just one-tenth of the share of the produce, but even did begaar at his palace in Bakhatgarh. I held regular meetings with them, trying to convince them that the times had changed and that they, not the Raja, could easily become the masters of all they surveyed. My perseverance paid off. One day I got all of them together, took them to Alirajpur, and filed for landownership rights under the relevant provisions of the Madhya Pradesh Land Revenue Code. With the help of a pro-active dalit IAS officer who was the then sub-divisional magistrate in Alirajpur we had the Raja of Bakhatgarh eating dust instead of the fruits of the toil of his tenants in no time whatsoever.

Moreover, in the same way as all work and no play makes Jack a dull boy, so also does all ideology and no fun make activists into dogmatic dodos! Living so closely among the adivasis, we could not but imbibe their love for fun and revelry. I used to say fondly that we were like Mac and his gang in the Nobel laureate author John Steinbeck's classic short novel Cannery Row, the only difference being that we were not members of the lumpen proletariat like them but committed social activists.

Life is full of problems and good things never last, especially for those fighting for the poor. Khemraj was married and his activist wife Anita was pregnant when I first met them in Tilonia. Anita had temporarily taken on work at the women's section in SWRC, as it was not possible for her to stay in Gendra with her pregnancy. But once her son began toddling, she came to Alirajpur in 1986. By then, we had built a bigger house in Attha, which was to serve as the office-cum-residence for us. But it was still not big enough to give Khemraj and Anita the privacy they needed. There was also the problem of expenses. Our funds were just not enough to allow Khemraj and Anita to bring up a family of even a simple middle-class standard. So after a while, it became increasingly difficult for Khemraj and Anita to continue in Attha. In the following year, Anita applied for and got a job in Rajasthan as the coordinator of a Government run centre for youth, the Nehru Yuva Kendra and Khemraj left with her to take care of the child. Khemraj was a sad man when he left, but he had to bow to the realities of life in the same way as later Amit and I would have to. In 1989, Amit met and married Jayashree who came to the valley as part of the massive mobilisation of youth from Maharashtra, carried out by the Narmada Bachao Andolan or the Save Narmada Movement in support of the anti-dam struggle. They too faced problems similar to Khemraj and Anita's and had to shuttle between Alirajpur and Delhi for quite some time. They would spend months in Delhi earning money and then come to Alirajpur and work there for some time. Then in 1995, they too had children and had to pull out of Alirajpur altogether. Some of the other non-adivasis activists pulled out for similar reasons and some others because they wanted to pursue other, more paying options, given the dead end to which mass organisational activism was leading at that time.

Shankar also got married in 1989 and had children soon. The non-adivasi activists could pull out of Alirajpur if they wished, but this escape route was not available to the adivasi activists. So we had to sit together and work out some formula for them. It was decided that the adivasi activists would take a stipend big enough to be able to look after the needs of their families and the non-adivasi activists like myself would continue to work without pay as before. If not in the society at large, within our group at least, we were able to implement the communist ideal of "from each according to his capacity and to each according to his needs." This meant an increased need of money for running the show in Alirajpur. Since SWRC was not prepared to foot the entire bill, we had to look for other sources of funds. At this crucial juncture in 1990, Baba Amte added his considerable moral weight to the Narmada Bachao Andolan by setting up residence in the submergence zone in the Narmada valley near Barwani town. He is a very perceptive person and having known activists for a long time, he knew that their main problem was always the lack of funds. He sent word one day that I should go and meet him. When I went to his riverside hut in Kasrawad village, he told me that he wanted to help us from time to time with some funds if we were amenable to this proposition. This was an offer I could hardly refuse.

Then SWRC threw a spanner in the works in 1993 by cutting off our funding altogether. This made the situation desperate; we had to look for new funding sources. Somehow we made ends meet for some time through ad hoc measures. This was when the agency Society for Rural Urban and Tribal Initiative (SRUTI) came to our rescue. SRUTI was already providing a fellowship to Khemla since 1987, but now they made a proposal to fund the organisation as a whole so as to provide it with some stability. SRUTI has played a stellar role by funding many of the adivasi mass organisations in the western Madhya Pradesh region, thereby ensuring that a widespread and sustained challenge in defence of adivasi rights could be mounted against the oppressive policies of the state and international funding agencies in the region.

Finally, much as I would have loved to continue my idyllic existence there, I too had to leave Alirajpur in 1994. I got married in 1993 to my colleague Subhadra Khaperde, who was an activist working with the mass organisation Ekta Parishad in the neighbouring Dhar district. Subhadra insisted that I break with the traditional patriarchal custom and leave my place of work to join her instead of vice-versa. But her colleagues did not like the idea of my joining them and objected to our staying in their area of work. So we had to move to Indore in 1994 to work out our future life and work plans. Things were complicated by the fact that I had become a chronic sufferer of malaria, which relapsed every two months or so. Doctors in Indore told me Jhabua was a malaria endemic area, and I had been deeply infected by the parasite. According to them, the only solution was for me to undergo a complete anti-malarial treatment and abstain from fieldwork for at least a year.

There was something else too. The Adivasi Ekta Parishad (AEP), an organisation of adivasis spanning the four western Indian states of Rajasthan, Gujarat, Madhya Pradesh, and Maharashtra, was formed about this time. The main thrust of the AEP was that the adivasis had had enough of being led by non-adivasi activists in their struggles. In the poetic words of Vaharu Sonowane, who was the co-convener of this new movement:

> We did not sit on the stage
> We were not called to do so
> We were shown our place on the ground
> We were told to sit there
> But they sat on the stage
> And talked about our sorrows
> Our sorrows remained ours
> They never became theirs.

Shankar was influenced by this movement and began demanding that we non-adivasis take a back seat or leave altogether so that he and other adivasi activists of KMCS could work on their own initiative. Fair enough, we said and withdrew.

This led to a new phase of work in my own life. I diversified into working with Bhil women along with my wife, in a new area, which finally culminated in the Bhil rebellion of Mehendikhera in 2001.

7   New Temples for Old

The six-year-old girl sat on her father's shoulder, eating a guava and enjoying herself, thrilled at the activity going on around her. It seemed to herald yet another exciting journey, like the one she regularly took, similarly perched on her father's shoulder, to the weekly market at Dhamtari in Raipur district of what is now Chhattisgarh state. There was something different this time, however, as the whole village of Dargahan was accompanying her in a caravan of bullock carts, laden with their household goods. Sometime before, a fleet of jeeps and trucks had brought government officials to the village, who declared that the gates of a newly built Gangrel dam on the Mahanadi river were being closed. The officials soon left, leaving only the police who stayed behind to ensure compliance.

As compared to many others, this girl Subhadra's family was luckier. Her father, though a "hali" (bonded labourer) in Dargahan, owned a small plot of land in the nearby village of Jepra, which was outside the submergence area. Incidentally, Subhadra's family belonged to the Mahar caste to which the great dalit leader Bhimrao Ambedkar also belonged. There is a curious history behind the Mahars' reaching this place.

The British had transported their Mahar ancestors to the jungles of Chhattisgarh to clear away the land for cultivation to raise revenue from agriculture. The local Gond adivasis of Bastar district, like the Bhils in western India, were averse to settled agriculture and resisted this intrusion. In 1910, the valiant Bhoomkal Revolt of the Gonds was put down with a heavy hand, after some of their own treacherous brethren betrayed the Gonds.

The British instituted a revenue taxation system called malguzari and extended it to the Bastar region. Under this system, revenue was collected from the malguzars, the Chhattisgarhi equivalent of zamindars or revenue agents. By the time of Subhadra's grandfather, it had become impossible to pay the tax by cultivation alone. He consequently had his younger son Devnath, Subhadra's father, employed as a bonded labourer with his brother-in-law, a malguzar. The malguzari system was abolished after independence, but Devnath had to continue working as a bonded labourer to pay off past debts. Although illiterate himself, he had the foresight to get his children educated, which he did by taking advantage of the state subsidised system. His eldest son chose to become a labourer at a young age, while the next one went up to high school and was working as a forest guard at the time of the displacement from Dargahan in 1971. Devnath spent the three thousand rupees, which he got as compensation for his house in the submerged village, on the wedding of this son. It turned out a bad investment since the son chose to live with his in-laws.

Subhadra's frolicking days as a carefree kid came to an end as the reality of the destitution, caused by the displacement, sank in. Their plot in Jepra had been lying fallow all these years. Enormous work had to be put in by the family to re-build the boundaries around the plot to form enclosures that could hold the water required for rice cultivation. In the absence of money to hire help, the children worked after school hours to build the Kharperde farm. This desolation was visible in the whole region, as not only the Khaperdes, but also most other displaced families were suddenly faced with livelihood crises that spelt the doom of the rural wonder that was Chhattisgarh.

The first thing that is bound to strike the eye of an outsider at any village in Chhattisgarh, even today, is the large number of tanks that dot the landscape. At times numbering up to as many as 147, as in the village of Bastar, which was the seat of the princedom of the same name. These tanks used to form the lynchpin of a socio-economic system that was amazingly sustainable in both economical and ecological terms. These tanks fulfilled the varied water-related needs of the village—ranging from drinking and washing to irrigation. The main purpose was the protective irrigation of the staple paddy crop, of which more than 17,000 varieties used to be grown resulting in Chhattisgarh being referred to as a "Dhan Ka Katora" or a bowl of rice.

These tanks and the agricultural system based on them were maintained through an elaborate communitarian culture. The celebration of the Agti festival in April every year used to mark the community expression of this sound ecological sense, distilled from centuries of bonding with Mother Nature. As soon as the festival commenced, the whole village turned out every day, until all the tanks were cleaned up and deepened. Yet another ritual of the festival was the exchange of seeds. All the farmers would pool their seeds in a common place. Thereafter, seeds of different varieties would be exchanged. Farmers from other villages were welcome to come and exchange seeds, too. This exchange supplemented the continuous practice of selection and conservation carried out in the field. In this way, a large genetic diversity was maintained and some part of the harvest always survived, come flood or drought. This community awareness and activity owed its existence to the unique medieval political history of Chhattisgarh.

Historically Chhattisgarh, "Chatar Raj" as it is popularly called, was the region of the upper Mahanadi river valley. A single dynasty—the Haihays—ruled this region from its seat in Ratanpur for nearly eight centuries, between roughly 1000 A.D. and 1757 A.D., when the Marathas overran it. The Haihays organised their rule around thirty six garhs or forts, which gave the region its name, as chhattis means thirty-six in Hindi. Each garh was the centre of administration for a chourasi or unit of eighty-four villages. These chourasis in turn were made up of seven barwahs or units of twelve villages. Each village had a gountiya as its head, who was responsible for revenue collection and general administration. The gountiya's powers, however, were not absolute, circumscribed as they were by the decisions of the gram panchayat or village council.

The Haihays were neither conquering as rulers, nor were they threatened by conquest by others. This minimised their military expenses. They were also not extravagant builders of palaces, monuments and temples like the Rajputs and Mughals. Consequently, the revenue they extracted from farmers was comparatively low. Thus, despite being the lowest rung of a feudal system, the village panchayats had considerable autonomy and could even regulate the trade within their jurisdiction. This naturally gave the farmers a lot of incentives to develop a prosperous farming system. This long period of peaceful rule, devoid of any wars, led to the development of a fairly egalitarian system that was both productive and ecologically sustainable. The demise of this system and the gradual eclipse of rural Chhattisgarh began with the downfall of the Haihays.

The Marathas sounded the first discordant note by substantially hiking the taxes. They ruled from Nagpur in the nearby Vidarbha region and took away all the revenue without spending anything on the region, apart from the bare minimum necessary for administration. In the first quarter of the 19th century, the British conquered this region by defeating the Mararthas. The colonialists promptly began implementing their oppressive system of land revenue maximisation discussed earlier. The Malguzari system of land revenue collection introduced by them effectively circumscribed the independence of the small farmer and also struck at the roots of the vibrant community partnership of the previous era. Most of these Malguzars were non-cultivating upper castes, brought in from north and central India, who had no interest in the development of sustainable farming practices. They were concerned only with the collection of revenue, just like their masters, the British. Moreover, a new trade route was opened up to link the region with the imperial capital in Calcutta. This further hastened the exploitation of the region's rich natural resources. Under the new dispensation, traders and moneylenders prospered at the expense of farmers. So much so, that the traders of Raipur, the capital city, financially supported the British in their fight to suppress the first war of Indian independence in 1857. And the malguzar class provided the imperialists with moral and logistical support.

Independence in 1947 only worsened the condition of the poor farmers. The formal abolition of the malguzari system was not accompanied by any far-reaching land reforms on the ground. The former malguzars became the new rulers and used a variety of stratagems to retain control over most of the land. In the 1960s, green revolution was set rolling in India, with the introduction of high-yielding varieties of rice and heavily irrigated, chemical fertilizer and pesticide based farming. A number of large and medium sized dams were built to improve irrigation facilities to meet the demand for water. Within a few years, a primarily self-sustaining agricultural system was changed into one producing for the national and international markets with external inputs. Traders and rice millers reaped the benefits. The most infamous of these cases was that of the Jain brothers who made millions initially by exporting rice, but later by "diversifying" into smuggling of foreign exchange and laundering of black money. They were subsequently implicated in a criminal case for laundering black money for many prominent political leaders. This exposed a big scandal that shook the political firmament in the 1990s. However, as happens with most such cases, this one too eventually came to a naught for lack of sufficient evidence.

Similar to what happened in the rest of India and especially in Punjab, the green revolution in Chhattisgarh too has only served to impoverish the small farmer in the long run. Today, with decreasing yields, proneness to pest attacks, and increasing costs of overheads such as chemical fertilizers, electricity and pesticides, it has become an albatross around his neck, leading to a virtual epidemic of suicides by farmers laden with debt. A maverick agricultural scientist, Dr. R.H.Riccharia, referred to his own field research to point out that there were indigenous rice varieties in Chhattisgarh, which were far higher yielding and pest-resistant than the foreign hybrids that were being introduced. However, his voice was a lonely and poor one, which got easily drowned out amidst the cacophony of heavy international funding in support of the green revolution. The introduction of profit motive among farmers and the monetisation of the rural economy have dealt a blow to the community spirit. Traditional consensus-based gram panchayats have lost their cohesiveness. The practices of voluntary labour to maintain the village tanks and the exchange of indigenous seeds during the Agti festival have gradually withered away, leading to a decay of the tanks and a serious erosion of genetic diversity.

Nothing is more symbolic of this all-round decay than the pathetic condition of the once thriving village tanks, which used to be the mainstay of the rural economy in the yesteryears. Many tanks have dried up. The few that remain have been subjected to heavier pressure than is healthy for them. Often, humans and animals bathe in the same tank. Pesticide and fertilizer residues, as well as human and animal wastes make their way into the tanks. Most deplorable, however, is the decrease in the protective irrigation potential of the tanks. This decrease has meant that in years of less-than-normal rainfall, crops fail, leading to droughts. One village elder recounted to me, with twinkling eyes, how in the summers of their childhood and youth they would go in teams from one tank to another, cleaning them of silt, while singing songs merrily. The operation had a festive atmosphere, and the youth looked forward to it. He lamented that the present day younter generation had become lazy and spent their time playing cricket in the dried up tanks, "Aaj kal ke korhiya laika man sukkha tariya me kirket khelthe"!

Industrial development only added to the woes of the bucolic Chhattisgarhis. It all started with the setting up of the Bhilai Steel Plant by the government in the 1950s. This was followed in quick succession by various other projects such as aluminium extraction plants, thermal power stations, cement plants and big-scale mining of iron ore, bauxite, coal, and limestone to provide raw materials. All this involved displacement of rural people without commensurate increase in employment for them. The operation and management of these industrial plants and mines required relatively high skilled people who had to be brought in from outside. The local Chhattisgarhis, especially the adivasis, either got low paid casual employment, or were left out totally from this process. Apart from these basic industries, there was little downstream industrialisation to utilise the products of these industries. Instead, the steel, aluminium, coal, cement and power were exported to Bhopal, Indore, Kolkata, and Mumbai for further processing. The iron-ore mined from Bailadila in south Bastar is not even converted into steel, but is shipped raw to Japan without processing. The region witnessed a stunted industrial growth without any significant forward and backward linkages that could create employment opportunities for a large number of people.

Prime Minister Jawaharlal Nehru was a great proponent of planned industrial development. While inaugurating the first chemical fertilizer plant of the country in 1954 in Sindri, Bihar, he hailed it as a temple of modern India and went on to say that India needed many more such temples. The first and most important such modern temple in Chhattisgarh was the Bhilai Steel Plant. To meet the plant's and its colony's huge water requirements, which, after some time, could not be met from local sources in Durg district anymore, another temple had to be built—the Gangrel dam on the Mahanadi river in Raipur district. India has a long history of religions competing with each other to build places of worship. Rulers have often taken part in such projects with gusto, producing some of the most breathtaking architecture of the world by using the surplus extracted from the toiling poor. There are also many instances of the kings of one religion destroying the existing places of worship of another religion, replacing them with their own temples, mosques or churches. In a way, Nehru's modern temple building, too, has followed this timeworn retrograde tradition.

The submergence zone of the Gangrel dam had been a highly productive and self-sustaining agricultural region, centred around the weekly market village of Chavar. The people of the region got the fascinating and addictive taste of the modern market economy for the first time when the dam's construction began. The people were initially very happy because they could sell their rice to the labourers and officers of the construction company at prices higher than the rates in the local markets at Chavar or even in Dhamtari. They could also buy novel consumer products that became available on the demand of the urban officers and the staff of the construction company. Thus, money began to play a much more important role than before. People were elated, oblivious of the fact that one day they would lose all their land. When the end came, most people were devastated as they spent the little monetary compensation they had received in the consumption of various things, primarily liquor. They even lost their sources of livelihood. A temple dedicated to the local goddess Angar Moti, literally meaning the ember pearl, stood in Chavar. The goddess was believed to be very powerful and capable of fulfilling the wishes of her devotees. People used to flock the site from far and wide to worship her and ask her for boons. However, this rural goddess too lost out to the new god of modern development. Her temple, along with her devotees, was sacrificed at the altar of this new god. Old Hindu superstition dictated that unless human sacrifice was made to the god at the time of erecting a new temple, it could not become functional. Nehru had no compunction in demanding and getting similar sacrifices from thousands of people for his own temple-building spree.

The rural people in Chhattisgarh have found a way out of the havoc caused by the lopsided and destructive development by either resorting to making bidis, or handmade cigarettes, or by migrating to other states in search of employment. In their search for work, they sometimes travel far and wide. In 1999, some Chhattisgarhi labourers were killed by armed separatists in the insurgency-ridden northern state of Kashmir.

Bidis are made by rolling tobacco inside leaves of tendu tree and tying them with string. This is a widespread cottage industry, operated through a system of putting out, whereby makers, mostly women, are supplied with the tendu leaves, tobacco, and strings by contractors. The women get paid by piece rate for the bidis they make. During the summer season, the rural poor also collect the tendu leaves on a piece rate basis. The bidi makers are totally at the mercy of agents who act as middlemen on behalf of the bidi factory and supply the raw materials to the makers, collect the finished bidis and make the payment. Despite this exploitation, the money earned from making bidis is much higher than the daily wages that come off agricultural labour.

Usually, exchanging old things for new items is a profitable exercise, which leads to greater productivity and happiness. But it's been another story altogether in the case of poor rural Chhattisgarhis. Chhattisgarhis, especially the region's adivasis, have suffered displacement and loss of livelihoods on a gargantuan scale. Expectedly, people here have not readily swallowed Nehru's exhortation to "suffer in the interest of the country". Countless clashes have taken place between the people and the state over the ill effects of this perverse temple building, in which both industrial workers and peasant masses have been ruthlessly crushed. Bastar itself has witnessed a large number of such atrocities, the most gruesome being the murder of the king of Bastar, Pravir Chandra Bhanjdeo, and his adivasi supporters. In 1966, they were killed in the king's palace in Jagdalpur by the police in what is one of the worst cases of callous extra-judicial mass killing of adivasis by the independent Indian state.

The adivasis of Bastar had been subjected to a raw deal ever since the suppression of the Bhoomkal rebellion in 1910. This increased with the vast influx of non-adivasis into the region for various developmental activities. This influx took place mainly due to the resettlement of Bengali refugees from the erstwhile East Pakistan after independence and the initiation of the iron-ore mining project in Bailadila. The king of Bastar, Prabir Chandra Bhanjdeo, was opposed to the new government that came into being in 1947 and organised the adivasis against the state, especially since the local Congress party was dominated by non-adivasi "outsiders." Disregarding the government's warnings, he set up a parallel administration in the area through his Adivasi Seva Dal. When the government threatened to deprive him of the privy purse being given to him for abdicating his princely rule, he responded by saying that in that case the adivasis under his leadership would derecognize the Madhya Pradesh government!

In February 1961, Bhanjdeo was arrested under preventive detention provisions and sent to jail. Immediately, the Adivasi Seva Dal launched an agitation for his release and began chasing traders away from the weekly markets, leading to a confrontation with the police. On March 31st 1961, a major conflict broke out in the market village of Lohandiguda, killing thirteen people in unwarranted police firing. Scores of others were arrested and indicted for armed rioting and attempt to murder. The Lohandiguda incident was to set the ball rolling for the final tragic act of rebellion of the adivasis of Bastar in the 1960s, before they began to mobilise two decades later under the leadership of the Naxalites.

Bhanjdeo was released from jail in April in 1961. He got a rousing reception on his arrival in Jagdalpur. Thereafter, he became even more strident in his demand for justice for the adivasis, especially with regard to formalising action against the officials responsible for the Lohandiguda massacre. In the 1962 general elections, six members of his organisation were elected as MLAs and one as the only MP from Bastar. They completely routed the Congress party. This was a time when the whole country was going through a food crisis due to successive failure of monsoons. In Bastar too, the price of rice, the staple crop, had begun to increase. The adivasis, led by Bhanjdeo, began an agitation demanding rice at subsidised prices. Their protests intensified as the situation deteriorated from year to year. The central government had to import grains to tide over the crisis, which had assumed nationwide proportions. However, since the distribution of these food grains was a time-consuming process and a backward and huge state like Madhya Pradesh faced severe logistical problems, in early 1966, the state government imposed a levy of rice on the cultivators with the intention of trying to procure as much as possible at the local level within the districts and obviate the need for allotments from the central government, which were hard to come by.

The adivasis of Bastar, who were already in a tight situation, found this unjust. A massive movement started for the repeal of this levy and Bhanjdeo himself launched into a prolonged fast in February 1966. In the villages and markets, people refused to give the levy and fought with the police to prevent its procurement. A remarkable fact about this struggle was the tremendous participation of women in the mass actions. There were innumerable rallies and demonstrations throughout the district against this unfair order. The government, instead of agreeing to the legitimate demands of the people, brought in additional police forces with the intent of crushing the agitation. The scene for a tragic end to a militant mass movement of Bastar's adivasis was thus set up. On March 25, 1966, a massive rally was planned in Jagdalpur and the people began collecting on the palace grounds, armed with bows and arrows. They clearly disregarded the prohibitory orders against public assembly clamped by the administration. The inevitable skirmish, given the tinderbox situation, started between the adivasis and the police in the afternoon and as in the case of Lohandiguda, it ended with the massacre of twelve people, including the king, in the police firing.

The devastation of nature and the decimation of populations living in harmony with it has been a singular feature of modern industrial development. This process began after Europeans began subordinating the peoples of the other four continents to facilitate their own industrial development through colonial plunder. This retrograde process of unsustainable exploitation of natural and human resources started with the landing of Christopher Columbus in the Bahamas in the West Indies in 1492; so it can be said to have been set in motion with this "Columbian Encounter." Indeed this trade-off between nature and the working masses on one side and industrial development on the other is such a fundamental feature of centralised modern industrial development that it is almost inevitable, whether the economy is capitalist or socialist in nature. The horrifying Gulag Archipelago of labour concentration camps and pollution of rivers and lakes in the Soviet Union was necessitated by the need for it to catch up with the development achieved by the Americans. America had itself created a few lesser Gulags of its own at about the same time to become an industrial power. John Steinbeck portrayed this poignantly in his novel "The Grapes of Wrath". The wholesale rape of Latin America, which still continues, provided the main resources for American industrial development. The British refined this process into an art in India. It is estimated that the Indian tribute contributed between twenty-five to thirty-three percent of the British gross domestic capital formation in the crucial four decades from 1765 to 1804, when the industrial revolution was getting off the blocks in England. Nehru and his technologists and administrators took it up from where the British left off and kicked off a process of internal colonialism to finance lopsided modern development.

Devnath and his wife were hard-working, which helped them recover from the body blow of involuntary displacement. They worked on their land and made it productive again. This, despite the fact that the increasing spread of mill-made synthetic cloth had put paid to the supplementary source of livelihood that Devnath earned off weaving. Relief was momentary, however.

Things went awry once again when at 13, Subhadra lost her mother to heart attack. Her mother was a strict disciplinarian and was feared by her children and even her husband. Her efficient running of the household was the main reason behind the family's swift recovery. Her death led to a new set of problems. Subhadra's eldest brother, who had been living separately all these years owing to a dislike of his mother's disciplining, came back and demanded his share of land and the house. Disregarding his father's obligation to bring up and marry off his youngest brother and sister, he beat up Devnath and forced him to accede to his demands.

All the household responsibilities now fell on Subhadra. She had to cook, wash utensils, wipe the mud floor with cow dung, and also help with the agricultural work. All this had to be managed on a smaller income than before. Even though her father helped with the housework, this sudden increase in workload ate into Subhadra's study time. As a result, she failed in her class eight examinations that year. Devnath, however, insisted that she continue with her studies because this, he felt, was the only lifeline that could bring them out of the sea of troubles in which they were immersed. However, the fact remained that after doing the entire household and field work, Subhadra hardly had any time to study. The government school system in India is such that it is possible to pass examinations the easy way—learning by rote and a clandestine helping hand from teachers. So in 1986, Subhadra managed to scrape through her higher secondary board examinations and joined the increasing force of educated unemployed Chhattisgarhi youth.

Subhadra's elder brother had secured a job immediately after passing out of school in the 1970s. What made this possible were the still expanding state system and the provision for reservations in government jobs. The need for educated dalit and adivasi people far exceeded the supply. However, by the time Subhadra entered the job market in the late 1980s, the structural adjustment policies of the International Monetary Fund (IMF) were in place as the Indian government had taken a loan to tide over a payments crisis. This initiated the reverse process of withdrawal of the state from direct participation in the social and economic spheres, which was a mandatory condition imposed by the IMF for advancing loans to governments. This limited government job opportunities, even as a rising number of applicants came out of schools. Subhadra's future looked bleak.

8 Gandhism as the last resort of the Hapless

By the time Subhadra completed her education in the late 1970s, things were changing, and it was no longer easy to get a government job without paying hefty bribes. Her sister was married to a wife-beating husband, and this discouraged Subhadra from getting married.

Subhadra, like many others in her village, took up the job of rolling bidis to earn money. The single harvest, which the land yielded, was just enough to provide food. One still needed money to provide for other needs such as clothes and travel. Subhadra's elder brother didn't have any steady employment. Even when he was employed, he did not contribute any money to the household. One day they had an altercation about bearing the household expenses equally. It ended with the brother slapping Subhadra. This was too much for her. She packed a few clothes and immediately left for Kodogaon village, some ten kilometres away, where her cousins stayed. She left without informing anyone at home. Once at her cousins', she did not tell anyone her reasons for coming. She just began working in their fields and staying with them. And of course, she continued to roll bidis. After some time, her father arrived there and pleaded with her to come back. But she refused, saying that she would not come back to the house until she had begun earning money independently.

A chance meeting with a Gandhian activist in Kodogaon was to lead Subhadra to work with a Gandhian NGO, Prayog, in Raipur district. Even though she did not fully understand what it was all about, the promise of a regular job that would pay her two hundred rupees a month gave her good reason to join the training.

Unlike Nehru, Gandhi was inspired by the Indian spiritual tradition embodied in the Bhagvad Gita, as well as western spiritualist traditions notably "Unto This Last" by John Ruskin and "The Kingdom of God is within You" by Leo Tolstoy. Inspired by an evangelical interpretation of Christianity, Ruskin's thought had led him to become a critic of industrial development, which, according to him, had to be jettisoned as it clashed with nature as well as human welfare.

His book "Unto This Last" gets its name from a parable in the Bible in which labourers are put to work throughout the day as and when there is an opportunity for them to be employed. At the end of the day, all are paid the same wage. When some of the workers who had been working from the beginning protest, it is argued that the last of the workers was prepared to work the whole day and it was not his fault that he got an opportunity only at the end, and so he too deserved the same wage. This is close to Marx's formulation of communism, but while Marx called for a violent overthrow of the capitalist system, Ruskin believed in spiritual conversion of the unbelievers.

In his book written after his conversion to Christianity, Tolstoy deplores the violence that is rampant in society because of the greed of human beings. He makes an impassioned plea, with an eloquence that only such a great writer could have displayed, that the way out of the sea of troubles in which human beings find themselves is to become completely non-violent.

Gandhi's ideas about development, society and politics were first conceived in his book "Hind Swaraj", written after his debates with various people in England in 1909. The main points of contention were rural versus urban industrial development and non-violent versus violent means of political action. Hailed as the "Sarvodaya Manifesto", this work critiques modern industrialism for the prominence it has given to greed, making human beings slaves of machines. It also inveighs against the resultant change in the education imparted, which has turned students away from sustainable occupations and trained them for professions based on greed. At the socio-political level, this has resulted in a centralised system of governance to facilitate the exploitation of human beings and nature. This system is democratic and participative only on paper; in reality it is controlled by powerful classes.

The book proposes an economic alternative, based mainly on rural industries, especially the charkha or spinning wheel and handlooms, to produce khadi or hand-spun and woven cloth. This, Gandhi felt, would gainfully employ labour and a minimum of modern industries. He envisaged a socio-political alternative based on participative and largely self-sufficient and autonomous village republics or panchayats in which sarvodaya or the well being of all would be possible. A political programme based on non-violence was proposed for achieving this. Gandhi argued that a truly just society has to be non-violent and to achieve that, the means employed must be non-violent, too. Civil disobedience and passive resistance, relying on spiritual power instead of arms are suggested as the modes of action and given the name "Satyagraha" or truthful pleading. Gandhi postulates that the aim of a satyagrahi or passive resister should be to bear repression passively so as to impress on the oppressor the immorality of his deeds and thereby win his heart over. According to him, an important part of the satyagrahi's programme is to resist unjust laws through civil disobedience or non-cooperation.

The adoption of a nationwide Sarvodayi programme of action after independence would have meant micro planning from the village or even hamlet upwards contributing to the macro planning of the country as a whole. Gandhi called this an Oceanic Circle to counter the image of a pyramid, which top-down planning conveys. In an ocean, water moves out in waves from an epicentre, which is the most powerful. So also the village republic was projected as the most powerful entity in Gandhian social dynamics.

Under the leadership of Jawaharlal Nehru, the majority of Congress members did not pay any heed to this proposal and went on to build further on the centralised state apparatus bequeathed by the British. It was only those who had already been engaged in rural reconstruction work in the many ashrams or retreats set up by Gandhi that continued to work on Gandhian principles, under the leadership of Vinoba Bhave. At his suggestion, a central body was formed in 1949 to coordinate the activities of all the Gandhian institutions. The body came to be known as "Sarva Seva Sangh" or the organisation for service to all. In an effort to get some legitimacy for his developmental efforts from the Gandhians, in 1951, Nehru sent a member of the Planning Commission to Vinoba Bhave with a draft of the First Five Year National Development Plan. After reading the draft, Vinoba reportedly said, "I have found only one useful thing in this bulky document. It is the pin holding it together. So I am taking out that useful thing and consigning the rest to the waste paper basket!"

One such rural reconstruction organisation was the Gandhi Ashram set up by S.N. Subbarao in Morena district in Northern Madhya Pradesh. Subbaraoji had launched a national youth project, which saw him touring across the country to hold camps for motivating the youth to take part in rural reconstruction work. The man behind Prayog, P. V. Rajagopal, popularly known as Rajaji, hailing from an upper middle class family in Kerala had joined Subbaraoji's Ashram in Morena. Later, he went on to set up the NGO Prayog in Tilda in Chhattisgarh, which was then eastern Madhya Pradesh. Initially Prayog was involved in the standard Gandhian rural development work, producing khadi textile and other handicrafts with grants and marketing support from the Khadi and Village Industries Commission (KVIC), a support organisation within the government, set up by Nehru to aid the Gandhian organisations in expiation for his sin of renouncing Gandhi's philosophy of development.

During the course of his activities, one day Rajaji discovered to his horror the existence of bonded labourers called kamiyas. Such labour had been legally abolished in 1947. Finding the district administration loathe to even recognize the problem, he filed a petition in the Supreme Court. After hearing all the parties, the Supreme Court took the Raipur district administration to task for having neglected its basic duties. The apex court directed that not only were the labourers to be freed, but that they also had to be rehabilitated with new occupations.

Such was the impact of this action that many more such cases came to light and a veritable movement, of freeing bonded labourers in agriculture and stone quarries, was set in motion. This experience made a profound impact on Rajaji and reinforced in him the need for political mobilisation to free the poor from oppression. He realised that rural development work alone would not do without mobilising the masses against exploitative economic and social relations. This required the participation of numerous village level animators who had to be trained in the Gandhian theory and programme of social and political action for the amelioration of exploitation and poverty. This was the genesis of the training programmes conducted by Prayog. There was also another side to the training. Bonded labourers who had been freed had to be rehabilitated and their families and children taken care of. So a Grameen Vikas Pratishthan or a village development institute was set up to provide training in alternative income-generating skills. The village animators were imparted training in running anganwadis or childcare centres.

After undergoing this three-month training, Subhadra and nineteen other young women were sent off to work in the villages of Saraipali Tehsil on the border with Orissa to work as village animators and also as anganwadi workers. While boarding the bus in Raipur they paid some coolies to put their iron trunks on the roof of the bus. But when they reached Saraipali, they found there were no coolies around. Since all of them were wearing saris, they felt uncomfortable about climbing up. This caused some tension as the bus conductor shouted at them to hurry up. Subhadra decided to throw all shame to the winds. Tying the pallu of her sari firmly around her waist, she climbed up to the roof of the bus and began handing down the trunks to the other women who had climbed up half the way. This was an enticing spectacle for the men at the bus stand, and they all gathered to gawk and pass vile comments. What surprised the men even more was the sight of the women putting the trunks on their heads and walking towards the village they had to stay in for a day or two before fanning out to their appointed villages. As they walked, they sang songs. Chhattisgarh had a tradition of travelling entertainers or damchaghas who went from village to village displaying their acrobatic, dancing and singing skills. Villagers welcomed them warmly as they were in high demand as entertainers in rural areas. The advent of television put paid to their art. Now, as the women seemed to echo that tradition with their singing, the village children began following them, shouting and singing along with them, mistaking them for damchaghas!

When they reached the village the headman showed them their halting place for the night—a hall adjacent to a temple of the Goddess Kali. Instead of a proper dinner, the villagers gave them popped rice and fried groundnuts to eat. In the middle of the night Subhadra woke up to a commotion. Apparently, a woman had been possessed by the spirit of Goddess Kali. She was swaying her head and singing songs in a trance. The other women poured water on her and made her smell cow dung smoke to abate her trance. This continued until dawn, when the woman finally came out of her trance and fell asleep. The next day, Subhadra left with her trunk on her head to the village of Bagaijor, where she was supposed to stay.

Her job was to run an anganwadi centre for small children, play with them, prepare some light breakfast and feed them. She also had to hold meetings in the nearby villages with the adivasis and find out cases of bonded labourers so as to be able to free them. She carried out the first task with aplomb. The adivasis were so poor that they happily sent their children to the anganwadis for the breakfast. The games and songs too were attractive to the children so they would turn up in large numbers. However, when it came to identifying bonded labourers, Subhadra hit a roadblock.

Ignorant of Rajaji's successful crusade, they were in no mood to rebel.

In the afternoons, Subhadra had to go out to the nearby villages to hold meetings and read out news from the monthly magazine published for the purpose called "Gaon Mitaan". The magazine carried details of Prayog's activities. The usual practice was to gather the children and make them play games and sing and dance. She became so popular with the children that whenever she entered a village, children would gather around her shouting "Mitaan awat he, Mitaan awat he" - Mitaan is coming, Mitaan is coming. While the children stayed with her to play, the elders drifted away when she tried to talk to them on the issues covered by the magazine. Back in those days in the late 1980s, there were no panchayats or elected village bodies. In the absence of grassroots democracy, the village elders held sway. These elders were both sceptical and suspicious of this bevy of young women who had suddenly descended on them with "unfavourable" winds of change.

Subhadra and her comrades were working on a salary of just two hundred rupees a month. She used to eat a heavy breakfast with the children; her next meal would only be in the evening after she returned from her tour of the villages. She did this to save on both time and money. Whenever possible, she ate even dinner at some villager's house! All the other young women too followed a similar routine. Once every week, they would gather in the central village where they had spent their first night. They came here to collect their rations which were distributed there. During one such gathering they woke up in the morning to find that a dog had eaten some amount of the jaggery they had bought the day before. Jaggery was an essential ingredient for making tea. They had no money left to buy some more. So the women deliberated that since the jaggery was to be used in tea, any germs left in it by the dog would be destroyed on boiling the jaggery while making tea. In the absence of an alternative (they did not have any money left to buy fresh jaggery), the women decided to use it. On hearing this one of the landlords commented, "Kutta ka prasad khake tuman ka samaj seva karbe" – "What social work will you do after eating the leftovers of a dog!"

Subhadra's sojourn in Saraipali was short lived; she had to leave soon. The Central Social Welfare Board of the Government of India, which had been funding the team of women of which Subhadra was a part, stopped the funds after one year. So the women had to pack their trunks, put them on their heads, and once again wend their way back to Tilda. There, most of the others were told to return home, but Subhadra and some others were asked to proceed to Durg district, where fresh work was getting underway.

After Vinoba's rejection of the draft Planning Commission's Development Plan, Nehru invited him for talks in Delhi. Vinobha responded to this by undertaking a padyatra, a march on foot, talking to the rural poor on the way. The talks with the Planning Commission failed, but this resulted in the launch of a new programme by Vinoba - thereafter he unrelentingly walked for more than thirteen years, until 1964.

Early on in the course of this walk he was confronted with the acute problem of concentration of agricultural land in the hands of a few. This was the main obstacle to rural development. Although land reform legislation had been enacted, it wasn't being implemented on the ground because of the power of the landed classes in the rural milieu. Vinoba felt that unless the landless masses were given the title to land, all talk of rural reconstruction would remain just that. He began mulling over a non-violent means to solve this intractable problem.

On April 18, 1951, he entered Pochampalli village in Nalgonda district of Andhra Pradesh. This village had been one of the nerve centres of the Communist Party of India-led Telengana uprising against landlords. The movement had just been quelled by severe police action. The dalits in the village came to him and said that they required only two acres of land per family, one dry and one irrigated, to break out of their poverty. Vinoba held a meeting with the upper caste members of the village and asked them what could be the solution to this demand of the dalits. One of the landlords who was sitting with Vinoba suddenly got up and said that he would donate a hundred acres of his land for this purpose. Thus began a veritable movement of land donation by landlords. Vinoba cited the first example to appeal to the hearts of the landed gentry, asking them to donate land for the landless. This was the genesis of the Bhoodan or land donation movement, which thereafter became the mainstay of Vinoba's long march.

The immediate post-independence period saw many stalwarts of the freedom movement opt out of mainstream politics to pursue Gandhi's vision of the establishment of Gram Swaraj or village self rule. The most notable among these was Jayaprakash

Narayan, who had started off as a communist and then became a socialist, before he finally converted to Gandhism to become a committed Sarvodayi in 1954. Thereafter, he devoted himself to Vinoba's Bhoodan movement. A vibrant spirit marked the work of the Sarva Seva Sangh, and it attracted many young men and women to its fold to work as village animators. Many years later Subhadra and I met one such worker, who served as the caretaker of the ashram or Gandhian rural development retreat in Machla in Indore. Radheshyam Bohre, then in his late fifties, spoke with a sparkle in his eyes about the first decade and a half of work he had put in as a village animator of the Gandhi Smarak Nidhi or Gandhi Memorial Fund. The high point of his working life was accompanying Vinoba Bhave on the Bhoodan Yatra in the Malwa region in the 1960s.

The Bhoodan movement and the larger Gandhian programme, exemplary as they were, could not realise even a small bit of their potential. This was because they were gradually pushed more and more to the periphery of the centralised parliamentary system, which stressed on the concentration of resources for modern industrial development. So the leaders and workers in the Gandhian organisations began losing their effectiveness after some time. The slide began immediately after the Bhoodan Yatra was over. According to Bohre, most of the lands that were announced as donated were never really redistributed, and the owners continued to retain control over them. The various sarvodayi organisations began losing their urge for grassroots mobilisation; instead they concentrated on producing and selling handicrafts and khadi or handspun and woven cloth with the subsidies and grants provided by the Khadi and Village Industries Commission (KVIC). Field workers like him were not only looked down upon, but also discouraged from going out into the field. He said that in the late 1950s and early 1960s he had been offered government jobs as a teacher and patwari or land record official on a number of occasions. Every time, he rejected these offers because he felt he had a mission to accomplish. But once the euphoria of the Bhoodan Yatra subsided, he found that grassroots mobilisation work was at a discount. Not only had the leaders of the Sarvodaya movement in Madhya Pradesh become disinterested to bring in fresh blood in the form of committed youth, but they even directed their own children into the mainstream job market to earn a good living.

The rot that had set in was deep. Things came to a head when in 1974, Jayaprakash Narayan launched his Sampoorna Kranti Andolan in Bihar. This was a vintage mass Gandhian mobilisation against the state to challenge the Indian National Congress party head on. There was a split down the middle within the Sarvodaya movement with some people supporting Narayan and most others, headed by Vinoba, against him. At that time, Vinoba had assumed a "maun vrat" and had stopped speaking. He declined Indira Gandhi's appeal to prevail upon Narayan. The leaders of the Gandhi Smarak Nidhi in Madhya Pradesh too decided to go against Jayaprakash Narayan.

Disillusioned with all this, Bohre resigned from the Gandhi Smarak Nidhi. In 1975, even before the government declared an internal emergency and curtailed civic rights for suppressing the movement, he went back to his ancestral land in Khategaon village to live the life of an ordinary farmer. He said he could have returned to his area of work and gone to jail but felt it was useless, as society had drifted far off the Gandhian dream and Narayan's final attempt to improve things would not succeed. Only after the lifting of emergency did he return to Machla on the request of Mahendrabhai, the coordinator of the Gandhian NGO that was in charge of the ashram. A sea change had taken place in the meanwhile; the ashram at Machla was no longer the hotbed of youthful activists with a desire for social change.

The bright young people had all left, some going abroad. The cooperative land movement that had once been so strong had fallen flat and the land distributed among the farmers was now tilled by the new owners. The ashram found it difficult to get students as well as trainers. This led to the abandoning of its training programmes. All work had stopped and its empty buildings were mute witnesses to the marginalisation of Gandhian thought and practice in independent India.

This is why the revival of the Sarvodaya movement in Madhya Pradesh, brought about by Rajaji, was a ray of hope for ageing Gandhians. Hundreds of young animators whom he had trained, including a whole host of women like Subhadra, were fanning out all over rural Madhya Pradesh, creating a new movement for rural reconstruction and empowerment. These youth had no idea of doing social work of any kind. They only learnt about such work during the training programme. The consequences were sometimes comical as we have seen and sometimes tragic since there was little security for the young women when they stayed alone in the villages. There were a few instances of the women being raped. Nevertheless, these young people did make an impact in the initial years, and the lethargic administration had to sit up and take notice of the issues raised by the young crusaders.

Bohre said that he felt like the caretaker of a graveyard, yet had agreed to become one because it reminded him of the early years of promise when things had seemed so rosy. He lamented that while in his own youth Gandhian work was greatly sought after and many youth would give up lucrative career prospects to join the Sarvodaya movement, now only those who had no other employment option chose to follow Gandhi's path (like Subhadra had done). "Majboori ka naam Gandhi hai", he said. *Gandhism is the last resort of the hapless.*

9 Mother Chhattisgarh is Calling

In 1989, Subhadra took up residence in the house of a Gond adivasi in Gotitola, an interior village in the Lohara block of Durg district of Chhattisgarh. She was one of four women activists who were there to mobilise the locals to stand up for their rights. The people, however, were chary of fighting for their rights and the women activists came up against a wall of apathy.

In time Subhadra understood the cause for such apathy. It wasn't as if the people were not aware of their rights. They were just not convinced that these young women, working alone in four different villages and trudging through the jungles, would be able to provide the kind of leadership required to stand up to their oppressors. In a way, it was the same credibility issue that a more seasoned activist like Khemraj had faced earlier.

Subhadra's village was about ten kilometres away from the town of Dalli, which was the nerve centre of the Chhattisgarh Mukti Morcha (CMM). The CMM had by then completed more than a decade of struggle and acquired a legendary status in the field of alternative social movements in India. Subhadra began attending the programmes of this organisation so as to learn more about the techniques of mass organisation and also to gain inspiration from its success. The Morcha had been tempered in its long struggle, waged since the late 1970s for the rights of adivasi contract labourers at the Dalli Rajhara captive mines of the Bhilai Steel Plant.

The unique feature of this struggle was that it broke out of the narrow confines of standard trade unionism and encompassed the whole lives of its members. Campaigns were carried out against the two most debilitating problems that beset poor labourers in India—alcoholism and debt bondage to usurious moneylenders. To alleviate these problems, women were mobilised to stop the brewing and selling of liquor and to form micro-credit groups. The outfit also began addressing the problems of patriarchal oppression. A hospital was set up with member contributions. Apart from providing treatment, the hospital also developed a community health programme to increase health awareness. On the cultural front, research was conducted to unearth instances of people's struggles in the history of Chhattisgarh that had been glossed over by the mainstream historians. New literature, in the form of songs and plays, was created and disseminated through repertory troupes to project a positive image of Chhattisgarh that could stand up to the modern urban culture propagated through the mainstream media. Inspired by its leader Shankar Guha Niyogi, the Morcha , began to fan out among the nearby villages as well as in the ancillary industrial units in and around Bhilai since the late 1980s.

The Morcha had been formed in 1982 against the backdrop of a misdirected and anti-people development and governance that had laid waste the native resources, both natural and human. The Morcha worked out a four-pronged strategy that incorporated getting environmental laws implemented; reviving traditional community and agricultural activities, including getting a better deal for farmers from corrupt traders; opposing corruption of the local bureaucracy; and declaring an ideological and cultural onslaught against modern development. The ideology of modern development had such a domineering impact on the masses that it was difficult to initiate mass action to challenge it.

Realising the importance of a comprehensive resistance against a well organised modern state, Niyogi formed a broader front with similar people's movements already underway in Madhya Pradesh. The Narmada Bachao Andolan and the Ekta Parishad, a mass organisation of adivasis and peasants, formed under Rajaji's initiative, were in full flow at the time. The Khedut Mazdoor Chetna Sangath in Alirajpur and the Kisan Adivasi Sangathan in Hoshangabad were two adivasi mass organisations that had established themselves as forces to reckon with. The mood was very upbeat among all these organisations, and together they did hold promise of better things to come at that point of time. This process of alternative mass movements had been set in motion earlier by the mobilisation against the Bhopal Gas Tragedy in 1984.

1989 is a watershed year in the history of the environmental mass movements in India. On September 28 that year, the first ever national rally and mass meeting against destructive development was held in the small town of Harsud in Madhya Pradesh. Thousands of people attended this rally, which ended with the resolve to launch a nationwide mass movement centred development and governance. The next day, an even bigger mobilisation was witnessed in Raipur under the aegis of the

Chhattisgarh Mukti Morcha. This one called for the establishment of a dream Chhattisgarh state, which would secure the interests of its poor citizens. The CMM's struggles had served to strengthen the organisation's basic understanding that just the creation of a separate state of Chhattisgarh without a radical change in the form of development and governance was not going to bring about an improvement in the lives of most of the people. Given the prevalence of a mass consumerist culture popularised by television that had enamoured both urban middle and lower classes, the environmentalist challenge perforce had to be mounted in rural areas. The peasants and not the industrial workers would have to be the vanguard of the environmentalist mass movements.

The Morcha had consequently intensified its participation in the politics of the village panchayats so as to strike at centralisation from below. These panchayats have lost their traditional character and have become a microcosm of the larger political arena that is beset by corruption. Present day panchayats act as nurseries for breeding cadres for the mainstream political parties. As a preliminary step in its battle against the present over-centralised system, the Morcha had begun a process of reversing this trend by reinvigorating the traditional consensus-based panchayat.

Kautilya, famous in Indian history as the political advisor to the first pan-Indian emperor, Chandragupta Maurya, had suggested to the young emperor that it was foolish to plunge one's hand into the centre of a bowl of hot rice and that he should instead pick the cooler grains on the side first. Centuries later, the Morcha followed a similar strategy and reaped rich dividends, as its adivasi leader, Janaklal Thakur, had been able to win the Dondi-Lohara assembly seat of the Madhya Pradesh Legislature in 1985. The CMM was unique in that it combined "sangharsh" - economic and political struggles with "nirman" - developmental and cultural renewal activities. It functioned democratically under a collective leadership, which had a clear political vision of an alternative social set up and the means to achieve it. Phaguram, a peasant leader of the Morcha and a folk singer who has created many revolutionary songs, which have become extremely popular, captured this buoyant mood of the time in his song -

"Chhattisgarh dai ke have ga gohaar

Sabho jan milke shoshan la tarbo"

"Mother Chhattisgarh is calling all her children,

Join together and overthrow the exploitative burden."

Subhadra drew a lot of inspiration from the CMM's struggles, but her own attempt at setting up an organisation reached a dead end. Her efforts to have women activists working in pairs rather than alone fell on the deaf ears of her male supervisor. Besides the feeling of insecurity that accompanies women in such remote areas, incidents of some women getting raped were not uncommon. Their powerlessness certainly did not provide them with an aura of being leaders for the local people. The people treat such lonely activists and their organisations as "bin pende ka lota" meaning a round vessel without a stand at the bottom to keep it straight in the event of a push from oppressors or the state. People have become so used to the system of patronage practised by mainstream political parties that they have lost faith in themselves and in their ability to fight. Disillusioned, Subhadra gave up her job and went back to Jepra in the spring of 1990.

Jepra had changed drastically since she had left. Her father—now too old to till the land—had rented it to a relative. Her brother was ill and jobless. Subhadra again looked for opportunities outside Jepra and renewed her contact with Rajaji in Tilda, who advised her to go to western Madhya Pradesh where work had begun anew. He also promised her the freedom that she needed to work effectively. This was a very good offer, and she immediately accepted it, despite having some inner misgivings about having to go to an unknown area and shoulder the immense responsibility of setting up the organisation there.

In the hot dry summer of 1990, Subhadra too hit the oft-trodden migrant's trail out of Chhattisgarh and took the Chhattisgarh Express train to head for Bhopal. There she met, for the first time, one of the stalwart Gandhian workers of Madhya Pradesh, Ramchandra Bhargava. Little did she know then that one day he and his wife Rukmani would act as her surrogate parents for the purpose of her court marriage with me. Bhargavji was in charge of the Gandhi Bhavan in Bhopal and also some other NGOs. Even though he or his organisations do not take part in any agitation activities, he always keeps his doors open for activists and organisations that do. That is why the Gandhi Bhavan in Bhopal has been the venue for many important national and state-level meetings of environmentalists. Since it is located very close to the legislative assembly, the chief minister's residence and the governor's residence, it is a convenient assembly point for launching agitations in Bhopal. When Rajaji had expressed a desire to expand his organisational work to the western Madhya Pradesh region to Bhargavji, he had enthusiastically agreed to help.

At a meeting of activists in Indore, Subhadra met Gandhian stalwarts Mahendra Jain and Kashinathji. The former, popularly known as Mahendrabhai, was the president of the the NGO that ran the ashram at Machla. Mahendrabhai had started out as a teenager activist of the Sarvodaya movement, going on to devote his life to people-oriented journalism and setting up the Sarvodaya Press Service on the way. He was jailed for eighteen months during the Emergency. His office-cum-residence in Indore had become a hub of the various mass movements afoot in the region. Kashinathji too was had led an exemplary life in struggle. A valiant freedom fighter, he, had been a frequent "guest" in British jails. Subsequently, he devoted his life to developing an alternative education system for the rural poor and adivasis. His ashram in Tavlai village in Dhar district houses a residential school for adivasi students.

It was decided in the meeting that work would be started in the Dahi Block of Dhar district, which had remained relatively untouched by both the Gandhians and also by the new breed of NGOs and social movements. This block was ideally situated because in the adjacent blocks of Sondwa in Jhabua district and Kukshi in Dhar district, the Khedut Mazdoor Chetna Sangath and the Narmada Bachao Andolan were very active and would be able to provide Subhadra good support. She went to the ashram in Tavlai. It was felt that children in the school from the Dahi block would be the right people to introduce Subhadra to the area and the people. Accompanied by a few teenaged adivasi students, Subhadra went to the villages of the block. Everything had been so hectic and exciting over the past few days that she had not had the time earlier to notice the change in the natural ambience. But as she walked in the blistering heat through the countryside, she was suddenly confronted by the drastic difference. The Nimar region was heavily denuded, and there were barren hills all around, which increased the heat. This was in stark contrast to Chhattisgarh, which, because of its tanks and irrigation canals and extant forests, remained green even in summer. The other change was in the food. Subhadra had been used to eating rice all her life. But here she had to eat thick maize rotis. The maize was of a hybrid variety and white in colour as against the yellow indigenous maize that was available in Chhattisgarh. This cereal tasted bland, as well.

Soon, she came across something even more revolting. The approach road to the villages was flanked by human excreta and stank like anything. Instead of going to the fields, people defecated on the sides of the roads. What was worse, she learned, was that the Bhilala adivasis did not wash themselves after defecation; instead they used stones to wipe their anuses clean. She learnt that the Bhilalas traditionally believed that washing their anuses was equivalent to washing their fortunes, however inconsequential they may be! The Bhilalas also bathed once a week on an average, given the acute shortage of water. So both defecating and bathing were challenging activities for her. She had to spend some time searching around for a can in which to take water for washing before she could go to relieve herself. Similarly, bathing became an elaborate ritual, as water had to be fetched from a hand pump or a dug well, which could be situated as much as a kilometre away. Chhattisgarhis always take a bath before lunch by taking a dip in the nearest pond. She learnt the hard way like I had earlier that living and working among the Bhils meant renouncing the transient pleasure of regular bathing.

The block was populated mostly by Bhilala adivasis. Only some of the villages, such as the market village of Dahi, from which the block got its name, had a substantial number of non-adivasis. The preliminary survey revealed to Subhadra a much higher level of illiteracy and lack of awareness than in Chhattisgarh, but also a greater willingness to listen to what she had to say about battling corruption through organised mass actions. She toured the whole block and secured the acquiescence of twenty households, which were to host the field workers who would come later. She was very happy to make some headway at last. There is the story of an activist visiting a village to address a meeting, only to find just two people there. Undaunted, the activist launched into his speech and thanked the two listeners for attending the meeting and listening to him so eagerly. The two people said that they had perforce to be present because the carpet on which the activist stood and gave his speech belonged to them, and they could not take it back until he had finished! Suffice it to say that great happiness warms the heart of an activist when people assemble in good numbers at meetings. Despite the alien climate, culture, and food, Subhadra spent a satisfying fortnight in

Dahi and went back to Tilda after making all arrangements for launching organisational work.

A training and selection camp was organised in Tilda for the recruitment of activists to work in the various new areas, including Dahi, in which mass organisations were to be set up. Twenty people were selected, and they came along with Subhadra to Dahi and took up their residence in the villages that had been pinpointed earlier. Within a short time, these young people were able to garner the support of the local adivasis, and people began to approach local authorities with various demands. As in the neighbouring Sondwa block, here too, a nexus between the traditional village patels, mainstream political party functionaries, and the bureaucracy ensured that corruption reigned supreme. Since people had already heard of the exploits of the KMCS and NBA in challenging this oppressive nexus in nearby areas, they associated these new activists in their areas with these organisations and began responding to their exhortations. Complaints were filed against officials who had taken bribes from the adivasis. Upon hearing of the positive response, Rajaji decided to hold a training camp for the local people.

This was an honour for Subhadra. Nowhere else had a local training camp been held so soon after the launch of operations, since usually the people took time to respond to the overtures of new activists. A training camp takes a lot of organising. But in this case there was an added problem. One of the basic tenets of Gandhian social work is that of inculcating cleanliness, especially the awareness of sanitation, among the people. This arose from the fact that in traditional Hindu society, the responsibility for cleaning the latrines lay with a particular caste, which had been branded untouchable. In an attempt to free these castes, Gandhi called them Harijans or the children of God. He made it compulsory for his followers to clean latrines in villages. Gandhi hoped by doing so he would be able to put moral pressure on the upper castes to either clean the latrines themselves or install hygienic water washed latrines and waste disposal systems like septic tanks. So there were periodic campaigns in which Sarvodayis went around cleaning latrines for a week.

The existence of a clean and hygienic village ambience was the acid test of successful Gandhian mobilisation. And the first thing Rajaji would notice on coming to the village where the camp was to be organised would be the excreta and its stench on the side of the road and he would conclude the activists had failed in one of their basic responsibilities. Since the people of the village were hardly bothered about this and were unlikely to participate in a cleaning drive so soon after their induction into Gandhism, the burden of cleaning the road fell on the activists. So on the morning of the camp, after the village people had duly relieved themselves, Subhadra and her team set about with shovels and baskets and towels tied round their faces cleaning the excreta. When Rajaji arrived, the village was spic and span and everyone was smiling from ear to ear and breathing stench-free air.

The camp was a success; it was attended not only by local people, but also by people and activists from the neighbouring districts associated with the NBA and the KMCS. A whole new enthusiastic cadre of adivasi youth was inspired to work for their community. However, before work could begin in earnest in the Dahi Block, a much more crucial battle—the struggle to save the Narmada needed support. The construction of the Sardar Sarovar dam had reached the bed level with the completion of its foundation work. It became imperative for the NBA to force stoppage of work at this stage before construction began on the superstructure of the dam. A massive long march—to be undertaken from Barwani in Nimar in Madhya Pradesh to the dam site at Kevadia in Gujarat—was planned, with the intention of forcing the government to scrap the dam altogether. This required massive mobilisation of people. The NBA requested Rajaji to spare his Dahi team of activists for a month to help in this mobilisation.

So Subhadra and her co-workers went off to mobilise people for the "Sangharsh Yatra" or struggle march of the NBA. They were no longer "bin pende ke lote."

10   Once Turbulent Flowed the Narmada

Today all is calm at Helkaria.

It was not always so. Today's calmness is the silence of defeat, the calmness of a tombstone that marks the taming of the thundering roar of the river Narmada that once majestically swept through a deep gorge in Sirkhiri Village in spate. Helkaria, a Bhil name meaning "tossing from side to side," has been submerged by the Sardar Sarovar dam. The now calm waters hide beneath them the story of the remarkable struggle waged by the NBA to retain the Narmada's pristine glory. The NBA's struggle has created many landmarks in the history of mass environmentalism in this country and the world over.

When I first came to Alirajpur, the construction of the main part of the Sardar Sarovar dam on the riverbed was in a limbo, held up by the lack of a clearance from the Ministry of Environment and Forests of the Government of India.

The history of the Sardar Sarovar dam is replete with happenings of the most bizzare kind. The foundation stone was laid at Navagam in Gujarat by Jawaharlal Nehru in 1961, and the first stage was to have a full reservoir level of 162 feet that would have submerged villages in Gujarat and Maharashtra, but not those upstream in Madhya Pradesh. Matters took a different turn when the Gujarat government envisioned a much more grandiose plan to raise the level to 425 feet, ambitiously targeting irrigation of areas like Kutch in north Gujarat. This necessitated the submergence of villages in Madhya Pradesh. Disputes arose between the different states involved, and in 1969, after Rajasthan also entered the scene, the Narmada Water Disputes Tribunal (NWDT) was set up to look into the disputes between states regarding the usage of the Narmada waters.

Much bickering took place for many years, mainly arising from the fact that the states inflated their claims regarding the irrigation and power benefits that should accrue to them and deflated the costs that they would have to bear. Finally, the NWDT came out with its award in 1978. It had to artificially inflate the design annual flow of the river at 75% dependability to 28 million acre-feet from the actually prevailing 22 million acre-feet to be able to appease all the states! Gujarat was apportioned 9 million acre-feet of the flow while Madhya Pradesh got 18.25 million acre-feet and Maharashtra and Rajasthan were given 0.5 and 0.25 million acre-feet respectively. The height of the Navagam dam, which had by then come to be named the Sardar Sarovar Project (SSP) was fixed at 455 feet and the height of the off take canal at 300 feet. The costs and benefits of the power to be generated also were apportioned between the three states.

In a peculiar topsy-turvy denouement, the planning of the use of Narmada's waters had to be carried out downstream upwards instead of vice-versa, as environmental logic would have suggested. The height of 455 feet for the SSP had to be fixed to allow Gujarat to draw its allotment of 9 million acre-feet of water. Since the reservoir to be created by the SSP was not capable of storing all this water, another mega dam, 860 feet in height, was planned upstream at Punasa, which later came to be called the Indira Sagar Project (ISP). Water was to be released from this dam and then stored in two more dams at Omkareshwar and Maheshwar before heading to the SSP. Another dam was to be built at Bargi to take advantage of the flow upstream of the Punasa dam. The heights of all these other dams were also calculated so as to be able to use the 18.25 million acre-feet that had been allotted to Madhya Pradesh. In reality, however, the estimation of a river's flow is a dicey game, based on the river run-off that is recorded every year at various measuring stations on the river. Different experts come out with different estimates based on the same set of data.

This is what happened with the flow of the Narmada, too. The estimate of 28 million acre-feet, decided upon in 1974, was more a political decision than a technical one. Current estimates put the actual flow at 75% dependability at 22.69 million acre-feet, which is closer to the value that the NWDT had arrived at in 1971. The extra flow value was necessitated to accommodate the exaggerated irrigation and power demands that were projected by the engineers involved. This led to an overambitious design of all the dams. The Bhakra dam on the river Sutlej in Himachal Pradesh, another, and perhaps the most famous, of Nehru's modern temples, also suffers from a similar faulty design. In that case, not just the states within the country, but the two nations of India and Pakistan were quarrelling with each other. Invariably, this kind of design, based on inflated demands for the waters of a river, later leads to more disputes between states. This is evident from the continual conflicts between Punjab, Delhi and Haryana over the waters of the Jamuna, Sutlej, Ravi and Beas rivers; and between Karnataka and Tamil Nadu over the waters of the Cauvery river. This is enough reason to assume that the same fate will befall the Narmada, too, in a few years' time.

The proper way to go about managing the surface and sub-surface water flows in a river basin is to start from the ridges of the topmost micro-watersheds that constitute the catchment of the river and then work down to the river itself. This process is economically much cheaper and environmentally a lot safer. Big dams should only be built to service the needs that cannot be met through in situ water conservation and extraction. However, since this decentralised water management requires very simple technology that has been around for thousands of years from the time of the ancient Harappan civilisation, it does not appeal to engineers and people like Nehru who like to think big and spend big even if it is with borrowed money. "Rhinang krittang ghritang pibet" - *borrow money to drink clarified butter,* as the ancient Indian saying goes. Such massively over designed dams create serious problems of submergence of forests rich in bio-diversity and communities rich in cultural diversity. Once these dams, canals and powerhouses are built, little money is left to compensate the environmental and social costs. Consequently, the displaced people themselves are left to bear these costs. No wonder that Nehru had to repeatedly use his rhetorical abilities in urging the displaced lots to suffer in the interests of the country, employing the religious symbolism of temples and sacrifices to delude a populace that was deeply bound in religious superstition. Even today, all public projects start with a religious "bhoomi pujan" ceremony to propitiate the gods, despite the Indian state being a secular one constitutionally.

However, all is not black in the NWDT award. It provides for the rehabilitation and resettlement of the displaced on the important legal principle of land for land as compensation, a first for this country. In the case of earlier dams like the one at Bhakra over the Sutlej river in Himachal Pradesh, the displaced people had been given short monetary shrift and mostly left to their own devices. That was what happened with Subhadra's family. The NWDT award went beyond the limited framework of the Land Acquisition Act, which only provides for monetary compensation in accordance with prevailing market rates of land in a particular area. Typically, in adivasi areas, the market rates for land do not reflect the immense value that it has for the adivasis' livelihoods, and so they get palmed off with pittances and are reduced to destitution.

The Madhya Pradesh and Maharashtra governments fought for and won exemplary rehabilitation provisions, the costs of which were to be borne by the Gujarat government. Each adult son was to be given a minimum of two hectares of irrigated land and villages were to be resettled together in one place as a community, with all civic amenities like parks, roads, electricity, and drinking water. All people who lost more than twenty five per cent of their land were to be so compensated and the determination of this submergence had to be according to the backwater level, which increases with distance upstream from the dam. Although the award had some drawbacks such as not having any provision for landless and encroacher families, overall it was vastly better than anything that had previously existed. Later on when the NBA went to the Supreme Court, more than all the arguments and facts marshalled by the NBA regarding the negative environmental and economic fallout of the dam, these solid legal provisions formed the basis for halting the construction of the dam for more than a decade.

In 1978, the World Bank sent a review team to assess the Gujarat government's application for a loan for the SSP, immediately following the NWDT award. The review team made suggestions for the conduct of various environmental and technical studies and also sanctioned a preliminary loan to the Gujarat government for preparing a detailed project plan. Finally, in 1985, an agreement was reached between the World Bank and the Gujarat government for the sanction of the loan. The novel feature of this agreement, like the NWDT award, was its stress on proper rehabilitation. It went one step further and stipulated that even landless and encroacher dispossessed would have to be provided land as compensation. A separate loan was sanctioned for the rehabilitation component to make sure that the rehabilitation of the displaced was not sacrificed on the plea of lack of funds. Finally, there was a condition that was to prove crucial later on in the struggle to stop the World Bank funding—the withholding of funding if the rehabilitation pre-conditions were not fulfilled according to schedule. The Japanese government, riding piggyback on the World Bank's approval, sanctioned a tied loan for the purchase of the hydroelectric power-generating turbines from Sumitomo Corporation.

In 1980, the Forest Conservation Act was enacted by the central government to control the increasing destruction of forests that had led to the forest cover coming down to just about eleven percent of the land mass of the country, as revealed by satellite imagery. This act made it mandatory for all development projects to have environmental impact studies carried out, on the basis of which these projects would receive approval from the newly constituted Ministry of Environment and Forests. So the SSP and also the ISP had to get this crucial clearance before work could be started on them. As late as in 1986, the Ministry of Environment and Forests circulated a note that was critical of both the projects. The note stated that their environmental impact assessments had not been completed and that the environmental problems arising out of these projects would be of a severe nature. It also said that a strong case could be made out for reducing the heights of both the dams. At about the same time, the kickback scandal in the purchase of the Bofors military field guns by the Government of India became public, considerably embarrassing Nehru's grandson and the then Prime Minister, Rajiv Gandhi. His earlier unassailable position as the Congress party's supreme leader was in jeopardy now. In an effort to muster political support within his party, he had to bend to the demands of his party members from Gujarat. He ordered the Ministry of Environment and Forests to give conditional permission in June 1987 to both the SSP and the ISP despite the lack of environmental impact studies, compensatory afforestation plans and catchment treatment programmes. What had been an obsession for the grandfather became a compulsion for the grandson. With finances and permissions under their belt, the authorities in Gujarat began construction of the dam with gusto.

In Gujarat, an NGO Arch-Vahini, had begun to organise the displaced people to demand proper rehabilitation and resettlement in accordance with the NWDT award, as some preliminary displacement had already taken place around the dam site. This NGO got in touch with us to start the same process in Madhya Pradesh and gave us the relevant documents. So in 1985 we began holding meetings in the villages that were going to be submerged. Around this time, we got a letter from Vasudha Dhagamvar of a Delhi-based NGO called MARG. Vasudha also wanted to do something about this issue. She wanted to tour the affected villages on the Maharashtra side and team up with us to launch a joint campaign for proper rehabilitation of the displaced. So in December 1985, I arranged for a meeting with her at my favourite bivouac spot on the banks of the river in Jalsindhi. Due to logistical problems, this meeting eventually took place in the temple village of Hapeshwar, just across the border from Madhya Pradesh in Gujarat. Medha Patkar accompanied Vasudha on this their maiden tour of the Maharashtra villages. The three of us sat down to discuss future plans over a dinner generously arranged by the temple's Mahant or head priest.

This was the humble beginning of the struggle, which was to rock the valley and the world so significantly later on.

We started off in sedate fashion by making the simple demand for proper rehabilitation for all the oustees and urged the government to prepare a rehabilitation package for the three hundred villages. Medha Patkar, who had earlier been working with another NGO in Gujarat, started working full time on this campaign. She soon unearthed a mine of information regarding not only the problems with the rehabilitation of the oustees, but also the overall cost-benefit analysis of the dam itself. The costs and benefits of the dam had been calculated by making baseless assumptions. The final results presented a rosy picture of the benefits, while showing reduced costs.

Within a year of the launch of this campaign by various mass organisations, it became clear that the government had no intention of rehabilitating all the oustees as mandated in the NWDT award. The Gujarat government's renewed pace of construction put more pressure on the organisations fighting for rehabilitation. These organisations had garnered a mass following and had organised large demonstrations to press their demands. Dissatisfied with the response of the state governments as well as the central government, in 1988, these organisations decided to form a common front and oppose the construction of the dam in totality.

The Narmada Bachao Andolan (NBA) was thus born.

With her indefatigable energy and mobilising powers, Medha Patkar managed to involve other mass organisations, NGOs and individuals in India and abroad who were not directly concerned with the struggle in the valley to form support groups for lobbying, publicity, and fundraising on a scale hitherto not seen in environmental mass movements in India. Medha composed the very popular theme song, which started in this way -

Narmada ki ghati mein ab ladai jari hai (The struggle is now on in the Narmada valley)

Chalo uttho, chalo uttho, rokna vinash hai (Rise up, Rise up and stop this destruction)

Throughout 1987 and 1988 numerous mass actions took place against the dam in Madhya Pradesh, Maharashtra, Gujarat, and even in Delhi. People repeatedly courted arrest breaking prohibitory orders clamped around high-security zones near the seats of power. The first major effort of the NBA to actually physically stop the work on the dam was in the form of a mass march in February 1989. Initially a two-pronged move towards the dam site was planned. Adivasis from Maharashtra and Alirajpur were to walk down the riverbanks to reach the dam site. And people from Nimar in Madhya Pradesh were to go by trucks via the highways and were to be joined by people from Gujarat.

I had some reservations about this plan. Since this would be well publicised, there was no way in which the Gujarat government would let these two massive groups of people reach the dam site; we would be arrested at a distance far from the dam site. My proposal—to have a third unpublicised phalanx of equal strength, which would secretly go by a route through the hills and reach the dam site at the break of dawn to surround the massive concrete mixer and stop it from working—was summarily rejected.

But we in the KMCS were an anarchistic lot—a group of headstrong individuals that operated with just the bare minimum of discipline and cohesion necessary to keep the group together. Moreover, apart from one person who later distanced herself from our happy go lucky ways and joined the NBA, none of us had any illusions that we would be able to eventually stop the dam. Nevertheless, we participated wholeheartedly in the mass actions of the NBA because they provided the thrill and fun of fighting the state and the World Bank on a much larger scale than would have been possible while working with the KMCS alone. I was not going to let such a golden opportunity of enjoying myself to the hilt go by so easily. At a meeting of our own, we decided to go ahead with my plan. What was the point in symbolically courting arrest like we had done so many times without actually stopping the work of the dam?

We surveyed a route through the hills that would take us to the concrete mixer without letting anyone know. We picked a spot at about two hours' walking distance from the dam site to camp on the night before the march. Then, we would make the sally to the dam site in the wee hours so as to reach the concrete mixer just when dawn broke. We ensured that none of us carried any weapons or canes whatsoever, as armed conflict would lead to criminal cases being registered against us, which would prove painful and expensive later, for in that case, we would have to repeatedly attend court hearings in Gujarat. So all we needed to do was to entwine our hands, surround the concrete mixer while shouting slogans, and wait for the police. For this, we would be arrested under preventive laws, which do not require court attendance, as the offences are compounded immediately by the executive magistrates.

On the appointed day around three hundred of us set off as planned; everything went like clockwork. Even as the two main phalanxes were stopped many kilometres away from the dam site, we managed to reach the concrete mixer and surround it at the break of dawn and stopped work on the dam. Immediately, there was a furore as the workers and officers of the construction company gathered there. The police had been deployed to tackle only the two main phalanxes, so none were available to deal with us. For the next two hours, we had the time of our life, shouting slogans and singing songs, keeping the concrete mixer inoperative. "Koi nahin hatega, baandh nahin banega" - *no one will move, the dam will not be built,* the most famous slogan of the NBA would rend the air, frequently interspersed with the song, "Narmada ni ghati ma amri larai chalu chhe" - *in the valley of the Narmada our struggle continues,* a Bhili adaptation of the NBA theme song.

The entire force of around five hundred people and all the trucks came to a standstill.

Finally a small force of ten policemen and a sub-inspector arrived with buses, offering to take us to the district collector to discuss our demands. Bava of Jalsindhi, who was later to become famous for writing a classical deep ecological letter to the Chief Minister of Madhya Pradesh in defence of his right to lead his natural lifestyle, rose in regal style and said that the collector did not have the answers to our problems and that the Prime Minister of India should come to talk to us, and that until then we would not budge an inch! He was greeted with a roar of approval from the rest of us, which reverberated through the surrounding hills.

We continued to maintain this grand attitude until two more truckloads of policemen arrived after some time. A tug-of war ensued as the police tried to forcibly load us into the buses and we rolled onto the road, entwined with each other. The police had to resort to baton charging and kicking us to drive some sense and fear into our heads. So after four hours of work stoppage, the construction of the dam began again. This was the only time when the work on the dam was stopped by mass action. Later, it would be stopped by a stay order of the Supreme Court during the hearing of a petition filed by the NBA.

We were taken to a stadium and kept there for two hours, fed snacks for our troubles, and then allowed to go free with a warning not to return again! We hired three buses and returned to Alirajpur with the satisfaction of having done a good job.

Another such memorable action took place in the spring of 1990. The construction of the dam had reached a stage where the possibility of submergence of land in the first village in Maharashtra loomed large in the approaching monsoons. Medha Patkar and three others launched into one of the many hunger strikes by the NBA in Mumbai. Their principal demand was that the Maharashtra government press for stoppage of work on the dam as rehabilitation of the oustees had not been completed. Some of our people and activists too went there to show support. It was decided in Mumbai that support demonstrations would be held in the Narmada valley to build up pressure. Upon returning, our activists said a rally and a rasta roko andolan - blocking of traffic on a highway, needed to be organised in Alirajpur. I said this was all right with me, but only if it was agreed that the rasta roko would not be lifted under any circumstances, thus forcing the police to take action against us. Moreover, since this time we were on home turf, we were not going to balk at giving back to the police with their own coin if they did try to remove us forcibly! I had, in the meantime, been implicated falsely by the police in Maharashtra in a case of murder and had just been released from jail on bail. So it was decided that I would be spared another sojourn in jail and left to handle things from behind the scenes, while the rest of our gang carried out the actual agitation.

I went to meet the sub-divisional police officer and give him the notice that we would be demonstrating in front of the office of the Narmada Valley Development Authority (NVDA) in Alirajpur on a particular day. Given our reputation for disruptive activity, he immediately asked me apprehensively whether we were going to organise a peaceful law abiding demonstration or not. I assured him with a straight face that it would not cause him any trouble at all. On the day of the agitation, a rally was taken out through the streets of Alirajpur. Then, all of the two hundred odd people entered the office of the NVDA and told the officers and staff to vacate the premises, as they (the activists) were henceforth going to stay there. Soon the office was cleared of its staff, and the KMCS ruled in it. Almost immediately the SDO Police arrived with police reinforcements, to be handed a charter of demands by the agitators. Once again, Bava, who had perfected his style by now, stated that only after the prime minister of India came and satisfied him, would he and his people vacate the premises. The activists spent the night in the office, shouting slogans and singing songs.

Early next morning, all the protestors reached the Indore-Vadodara highway that ran in front of the office. The rasta roko andolan began. In next to no time, traffic began collecting on both sides. The SDO Police had to jump out of his bed and come rushing to the spot with truckloads of policemen. He pleaded with the agitating people that he had already sent their charter of demands to the higher authorities and that they should desist from inconveniencing the public. At this, Bava launched his tirade on the inconvenience that the government was causing to thousands like him, which, he said, made no difference to those in power, preoccupied as they were with the inconvenience of city people. He ended grandiloquently with his standard refrain about the summoning of India's prime minister.

Obviously things could not have continued for long in this fashion. Suddenly, a company of mounted police was called into action. Along with the rest of the police, they charged at the protestors. As planned, the agitating activists and people had a go at the police and a free for all ensued, which was naturally won by the police. The activists were arrested and the rest of the people dispersed. Watching the action from a hidden location, I saw a grand sight, which will forever remain etched in my memory. Khemla's father Chena, by then a venerable old man of over seventy years, was also among the protesters sitting on the road.

As soon as the police action began, he stood up, a lean figure dressed only in a dhoti tied around his waist, covering the traditional "kushta" or loin cloth and a pugree round his head, and started beating his chest with his fist and shouting abuses at the police to come and kill him, the louts, as there seemed to be no place in this country for the adivasis. "Bomgola nakhin mari nakh tuhri ******* " he shouted repeatedly as if in a trance - " Bomb us to extinction you ******". The sight was awesome and it must have had some effect on the police, too, because they did not touch him even as he went on in this fashion while all hell was being let loose around him. Finally, he walked off in a dignified manner after the activists, including Khemla's wife, had been arrested. Chena is no more, but that one act of insouciant defiance capping his earlier career of rebellion in his youth, has made him immortal to me.

Khemla and I had been given the responsibility of managing things after the dispersal. We had already planned that the people should regroup at a location on the outskirts of the town where we would cook and eat a meal and then take out yet another rally protesting the police action. We had also arranged for photographers to take pictures of everything that happened that day from hidden locations so that we would have a good story for the press. While the cooking was in progress, I came across yet another example of the insouciance of the Bhil adivasis that made my day. One of the men was stretched out on the ground under the searing summer sun in his kushta covered from top to toe with his dhoti. He was busy taking forty winks. Here we were taken to the cleaners by the police, and there was every possibility of us being beaten up again when we went back into the town with a rally in a few hours. Yet, this man thought it more prudent to catch up on lost sleep than to worry about the police! The repeat rally passed off peacefully, mainly due to the fact that the IAS officer who was the Sub-divisional Magistrate was good at heart. He gave strict orders to the police that unless we created any law and order problem, no action should be taken against us. The next day, the papers were full of our story. As a result, the Inspector General of Police had to come down from Indore to assess the illegality of the administration's actions.

The whole exercise turned out to be a roaring success from our limited local point of view. But this demonstration; a similar one in Barwani led by no less than Baba Amte, the great man, who, despite his spinal disability, stood heroically for seven hours with his arms locked round the gate of the Sub-Divisional Magistrate's office, which had been padlocked by the NBA and the hunger strike in Mumbai could not stop the work on the dam. Medha Patkar and others withdrew their hunger strike after a few days on being assured by the Maharashtra government that no one would be allowed to be submerged without proper rehabilitation. But later the government of Maharashtra backtracked on its assurance and refused to seek the stoppage of work on the dam.

In Gandhian political action, hunger strike is the ultimate strategic action of the satyagrahi. It is a do-or-die action and leads to either the victory or the death of the striker. A crucial requirement for its success is that there should be a massive mobilisation of people in support of it to put sufficient moral pressure on the state. As we shall see later, despite mass support, the hunger strike has been successful in getting demands fulfilled only on a few occasions. Thus, this strategy shouldn't have been adopted at such an early stage when mass support was not available. The hunger strike is an additional action that complements and reinforces the mass mobilisation process and cannot be a substitute for such mobilisation. Going for the hunger strike at the very outset, substituting it for a process of building up a wider and stronger mass movement, underlined the weakness of the anti-dam movement vis-à-vis the state. This was to set a trend for the NBA later on, with the further reduction of mass strength, of numerous hunger strikes and jal samarpan or drowning in the river agitations, which were always withdrawn either on some assurance, or ended in the participants' being arrested by the state.

On September 28, 1989, the first ever national-level mass rally against destructive development had been held in Harsud, a town that has since been submerged by the ISP. This marked a watershed moment in the history of the environmental movement in this country since previous environment struggles, such as Chipko and Silent Valley movements had been single-issue agitations that did not comprehensively challenge modern development. For the first time, thousands of people from all over the country had gathered at one place to declare their resolve to fight for the initiation of people-centric governance and development, which was environmentally sustainable, as against the prevalent paradigm in which the vast majority of the people and the environment had both been devastated.

The arrival of Baba Amte, a life-long fighter for disabled leprosy patients, elevated the proceedings to a higher moral stage. This modern sage who had straddled the sphere of mass agitation work with as much authority as in the sphere of charitable work, for which he was more well known until then, declared that he found the adivasis to be in a worse state than the leprosy patients he had worked with. He decided to devote himself to the cause of the NBA. Shivarama Karanth, the noted Kannada novelist, was also present at this rally as was the noted film actress and social activist Shabana Azmi.

Fittingly, Baba Amte himself set the independent tone for this new mobilisation by candidly asking two uninvited leaders of national political parties to step down from the stage that they had ascended uninvited. He asked them to sit on the ground alongside the masses. This illustrates the seriousness with which a new kind of mass political activism was being initiated.

In a follow-up meeting of activists on the night after the mass meeting, it was decided that a two-day convention would be held in Bhopal in early December 1989. This was to coincide with a public meeting that is held every year by the Bhopal Gas Peedith Mahila Udyog Sangathan on 3rd December to pay homage to the people who died in the fatal gas leak from the Union Carbide factory on that day in 1984.

It was also an indication that Madhya Pradesh, one of the most backward states in the country, had emerged as the epicentre of the surging new environmental mass movements.

11 Following the Heart

Originally, Bhopal was an old world town with the laidback ambience of nawabs or Muslim princes. It was situated between the two lakes that had been presciently built by the nawabs to cleverly harvest the rainfall in the nearby hilly catchment, in order to fulfill the town's water requirements. Bhopal's only claim to fame at the time of independence was its cricket-playing debonair nawabs.

The decision to make it the capital city of Madhya Pradesh, following the reorganisation of states in the mid nineteen fifties was a compromise, given its low profile as compared to the other more warring contenders such as Indore, Gwalior and Jabalpur. Today, Bhopal carries both the old and the new worlds, as the old town of the nawabs is surrounded by the modern abodes of the netas or politicians and the babus or bureaucrats, who are the rulers of present day India.

A large, heterogeneous state, Madhya Pradesh is rich in natural resources such as forests and minerals. Politicians and business magnates enjoy a symbiotic relationship here— politicians make the natural resources available to businessmen and industrialists at hugely subsidised rates, and the latter return the favour by funding their political campaigns. It is no accident that one of the largest industrial houses in India, the Birlas, has built a temple at the highest point in Bhopal next to the seat of power on land given to them free of cost by the government. This, even as the poor adivasi construction workers live in roadside shelters.

Such disparities have naturally spawned mobilisations of the poor. Initially these were led by the Communist Party and the Socialist Party, both of which managed to send legislators to the state legislature and Parliament. However, over time, the mass organisations of these parties were marginalised in the face of heavy state repression, while the legislators were absorbed in the reigning political culture. The peasant movements were crushed and the trade unions lost their political character, remaining content to agitate with just better wage demands. The Congress proved to be a worthy successor to the British in using a carrot-and-stick policy to entrench its rule.

The 1970s saw the emergence of groups like the Vidushak Karkhana in Shahdol district and Kishore Bharati in Hoshangabad. They challenged both the development paradigm as well as the models of social and political action followed by the communists and socialists. Following a decentralised, participatory model, these organisations began experimenting with a bottom-up approach to the problems of poor people. This upsurge was, however, short lived. It soon dissipated without making any significant local impact. However, the theoretical output generated from this brief foray into mass politics by intellectuals and scientists from some of the best educational and scientific institutes from India and abroad has proved to be of lasting value. Later, this provided a base for the environmental movement to develop a broader ideology of mass environmentalism in the country.

It was against this backdrop that Bhopal as well as Madhya Pradesh made their debut on the international media scene with a dubious distinction in 1984. On the night of December 3 that year, a lethal gas leaked out from a pesticide factory of the U.S. multinational corporation (MNC) Union Carbide Corporation (UCC), situated in Bhopal's outskirts. The spillage killed thousands of people. The chairman of UCC, Warren Anderson, was arrested by the government of Madhya Pradesh when he came to visit the site immediately after the disaster.

The government of India in its wisdom, however, decided to release him within a few hours on a paltry bail of rupees twenty thousand. Anderson seized the opportunity to wing back to the U.S. and has since been absconding from the hearings of the criminal cases that were filed and are still pending even more than twenty years after the massacre. Given the fact that the government has not been able to extradite relatively less powerful people from the underworld like Dawood Ibrahim, there is little possibility of its being able to bring Anderson to book. Displaying even greater wisdom, the government enacted an act in parliament delegating to itself the responsibility of filing the tort case for damages against UCC in the U.S. on behalf of all the affected people. Then it proceeded to file a claim of just 3.3 billion USD and made a hash of its legal representations before the U.S. trial court, which finally directed that the case should be heard in India itself, and the decision by the Indian court would be binding on UCC. By doing so, the U.S. washed its hands off the enormous costs they would have had to bear in the form of the bankruptcy and liquidation of a star MNC like UCC, had the case been decided in the US.

The Indian government settled for a measly one-seventh of the amount originally claimed. The Bhopal gas tragedy was an explosive eye opener to the fact of multinational corporations transferring hazardous activities and wastes to third world countries. Indeed, some years later, the Chief Economist of the World Bank was to say in a note circulated among some of his colleagues "Just between you and me, shouldn't the World Bank be encouraging more migration of the dirty industries to the less developed countries?" The reasons advanced in support of this argument were that the costs of losses due to pollution in the Third World were low because the wages there were low and that since their environments were cleaner than the First World, they could absorb more pollutants.

The Economist magazine, which exposed this note, supported this argument stating that since third world governments wanted to develop their economies and there was no way to do so without polluting their environments, they might as well take those industries that could not be economically run in the first world anymore due to stringent environmental regulations. This is exactly the logic that had earlier resulted in the UCC plant being set up in Bhopal and its operating with far lower safety standards than what the corporation was following in the U.S. All this reflects very poorly on the Indian government, which has failed to protect the lives and entitlements of its poor citizens, so as to provide benefits to the Indian capitalist class, which sees its profit in playing second fiddle to the MNCs.

On the contrary, the civil society's response to the gas disaster has been one of the most remarkable examples of environmentalist political action in India, which set off a series of new, more militant and effective mass environmental mobilisations throughout the country. The activists of Kishore Bharati immediately came down to Bhopal and joined hands with trade unions to form the Zahreeli Gas Kand Sangharsh Morcha. This organisation began agitations demanding proper relief to the affected persons and adequate legal steps to pin down the responsibility on UCC. Since the government was clearly bent on abdicating its responsibility of cornering UCC, this organisation built up links with civil rights organisations in the U.S. to put pressure on the government there and also to pursue legal action in the courts. Later, the Morcha, along with a few other organisations set up a clinic to provide treatment to the survivors. One of the blackest acts of the government in the early days after the gas leak was to obfuscate information regarding the nature of the gas that leaked from the tanks of the factory. This was done at the behest of UCC because the graveness of its culpability depended on how lethal the gas was. The less lethal the gas and its effects on the people, the less would be the degree of UCC's culpability. So there was a continuous effort to deny that the gas that leaked was methyl iso-cyanate, which is extremely lethal. The treatment for those exposed to the gas would naturally also vary according to the nature of the gas. Since the government was denying that the gas that leaked was methyl iso-cyanate, the treatment being provided by the government hospitals was also faulty. The Morcha clinic, however, began providing treatment in accordance with the assumption that the gas was methyl iso-cyanate. Not surprisingly, the results of their treatment were rather good. The government responded by closing down this clinic and arresting its doctors. Small wonder that the results of the epidemiological studies conducted for more than a decade by the ICMR before being abruptly stopped have not been made public.

Faced with repression and apathy from the government and beset with internal problems leading to a split in the Morcha, it gradually lost its mass base. Once the settlement was reached with UCC in 1989, the payment of claims began. The affected people got involved with this process and lost the urge to agitate further. However, a splinter organisation named Bhopal Gas Peedith Mahila Udyog Sangathan continued to fight for a better deal in the courts in this country, abroad, as well as on the streets. The indefatigable efforts of two affected women from Bhopal— Rameeza Bee and Champa Devi—are a testament to the fighting spirit that lies hidden in our masses. They not only kept their struggle and the memory of the mass murder alive by organising a rally and a meeting on the anniversary of the gas leak every year, but also led their organisation to participate in all the other mass environmental struggles that were taking place in the country and played a stellar role in putting up a joint front against the destructive and iniquitous development policies of the government. It was ably supported by activists, both Indian and American. One particularly valiant ongoing effort has been the "Jharoo Maro Abhiyan" - broom and sweep clean campaign. They have consistently gone to various fora in the world with their brooms as symbols of their demand that UCC and now Dow Chemicals, which bought it and made it into its subsidiary later, clean up the environmental mess around the factory in Bhopal and pay a proper enhanced compensation to the victims.

These ladies had the crucial last laugh when they put one over the government in a telling manner, two decades after the disaster. Wont to cheat the masses at will, the central government had disbursed paltry amounts as compensation to the affected people from the money given by UCC. In the meantime, the remaining corpus, deposited at the Reserve Bank of India in a dollar denominated account, had accumulated compound interest as well as appreciated in rupee terms and become a whopping fifteen hundred odd crore rupees. Despite repeated representations that this money should be disbursed in full to the affected people, the government refused to do so. The two women petitioned the Supreme Court on behalf of their organisation, demanding that the entire amount be disbursed to the affected people. To create public opinion during the pendency of the case, they held several sit-ins and hunger strikes in Delhi and Bhopal. In a landmark judgment, the Supreme Court allowed this petition in 2004, forcing the government to backtrack and begin giving the people their due.

Moreover, this judgment put its imprimatur on the findings of the Bhopal Gas Tragedy Relief and Rehabilitation Department that the number of deaths due to the gas leak have been 15,310, with 5,54,895 other casualties. The settlement with the UCC in 1989 had been on the tentative estimate of just 3,000 deaths and 1,02,000 other casualties. In truth, a five-fold increase in casualties has taken place, thus giving a strong legal basis to the demand that Dow Chemicals pay more compensation. The significance of this victory, resulting from the doggedness with which two women have pursued this struggle sunk in to me the other day, when my neighbour's wife in Indore said that she was going to Bhopal to receive her second instalment of compensation as someone affected by the gas leak. She was a teenage girl residing in Bhopal when the gas leak took place and had been registered as an affected person. This brought her some token compensation earlier. Now, because of the Supreme Court order, she was getting another instalment. She was extremely happy and was all praise for the government for being so considerate as to pay her this huge sum of money! In 2004, Rashida Bee and Champa Devi were jointly awarded the prestigious Goldman

Environmental Prize for their tenacious battle for environmental justice. Earlier in 1992 it was awarded to Medha Patkar for her battle to save the Narmada.

This then was Bhopal, the heart of the country and home to one of its best and longest surviving environmental movements, where we were to congregate for drawing up a blueprint for a countrywide movement against destructive development. We couldn't do better than follow the heart when its people had fought so valiantly against the worst manmade environmental disaster the world has ever witnessed. The meeting went off well and was attended by NGOs and mass organisations from across the country. Its culmination saw the launch of the first nationwide environmental movement, Jan Vikas Andolan, the election of its executive committee, and the chalking out of a plan of action. Although it started with a great deal of euphoria, the Jan Vikas Andolan failed to fulfill its initial promise as too many anarcho-environmentalist cooks spoilt its socio-political broth! On the concluding day of the meeting, news came that a World Bank team was in Bhopal to conduct meetings with the Madhya Pradesh government regarding the latter's loan application for funding the construction of the Indira Sagar Dam at Punasa. This prompted the activists to call a secret conclave, where it was decided that the World Bank team would be surrounded by a select group of activists the next morning as it left the hotel to attend the official meeting.

Early next morning, we were at the hotel. One of the activists in our group knew the Indian member in the World Bank team, so he and I went inside the hotel, while the rest of the group waited outside. I discreetly found out which car had been reserved for the World Bank team and stationed myself near it. My activist friend who knew the World Bank team member went inside and struck a casual conversation with him to find out the time the team would be leaving the hotel. Then, he joined the rest of our group outside the gates. As soon as the World Bank team got into their car and the vehicle moved out of the porch, I began waving my sweater as a pre-determined signal to those at the gate. The car had just crossed the gates where it had to slow down to negotiate the cattle trap, when our group surrounded it while shouting slogans of "World Bank Go Back." I sprinted behind the car and jumped on to its roof to do a jig so as not to be left out of the shindig! Within twenty minutes, the police appeared on the scene in full force. We were all packed into a bus and taken to Bhopal jail. Such arrests are usually a formality, and the arrested people are let off soon. However, the administration did not want to take any chances, and we remained imprisoned for all the three days of the World Bank team's stay in Bhopal.

Our outing in the Bhopal Central Jail proved to be a very entertaining and educative one. We were around thirty people from all over India—all activists of various mass movements. Since Medha Patkar was the only woman amongst us, she was locked up alone in the women's ward. A special barrack was opened for the rest of us. We had hardly settled down when we got the news that Medha had gone on a hunger strike. We decided to follow suit and refused to eat the lunch offered to us. With so many headstrong and quirky individuals—who did not know each other very well—cooped up together in one room, fireworks were inevitable sooner or later. The first serious altercation ensued in the afternoon when a regular inmate of the jail came with a big cauldron, full of hot steaming tea. The cup that warms but does not inebriate was particularly desirable in the biting cold within a prison surrounded by dank walls. But a debate at once ensued as to whether tea was allowed during a hunger strike or not. Now, this was a hodgepodge combination of people holding allegiance to various ideologies, including hardcore Gandhism in which the hunger strike is a potent action of satyagraha, and except for water, everything else is forbidden. So while the Gandhians insisted that tea could not be taken, others argued that only solid food was prohibited in a hunger strike and tea was allowed.

There seemed to be no signs of either side compromising. Even as the tea went cold, the heat of the debate wouldn't subside. Suddenly, the jail inmate who had brought the tea and left when the debate started, came back and intervened to say that drinking tea was allowed in a hunger strike. At once those in favour of tea gave a shout of victory and said that even this ordinary jail inmate knew the basic fact that tea was allowed in a hunger strike, so the Gandhians should relent. But the latter were not going to give up so easily and asked the jail inmate as to what his source of knowledge was regarding such a weighty matter. The inmate said he had gone to inform the jailer about the debate, lest the latter accused him of neglecting his duties. Upon hearing the problem the jailer told him to inform us that in his opinion, drinking tea was all right in a hunger strike. At this the Gandhians preened themselves, looked at those in favour of drinking tea with contemptuous glances and said that if they wanted to follow the jailer's advice, they were welcome to. This finally brought the debate to an end; the tea drinkers had to do without their favourite beverage.

One of those imprisoned with us was a Marxist, and drinking both tea and the somewhat more inebriating drinks were part of his routine. To do without either was a bit too hard for him. Though he gave in with the others and abstained from the tempting cup of steaming tea, it was only his training to follow party discipline that made him do so. "Since us Marxists have no God", he remarked, tongue in cheek, "we have to rely on more materialist escapes like drinks to drown away our sorrows, which are many in the absence of the Indian Revolution."

According to him, the CPI in India, unlike the Communist Party of China, had not been able to analyse the Indian society properly and had consequently failed to formulate an appropriate mass revolutionary programme of action in the crucial decade of the 1930s. This had contributed to its becoming marginalised with time, especially in a highly feudal state like Madhya Pradesh. Fed up with the sort of dead-end the CPI had reached, he resigned from it and began seeking some action in environmental movements instead.

As a relatively young and enthusiastic activist, I found the internal bickering in the discussions between the various factions of the Bhopal gas movement within our small jailbird group disconcerting. Each would blame the other of sabotaging the movement and collaborating with the government. Later, while studying the history of similar movements in the state, it dawned on me that this was not unusual since the communists and the socialists had split, as had the naxalites whose numerous splits would put even amoebae to shame. The first environment movement, Chipko, had split after sometime, and the NBA too would do so soon, although the leaders of the dissenting factions had the maturity to keep a joint public front, thus saving the NBA from losing face.

There was a serious altercation with regard to the hunger strike on the third and final day of our stay. Our supporters outside, unaware of the hunger strike, had sent in fruits and tasty snacks on the second day, which were routed to us by the jail administration. These fruits and snacks were given for safekeeping to the negotiating committee of seniors we had chosen so that no one breached the hunger strike. The committee in turn had secretly decided to keep the tempting foodstuff under the surveillance of a senior leader from the movement against the Indira Sagar Dam at Punasa. We were in for treachery on part of this leader, who soon began polishing off the booty with some "like-minded" comrades. It turned out that this gentleman was a local Congress leader, who had joined the environment bandwagon only because his large lands were slated for submergence by the dam.

The group around him, however, began to get bolder and tried to "recruit" some of those who were dressed in more modern outfits like jeans and T- shirts, wagering that they would be more amenable to breaking the fast than us kurta pajama wearing hardcore activists. It was a revelation of sorts when the jeans wearing youngsters turned out to be more steadfast Gandhians than the Congress "leader." There was a furore and a tussle ensued, and if it did not end with blows among ourselves, it was because of the jailer deciding to release us.

Our Gandhian political action was immediately followed by a "un- Gandhian" one—a sumptuous non-vegetarian meal and the purchase of a ticket to Baba Amte's ashram in Anandwan in Maharashtra—all courtesy the jail authority that is supposed to provide travel fare to prisoners on their release from jail. Since my friend Jacob Nellithanam and I had put the ashram as our residence address, we got the fare to the place we had long been unable to visit due to lack of funds. With a little cleverness, the state too can be made to fund anarchist aspirations!

The events that transpired during those three days in the jail, where almost all the leading lights of environmental mass movements of the country were together, seem to me to have borne the seeds of the present marginalisation of these movements. Unlike the gods of Hindu mythology who, in order to make themselves immortal, had churned nectar from the oceans, we anarchists are pulling in so many different directions that there is little chance of us being able to churn a nectar of any kind, mortal or immortal, to save the world from the stormy tides of destructive development.

12 Grand Old Men of Anarcho-environmentalism

Sisyphus, of whom we shall discuss more later, is not just a mythical Greek hero who fought stoically against adversity by rebelling against established hierarchies. Over time, he has come to personify the spirit of rebellion that is extant in all humans who refuse to give up the struggle in the face of daunting hurdles. In the long and tenuous battle against modern development that is being waged today, it has been my good fortune to have encountered some modern Sisyphuses in flesh and blood.

Baba Amte was certainly one of the most inspiring persons that countless idealistic young men and women looked up to, and whom he, in turn, nurtured. In the mid-1950s, Baba Amte began his work in the middle of a jungle in Anandwan in Chandrapur district of Maharashtra. There, he would treat leprosy patients, a work that later blossomed into a full fledged rehabilitation programme, leading to a productive community for these patients, who were hitherto virtually treated as outcastes, if not worse. For apostates from the false religion of modern development, like Jacob and I, Anandwan and the other two centres in Somnath and Hemalkasa, deep in the jungles of Chandrapur and Gadhchiroli districts, home to the Gond adivasis, are places of pilgrimage. Baba Amte did not just rest on his laurels from caring for the leprosy patients, but strode further ahead to do something for another set of developmental outcastes in India – the adivasis. To extend Baba Amte's motto for the leprosy patients, the adivasis in India are not disabled but quintessentially differently-abled victims of the perverse logic of modern "temple-building".

Strangely, he calls himself a spineless man!

He refers, of course to his spine that was once replaced by the bones of an animal, after he sustained an injury. In his characteristic jocular style he remarks that the bones must have been that of an ox since he felt stronger and more obstinate after they were put in. He ignores the fact that the operation had incapacitated him to the point that he could only stand bolt upright, or lie down, he could not sit. Despite having a pace maker attached to his heart, he undertook two Bharat Jodo or Knit India yatras to inspire youngsters to work for the disadvantaged. His stubborn persistence would have done the ox - still the mainstay of Indian agriculture, proud.

I met him for the first time in Harsud and introduced myself. Imagine my surprise when he gave a hearty laugh from his supine position and said, "You look so frail and innocent to be a murderer; the police must have made a mistake". I later learnt that he had come to know of my arrest on the charge of murder immediately and then phoned people to ensure that I got released on bail as soon as possible. That is the level of concern that this great man showed for activist youth who he felt are the torchbearers of a more humane society than the one we live in at present. He laid his hand on my shoulder in that first meeting and said, "From now on I shall call you my 'badmash dost' - mischievous friend."

In the early 1980s, a dam was planned on the river Godavari in Andhra Pradesh. The dam would inundate most of the jungles and adivasi villages in Gadhchiroli. Baba Amte gave a clarion call to the adivasis to rise up in protest. In response, thousands of them gathered on the banks of the river. The then Prime Minister, Indira Gandhi, heard of this and ordered the project to be shelved like she had done with the Silent Valley dam in Kerala earlier. But that did not make Baba rest on his oars. He decided to take up the issue of the large-scale wanton destruction of nature and the involuntary displacement of its children, the adivasis, by dams. By this time, the movement against the Sardar Sarovar dam had begun to pick up momentum, and it attracted his attention. So he called a meeting of environmentalists from all over the country in Anandwan to search for alternatives to big dam building in 1988. This was the first such meeting, and it came up with comprehensive recommendations regarding a more people-friendly water resource utilisation policy than the one that was being pursued by the government in the Narmada Valley. This was how he came to be associated with the struggle in the Narmada valley in particular and the more widespread struggle against destructive development in general.

Baba and Sadhana Tai came to the Narmada valley in 1990 and set up a centre on a piece of barren land on the banks of the river in village Kasrawad in Barwani district, which was at that time the nerve centre of the NBA, and both became part of the struggle. In 1993, when I was convinced that the battle against the dominant paradigm of modern development could not be won, I turned to them. Sadhana Tai offered me traditional sweets made of sesame seed and jaggery, and Baba and I got talking. He sensed the turmoil in my mind and the boredom in my life and commented in his characteristic style, "Tum janmei ho badmashi karne ke liye aur jab tak jinda rahoge tumko badmashi karte hi rahena hoga - you have been born to do mischief and so as long as you are alive you have to go on doing mischief!" A simple inspiring exhortation to never say die as he himself hadn't. With his passing away we have lost one of the great fighters of post-independent India.

Another such mentor whom I often looked up to and who dominated the political firmament of Western Madhya Pradesh for over half a century was Mama Baleshwar Dayal Dixit. He had led an adventurous life: starting his political career as a sixteen-year-old in 1923 by thrashing his British school teacher who had spoken ill of Gandhi. Rusticated and fearful of his father's wrath, he ran away to his maternal uncle's place in Khachrod near Ujjain. Inspired by Gandhi's satyagraha for sanctioning temple entry to dalits, he had prasad distributed to devotees by some dalits at the local temple. On the run once more, he was invited by the mother of the renowned freedom fighter Chandrasekar Azad to run a school in his hometown in Bhabra in Jhabua district. Later, he became the principal of a school in nearby Thandla.

Mamaji was well- known for his novel and practical forms of protest. When he learnt that Brahmins and Kshatriyas, unlike the Bhils, were exempt from begaar or forced labour, he got the sanction from Shankaracharya of Puri, one of the four high priests of Hinduism, to perform a "shuddhi" or purification ceremony. In this, he had the adivasis wear the janeyu or sacred thread, thereby converting them into Kshatriyas. Given the religious prestige of the Shankaracharya, the princes could not question this and had to free the Bhils from begaar, raising the movement to an altogether different level.

In the course of his struggles for the abolition of feudal rights of princes and jagirdars, Mamaji came into contact with the stalwarts of the socialist movement—Rammanohar Lohia and Acharya Narendra Dev—and embraced their ideology.

Even after embracing socialism, he remained rooted to the Bhil homeland and went on to lead the Lal Topi Andolan, certainly one of the greatest peasant movements in the history of Madhya Pradesh. The Andolan, however, was put on the back burner as the socialist leadership increasingly stressed on participation in electoral politics at the cost of the cadre-based mass mobilisation of the movement. With the waning of the influence of the Socialist Party and its numerous splits, many of the local leaders of Jhabua defected to the Congress party, falling prey to the many temptations of wielding power.

Mamaji consistently refused to be drawn into national politics and only reluctantly accepted the president's post of the All India Socialist Party in 1962 for a year after being pressurised by Lohia. Then, following the 19-month incarceration during the Emergency, between 1975 and 1977, Jayaprakash Narayan forced him into becoming a member of the Rajya Sabha in 1978. He used to term the proceedings in the Rajya Sabha a farce and was particularly peeved that the right to work had not been made a fundamental right in the Constitution. He once related to me in hilarious detail how he had tried his level best during his six years in Parliament to get this done and how members of his own party had not responded and had started avoiding him altogether to escape from his persistent harangues. He found himself sitting alone in Parliament, as by then, the Janata Party had split, and his fellow MPs were all busy defecting from one party to another.

He was, however, a contradictory person, and despite his disillusion with parliamentary politics, he continued to campaign for Janata Dal candidates even in his late 80s.

Mamaji declined the freedom fighter's pension and privileges, saying it was absurd to accept monetary return for patriotic deeds. He carried his simplicity to the grave as it were, declining treatment at the All India Institute of Medical Sciences when he was seriously ill towards the end of his life in 1998. While he lived, his Bhil Ashram in Bamnia was a small hut situated on a tiny plot of agricultural land that had been made by soil deposits resulting from blocking a gully with stones at a point where it took a wide turn. His meagre personal needs were met from the produce of this patch of land. He will forever remain a beacon for all those who believe in fighting for lost causes.

Another erstwhile socialist whom I had occasion to meet at a meeting of the human rights organisation People's Union for

Civil Liberties (PUCL) in 1987 was Om Prakash Raval. He was elated to find that I was an engineer from IIT who had turned to activism. Patting my back he said, "Well done, my young man; the sight of you warms the cockles of my old heart." As chance, and little else, would have it, he had been the Minister of Education during the brief Janata Party government in 1978, before the party split and the Madhya Pradesh legislature was dissolved. He later threw in his lot with the Bhopal Gas Andolan and later still went on to become the mainstay of the NBA in Indore. We lost him in 1993 to a sudden heart attack, just when we needed him the most. A considerate and honest man like I had never seen before, his inspiration keeps me going in the face of heavy odds.

Ravalji had started his career as a teacher and was a crusader for the rights of teachers in an era when they were badly paid and worked in pathetic conditions. After independence, he spurned an offer to work in a government job and instead continued to pursue his political interests, broadening the scope of his struggles to include that of agricultural and industrial workers. In 1951, he joined the Socialist Party. He was among the more promising younger leaders of the Socialist Party in Madhya Pradesh.

Early in his career in the Party, he went to the town of Barnagar near Ujjain on one occasion. Along with the local party activist there, he went around the town with a hand cart and a battery-powered public address system, announcing that in the evening there would be a mass meeting of the Socialist party to be addressed by its young leader from Indore - Om Prakash Raval!

He told me once with a mischievous smile that he knew that his days as a minister were numbered, so he wasted no time in pushing through a legislation that granted various benefits and economic security to teachers in private schools and colleges being run with government funds. Although he used the four-month-long flirtation with power as Education Minister to make up for his unsuccessful struggles for teachers' rights, he was disillusioned by the internal bickering within his party and parted ways with mainstream politics forever.

He came into his own as a major supporter of the NBA. He would take part in its rallies, visit remote villages to hold grassroots meetings, garner support in Indore, and write in the press. Later, when, after the Harsud rally, the Jan Vikas Andolan was formed in Bhopal, he became a member of its national executive. On one occasion, we were returning from a meeting of the JVA in Bangalore by train. In his mid-60s then, he was the oldest member in the group, but he participated in our revelry as if he was the same age as us. We were singing Hindi film songs. Someone began singing the song – "aa chal ke tujhe, main le ke chalun ik aisi gagan ke tale, jahan gham bhi na ho, aansu bhi na ho, bas pyar hi pyar pale" – Come, let me take you to that heaven where there are no sorrows and tears, where only love prevails. He also joined in, and when the song was over, he said smugly that true love and sorrow are inseparable so how could there be pyar without gham. According to him, this song was as utopian as our own dreams and plans for a better India that we had just worked out in Bangalore!

The PUCL meeting in Indore in 1987 was also where I met Mahendrabhai Jain. A died-in-the-wool Gandhian of the old school, he joined the Sarvodaya movement when Vinoba Bhave passed through the Malwa Nimar region as part of his Bhoodan Yatra. Vinoba prevailed upon him to choose a mission in life and stick to it throughout, notwithstanding any obstacles. So he chose to start a press service devoted to publishing news and features related to Gandhian values; Sarvodaya Press Service. Additionally, he also worked as an activist of the Gandhi Peace Foundation. At that time there wasn't any press service exclusively devoted to the propagation of Gandhism, and the mainstream press did not have much space for such issues. Yet Mahendrabhai laboured on urging people to write and pressed editors and journalists to carry the articles he sent out. Working on a shoestring budget, he handled everything—from editing to typing and then cyclostyling the press notes by himself—he eventually succeeded in establishing the Sarvodaya Press Service as an internationally renowned supplier of quality articles and news on environment and alternative development issues. He achieved this solely on his own meagre salary as an activist of the Foundation and the resources generated by the payments made for his press notes by newspapers and magazines. He never accepted any external funds.

Many years later, a representative from PANOS, an international news agency for environmental issues, working out of a modern office equipped with computers, scanners and printers, was floored to see Mahendrabhai sitting in a small twelve-foot by ten-foot room, labouring over a typewriter and a cyclostyling machine surrounded with piles of books, magazines and papers.

His opposition to the draconian measures brought into force during the Emergency and subsequent imprisonment during those dark months led him to become a prime mover for the formation of the PUCL in Madhya Pradesh, after his release. Mahendrabhai felt that the neglect of confrontational grassroots politics by the vast majority of Gandhians had been a major faux pas. Since his responsibilities with the press service prevented him from actively participating in grassroots movements, he decided to help them as much as possible by providing support service. Thus, Mahendrabhai's residence became a clearinghouse of information about the various movements going on in the Malwa region.

The NBA especially benefited from his help, since it had to rely heavily on instant communications of its actions or the repressive actions of the state to the outside world. In those days, in the late 1980s and early 1990s, the Internet was non-existent in our part of the world. So desperate phone calls would be made from some remote place in the interior, and Mahendrabhai would take down impromptu notes. Based on these, he would type out a press note and circulate it all over the world! The coordination of the movements of various people coming from outside to the valley would also be done through this efficient one-man exchange.

Subhadra and I will forever remain indebted to him for allowing us to drop anchor in the ashram at Machla at a time when we were penniless, and I was seriously ill. We spent nearly a decade in the serene, natural and tree-clad environs of Machla and were frequently in touch with Mahendrabhai during this time. Every time we met, he would relate some joke or other, cleverly playing on the words he used. Once he chuckled and said "Tum aur ham jaise *a-sarkari* kshetra ke log isliye sarkar ki aankh ki kirkiri bane hue hai kyunki ham unse jyada *asar-kari* hain! - people like you and me in the non-governmental sector are detested by the government because we are more effective". It was, of course, a play on the words a-sarkari and asar-kari, which have the same pronunciation, but different meanings.

Another instance of such word play was when I was arrested on the wrongful charges of being a Naxalite after the Mehendikhera confrontation in 2001. When the Divisional

Commissioner informed him that I had been suspected of being one since I held surreptitious meetings in the night like Naxalites do, he told her: "Aap log raat aur din ka antar nahin samajhte hain isliye aap aur hamare beech raat aur din ka antar hai - You do not understand the difference between day and night, and so there is a difference of day and night between us!"

Yet another Gandhian who has played a stellar support role for the movements in this region is Ramchandra Bhargava. Bhargavaji is positioned in an enviable place as the Coordinator of the Gandhi Bhavan in Bhopal. The Bhavan is so centrally located that it is always rented by various organisations for holding seminars and conventions. Nevertheless, it has always been available to the grassroots movements free of cost for their meetings and conventions. There have even been occasions when commercial bookings by outside people have been cancelled to accommodate some last minute convention to be held by the movements. On many occasions rallies to block traffic in the high-security area of Bhopal just next to the Gandhi Bhavan have been planned and begun there, yet Bhargavaji didn't flinch under pressure and always welcomed people like us with open arms.

Bhargavji came into his own during the Bharatiya Janata Party government under the chief ministership of Sunderlal Patwa, from 1990 to 1992. The BJP government took it into its head to crush the burgeoning social movements in the state. So there were continous protest rallies or meetings in Bhopal. These were all organised and planned at the Gandhi Bhavan. Despite pressure from the government, not only did Bhargavji not relent, but was able to convince the chief minister to at least agree to meeting and talking to the activists of the social movements, instead of unleashing repressive action unilaterally.

When Subhadra and I decided to get married, we chose Bhopal as the place to tie the knot. The Indian Marriages Act stipulates that at least one of the two people applying for registration of marriage must be a resident of the area of jurisdiction of the court where they file their registration. Moreover, we had to provide proofs of our ages, which we did not have, as we had both misplaced our school-leaving certificates. Bhargavji not only arranged for the affidavits and certificates at a short notice, but also bore the expenses of the marriage, and blessed us as the surrogate father of the bride.

On a searing summer afternoon in 1986, we were holding a meeting of people from all the submergence villages in Alirajpur in the village of Anjanbara on the banks of the Narmada. Suddenly we saw a towering old man, dressed in a traditional dhoti and kurta, huffing and puffing his way to our meeting spot. Barely able to walk, he was supported by two men. This was Dr. Brahmadev Sharma who was, at the time, the Commissioner for Scheduled Castes and Scheduled Tribes of the Government of India, a constitutionally mandated post for the protection of the rights of the scheduled castes and scheduled tribes, which has since been replaced by the National Commission for Scheduled Castes and Scheduled Tribes. He had heard about our meeting and had made his way to it, walking up hill and down dale for a stretch of five kilometres that had no motorable roads. Sharmaji is a legend and has done much to ensure that activists like me retain some relevance in a milieu that is becoming increasingly hostile to the mass mobilisation of adivasis. A PhD in mathematics, he joined the Indian Administrative Service in 1956 and soon made a name for himself for his strict actions as the District Magistrate of Bastar against the government functionaries and traders who were exploiting the adivasis in the region. His tenure in government service up to 1981, when he resigned due to differences with the government over the way in which the welfare of adivasis should be ensured, was a single-minded pursuit of justice for the children of nature.

In 1986, as Commissioner, Scheduled Castes and Scheduled Tribes, his statutory reports to the President of India scathingly indicted the government in not meting out justice to adivasis. He filed a petition in the Supreme Court, demanding government action on the report. After retiring from his post in 1991, he went back to the villages of Bastar, from where he had begun his crusade for the adivasis to start a grassroots movement of the people for village self rule. This was the phase in which he came up with the famous anarchist slogan - "Hamara gaon mein hamara raj" - *our rule in our village*, which has now become common currency in adivasi areas. Around this time, a proposal came up for setting up a steel plant in the villages in which Sharmaji was working, and he spared no time in launching a movement against this. Goons hired by the company tried to humiliate him by stripping and parading him in the streets of Jagdalpur, creating a furore all over the country.

My association with Sharmaji, which began with that meeting in Anjanbara, continued well after that. Throughout his term as Commissioner, he continually helped the KMCS and the NBA in their mass actions by mediating with the administration to adopt a more positive approach. Following his retirement, he became the prime mover behind the formation of the Bharat Jan Andolan, a forum of mass movements fighting for just and sustainable development and governance. Not only has he led this forum from the front, but he has also written copiously on the problems of rural and especially adivasi development and their solution. He set in place an organisation called "Sahayog" or assistance, a fairly efficient system for the mobilisation of resources from society at large to help out young activists in their work and struggles.

As a member of the parliamentary committee set up to draft the bill for this purpose under the chairmanship of the then MP from Jhabua, Shri Dilip Singh Bhuria, he was instrumental in bringing out a set of radical recommendations for the establishment of true democratic control by adivasis of their lives and habitats, thus extending the provisions of the 73rd Consitutional Amendment for Panchayti Raj to adivasi inhabited areas.

Later, it was through his persistent efforts as Chairman of the Bharat Jan Andolan that the Panchayat Provisions Extension to Scheduled Areas Act (PESA) was passed in 1996. Despite its later dilution, it is a very powerful instrument for assertion of adivasi supremacy in Scheduled Areas. Unlike the equally commendable provisions of the Fifth Schedule, whose implementation is left to the discretion of the state governments, this Act gives the adivasis powers to act and secure their rights and entitlements. As we in the case of the Mehendikhera confrontation, mobilisation by adivasis around the implementation of this Act can only be crushed by the state through the adoption of wholly illegal repressive measures. Sharmaji came to meet me after the Mehendikhera incident when I was in jail on the usual trumped up charges. He commended me for so purposefully manifesting on the ground what he had conceived on paper.

Concerned about the safety of Subhadra and our small seven-month-old child, he provided me the much needed support and the healing balm of words of an elder who had seen the world and knew its ways- "Fikr mat karo, kuch dinon ki hi to baat hai, ham tumhare saath hai" - don't worry, its just a matter of a few days, we are with you.

13 Things Fall Apart: The Long March and its Failure

By 1990, the NBA had a wide network of supporters in India and abroad. On December 25 that year, the NBA put this support to effective use in organising the biggest mass mobilisation ever by environmental groups against the construction of the Sardar Sarovar dam. The long march to the dam site, Sangharsh Yatra, was launched from Rajghat on the banks of the Narmada near Barwani, where people from Nimar and outside the valley flagged it off. They were to be joined by adivasis from Maharashtra and Jhabua in Alirajpur. Baba Amte was to lead the march in his special van.

Subhadra and her teammates spent the last twenty days before the start of the march going from village to village in Nimar, exhorting people to turn out in large numbers on the appointed day with appropriate preparations. The march was to be undertaken in biting winter cold and could last up to a month or more. Provisions such as warm clothing, wood for burning and rations for cooking had to be taken along. These were to be taken on tractors that would accompany the marchers.

I joined the march with the adivasis from Maharashtra and Jhabua in Alirajpur five days after it had hit the road. The next day, early in the morning, the march started from Alirajpur. By the end of the day, it reached Ferkuva on the Gujarat border. At Alirajpur, we had come to know that the Gujarat government had posted its forces along the border. Behind the forces, a mass of people squatted on the road, keeping vigil. Led by Urmilaben, the wife of Gujarat's chief minister, they had been pressed into service to prevent us from reaching the dam.

That night at Ferkuva, the Nirnayak Dal, the organising committee for the march, mandated that a small band of the marchers led by Baba Amte will cross the border to test the waters. As expected, they were stopped by a posse of policemen who respectfully asked Baba to turn back as they expected confrontation ahead. Baba refused to budge and immediately began a dharna then and there. It was a piquant situation with the

Gujarat police sandwiched between us and those on the Gujarat side of the border.

The Gujarat politicians, assisted by the chambers of commerce, intelligentsia, NGOs and the Press, had built up a hysteria favouring construction of the dam, seen as the "Jeevadori" or lifeline to bring water to the parched areas of the state. The debate was thus cleverly manipulated and shifted from the plane of environment, social and economic concerns to a Gujarat versus Madhya Pradesh confrontation. Tremendous amount of data against the sustainability of the dam and examples of sustainable alternatives of water resource management were summarily rejected by the Gujarat government. It had instead mobilised both people and police on its side of the border for a showdown around what it had converted into an inter-state confrontation.

Fanatical commitment to the SSP saw the Gujarat government resisting every move to disrupt the dam's construction. Jayaprakash Associates, the company constructing the dam, had brought in labourers from Uttar Pradesh and Bihar. Enigmatic as its presence in this area is, it so happened that a Trotskyite-led workers union- Vadodara Kamdar Union (VKU) took up the cause of the workers. The union immediately organised a strike by the labourers, bringing the construction work to a halt.

However, with the aid of the Gujarat police, Jayaprakash Associates cordoned off the striking workers in their hutments and brought in fresh workers to continue the work on the dam. Goons were hired to intimidate activists of the VKU. The organisation's president was even stabbed, though not fatally. After a few months, the strike broke down under severe repression sanctioned by the Gujarat government, despite the demands of the workers being legitimate ones. No legal and humanitarian scruples were heeded if they came in the way of the construction of the dam.

We met the situation arising out of the stalemate by camping on the border and setting up a "Sangharsh Gaon" ("Struggle Village"). Each village contingent from Nimar would have its own place around its tractor where food would be cooked. At night, there would be log fires around which singing or story-telling would go on. The adivasis huddled inside massive tents mounted for them and for the visitors from outside the valley. Failing to make any headway in trying to break the police barricades, seven men and women, including Medha Patkar and an oustee from Maharshtra, Khajiabhau went on strike on January 7, 1991, demanding a comprehensive and independent review of the SSP policy. The rest of the thousands of people sat down in support of the hunger strikers.

One of those who were on hunger strike with Medha happened to be another Kolkata native, Meghnad, an old friend and fellow activist working with adivasis in Jharkhand since the 1970s. He also faced a false charge of murder like myself. However, the similarities ended there, and he scored head over heels over me when it came to singing and entertaining. He later took to filmmaking and has now become the accomplished maker of documentary films on environmental and indigenous matters.

Meghnad, possibly because of his Jharkhandi militancy vintage, had been given the responsibility of organising the security of the Yatra and especially of its prominent leaders, Baba Amte and Medha Patkar. At the beginning of the sit-in at Ferkuva he came to me one day and said ruefully that Medha had ticked him off for standing close behind her during a press conference, misconstruing his presence as trying to get photographed with her to get attention. He gleefully resigned as head of security for the Yatra citing his unsuitability for the post in the light of Medha's admonition and instead got back to his forte—singing songs and doing skits.

Meghnad, perhaps because of his experiences in Jharkhand, recognized the limits of Gandhian mass action in independent India. A hard drinker, subsisting on a diet of water in Fekuva must have been harsh on him. He sheepishly remarked that he was in Fekuva seeking a change of air from Jharkhand and using this opportunity to expiate for his many sins!

The Gujarat government was in no mood to relent, but the international press coverage and tremendous goodwill that the NBA had built up tilted the balance as far as the World Bank was concerned. The World Bank announced the setting up of an independent commission to review the SSP. This was unprecedented for the World Bank. The hunger strike ended on January 28, and Medha announced that everyone would return to their villages and continue the fight there. But while Sharmaji's slogan that Medha used- "Hamara gaon mein hamara raj" made good sound bites, it was mere rhetoric for most of the people who had been mobilised for the march. They felt that turning back from

Fekuva without the government acceding to their demands was defeat. This marked the start of the crucial downturn of NBA's mass mobilisation.

This denouement, unfortunate as it was, highlighted the inherent contractions within the NBA that had developed a layer of generally urban, middle-class idealistic youth romanticising the NBA as a force against modern development. The NBA relied on these youth to challenge the World Bank and the many other institutions that it was ranged against. The masses—Bhils and other peasants from "backward" castes—on the other hand, had more pressing needs and expectations from the movement. These included saving their lands and livelihood. They had little understanding of the forces that had brought them to such a pass.

The NBA worked on two planes. One was that of mass struggles and demonstrations involving the oustees in the valley and in the major decision making centres such as Bhopal, Mumbai and Delhi. The other was that of lobbying and advocacy with the urban public, press and decision makers, both national and international. While the oustees played a major role in the first kind of work, they invariably got marginalised in the second kind of work, and it was left to the activists to take on the brunt of this work. Naturally, to the world at large, these activists appeared as the leaders and the most charismatic and hard working among them, Medha Patkar, became the main leader of the NBA. Things went fine as long as the oustees felt that this dichotomy and the resultant leadership of the activists would result in the stoppage of the work on the dam. For this reason, the Sangharsh Yatra saw tremendous mobilisation and involvement of the outsees on an unprecedented scale. They believed the activists' claim that this mass action would definitely tilt the scales in their favour.

However, things went awry when a majority of the indigenous oustees in Madhya Pradesh and Maharashtra did not buy the "hamara gaon mein hamara raj" rhetoric and perceived the withdrawal of the hunger strike and the retreat from Ferkuva as a crushing defeat.

Immediately after the setback to the Sangharsh Yatra, there was a mass exodus from the NBA. Co-option by the governments of all states in the form of rehabilitating the oustees also accelerated the exodus. Even Khajiabhau who had sat on hunger strike for twenty-two days with Medha Patkar, opted for the alternative land offered by the government.

When the displaced people perceived that they could not stop the dam, a perception that has been borne out by later developments, they opted for the next best option of resettlement on land offered by the government. Despite the tardiness of the rehabilitation process, these people have nevertheless felt that it is better than being submerged and left with nothing at all. "Agar gaon hi nahin rahega to raj kahan karenge" – *what will be there to rule if our village ceases to exist!* as one oustee, Dhankia, commented wryly.

After this, the government let loose repression on the remaining loyalists. The NBA was wholly unprepared for this. Major local leaders were taken to police stations and stripped before being beaten up and sent to jail. This severely reduced the efficacy of the NBA; the number of people prepared to undertake mass actions or even attend rallies began to dwindle. Coupled with the rehabilitation policy, the famed carrot and stick policy of the British that had been used to marginalize the Lal Topi Andolan and the Zahreeli Gas Kand Sangharsh Morcha, was now used to decimate the NBA.

The KMCS too was not spared. A problem had cropped up during the Sangharsh Yatra, with the Forest Department trying to close in traditional pastureland for plantation purposes in Kiti village. Things reached a head with the government bringing in police forces in support of the Forest Department staff. The people refused to give ground. Shankar and I, along with some of the people, were called to Alirajpur by the administration for discussions. This was just a ploy, and we were arrested under provisions for preventive detention in the CRPC and sent to jail without much ado. In midnight swoops, all the other activists who were scattered in different places were arrested, too, and sent to jail. Fortunately, this did not serve the administration's purpose because the people still resisted the police forces and coerced a showdown in which the police opened fire. In the meantime, our lawyer in Indore and some other activists who had escaped being arrested filed a habeas corpus application in the High Court for our release. This sobered up the administration. Giving up enclosure of community pastureland was a far less serious loss for the government than stopping the construction of the dam. So ultimately, the Forest Department abandoned its ill-advised plan under pressure from the administration, which baulked at killing adivasis to implement it.

Meanwhile, the NBA got a shot in the arm when the World Bank appointed Review Committee recommended unequivocally that the World Bank step back and consider the project afresh. The Committee confirmed the apprehensions expressed by the NBA regarding the violation of environmental stipulations, the submergence due to backwater effect, and the extent of displacement, which was so massive that it could not be compensated under the existing laws and policies. The victory, however, was largely symbolic because the World Bank refused to step back and instead stipulated a six-month period of monitoring to verify the Committee's findings. This put pressure on the Indian government to ensure that all data regarding the oustees was collected and a proper rehabilitation plan put in place. Catchment treatment and afforestation plans, pending ever since the conditional clearance given by the Ministry of Environment and Forests in 1987, were also to be readied in six months' time. All this meant that the submergence area would have to be surveyed in detail.

The Alirajpur villages where the KMCS was active were to be the first to be submerged in Madhya Pradesh. So from October 1992, the government of Madhya Pradesh stepped up its campaign to get these surveys done and wean away the people from the NBA. The District Magistrate of Jhabua held a so-called "Problem Mitigation Camp" in Kakrana village on October 30 to talk to the people about the benefits of resettling in Gujarat. He not only exhorted the people to move to Gujarat, but also warned them of dire consequences if they continued to associate with the activists of the KMCS and defy the might of the state. Khemla was present in that meeting along with a lot of people. Irascible that he is, he immediately got up and began taking the District Magistrate to task as to why he was forcing people to go to Gujarat when the NWDT had provided that people would have to be resettled in the place of their choice in Madhya Pradesh. The police who were present there in large numbers arrested Khemla and brought him to the District Magistrate who slapped him repeatedly and ordered that he be arrested and taken along to Alirajpur. This angered the other activists of the KMCS and also the people; a confrontation ensued, which ended with the police arresting four more people, beating them up and taking them to Alirajpur while dispersing the rest of the crowd.

Khemla was tied up with his hands arched over his back to his ankles and thrashed severely with canes in the Alirajpur police lockup by no other than the Subdivisional Magistrate, an IAS officer, who told the police that they did not know how to beat up people and he would teach them how! The others too were beaten up mercilessly, and all of them were humiliated by being made to catch their ears and do sit-ups. As is the norm in such cases, false charges were cooked up against them and they were sent to jail. Khemla never recovered from the beating fully; his back gets paralysed with pain quite frequently. Following this, temporary police camps were set up in a few villages along the Narmada, which were approachable by road, and forcible attempts were made to survey the villages. This resulted in more confrontation as the people uprooted the tents in these camps, overpowering the limited police presence in them. This brought things to a head, and the administration responded by bringing in more police and setting the camps up again.

The process of forcible survey of villages commenced once again in January 1993 with augmented police escorts for the survey teams. Village after village was surveyed and those protesting were severely beaten up. The villagers in Anjanbara village were celebrating the important religious festival of Indal at their Patel's house on the January 29. There were a lot of people there from neighbouring villages, too. In the midst of the festivities, the survey team arrived and the policemen began misbehaving with the women. This proved to be the last straw. The villagers confronted the police and being in much larger numbers forced the team to retreat. News of this was sent to the higher ups; the next day, a much bigger police team of some two hundred came to the village and began beating up people, breaking their utensils and looting their household goods. After some time, the men were forced to flee. Taking advantage of this, the police arrested some women and began taking them along. This sparked off another confrontation between the men and the police, resulting in one person being injured in police firing. Once again, the police implicated scores of people and all the activists of the KMCS in false criminal cases and arrested them one by one, beat them up in police lockups, paraded them in the streets of Alirajpur in handcuffs and sent them to jail.

The administration even organised a rally of the people of Alirajpur against the KMCS, branding it as an anti-national organisation for opposing the World Bank! Despite this heavy repression, the KMCS took out a counter rally in Alirajpur to protest against these grossly illegal activities. The attendance in this rally, however, was only in hundreds as opposed to the thousands that normally take part in such demonstrations. This was due to fear of further arrests. The rally was well covered by the national and international media as was the heavy repression unleashed on the people in the course of the surveys. This went a long way in persuading the World Bank to withdraw from the SSP. Ultimately, in a face-saving arrangement, the Indian government announced on March 30th 1993 that it would not avail of the remaining amount of the World Bank Loan. Even though following this development the Japanese Government, too, withdrew its loan for the turbines of the powerhouse, this did not in any way deter the Gujarat and central governments from proceeding with the construction of the dam.

The same process had also started in Chhattisgarh, with the CMM being exposed to heavy police repression. Shankar Guha Niyogi had begun organising the workers of the various factories in and around Bhilai that had been set up to utilise the steel produced by the steel plant for downstream manufacturing from 1990. There was gross violation of labour laws in these units; the workers were working on pittances without mandatory welfare provisions like permanency of tenure, house rent allowance, and pension benefits. The struggle had picked up in strength, and there were widespread strikes in most units in the area demanding the implementation of labour laws. The mobilisation spread like wildfire, leading to the unionisation of workers of almost all the units that employed labourers on an ad hoc basis. This was when the owners of these units decided to gang up. They hired a professional assassin from Uttar Pradesh, Paltan Mallah, to kill Niyogi. This man shot Niyogi dead in his sleep at night at his residence at Durg on September 28. The immediate response of the BJP government was a negative one in that it did not even acquiesce in the legitimate demand that the police register the names of those being accused by the CMM in the FIR. However, there was a countrywide furore over this, and under pressure from the central government, the state administration had to order an investigation by the Central Bureau of Investigation (CBI).

Meanwhile, the agitation of the CMM continued for the implementation of labour laws in the units in and around Bhilai. The government, under pressure from the factory owners, was not prepared to implement the demands of the workers that they be made permanent and given proper benefits. Finally, the CMM workers sat in dharna near the Powerhouse railway station in Bhilai. This movement for regularisation of workers in Bhilai was taking place at a juncture when a whole new era of globalisation, characterised by off-shoring of manufacturing to low labour cost locations, was just taking off worldwide. The new watchword for global capital at that time and ever since has been that of "labour market flexibility," involving the right of the employers to hire and fire labourers at will, pay them subsistence wages and not provide any accompanying benefits that the regularisation of employees entails under labour legislation. These labour laws had been put in place as a result of more than a century of trade union struggles and a clear realisation by the capitalist states in the wake of the Great Depression of the 1920s that unrestricted capitalism without welfare measures for the labour class would lead to demand collapsing and to markets being flooded with goods that no one could buy.

Marx had pointed out that this situation arises from a fundamental contradiction that has plagued capitalism right from the beginning—that of falling rates of profits due to increasing competition and technological advancement. To keep the profits rolling in, production and sale of commodities have to be expanded continually with the introduction of newer technology while the wages of the labourers have to be suppressed. But there is a limit to how much of this can be done within one country. A stage comes when there are too many products to sell and too few buyers with the wherewithal to buy them. In the early stages of capitalist development, this problem was solved by imperial control, which allowed the European nations to export their excess labour and goods to the colonies. In the immediate post World War II years, too, the capitalist firms of the developed west could provide good wages and considerable benefits to their labourers at home, thus keeping demand high by extracting super profits from the exploitation of the labour and natural resources of developing countries. However, as these developing countries began to develop industrially, competition grew to the extent that it became uneconomical for companies in the developed world to employ regular labour with good wages and side benefits. This forced the shut down of manufacturing units in developed countries. These units were relocated in places closer to cheap natural resources and labour in the developing countries.

China in particular and East Asia in general were becoming the favoured destinations for the off-shoring of developed country manufacturing units. Within India, an exodus of manufacturing had begun from traditional centres like Mumbai and Kolkata to places like Bhilai or even less developed locations in search of cheap and unregulated labour markets. Under the circumstances, the industrialists in Bhilai would have to cut down on their profitability and global competitiveness considerably to accommodate the demands of the CMM. So they put pressure on the government to crush the movement once and for all, instead of negotiating with it. When, even after a few days, the demands were not met, the workers went to the railway track and stopped the running of trains on the trunk Howrah-Mumbai rail route on July 1, 1992. The government was in no mood to find a solution through discussions. Suddenly in the evening, police began firing on the protesters, killing seventeen of them. A severe crackdown followed, in which anybody connected with the CMM was arrested and beaten up in the police station before being sent to jail. A false case of murder of a police inspector was foisted on the major leaders of the CMM, prompting them all to go underground. The whole process of mass mobilisation in the Bhilai region was set back greatly, and never recovered from this body blow.

This had its effect on the Dalli unit of the CMM, too. The deposits of iron ore in Dalli were slowly coming to an end. The Bhilai Steel Plant management wanted to introduce machines and mine out whatever was left. They proposed to the CMM that they would give a golden handshake and lay off most of the workers and retain some as permanent staff. Sensing that in the changed global environment there was little possibility of a successful mass agitation against this proposal, the CMM agreed to this offer. Over the years, the main Dalli mass base of the CMM has been dissipated. With the closure of the mines due to the exhaustion of the ore, the once vibrant town and worker's bastis, where one of the most inspiring mass movements had taken roots, now wears a ghost town look.

The various activists associated with Prayog, which in 1991 had consolidated all its mass units under the umbrella organisation Ekta Parishad, too, had to bear the brunt of police repression. One particularly militant activist, Sitaram Sonowane, was abducted by the Forest Department in Raipur district where he was working with adivasis for their right to continue to till forestland as they had been, for ages. There was no news of him for almost a week. Only after national human rights organisations raised a hue and cry did the Forest Department staff produce Sitaram before a magistrate. A meeting held by some members of Ekta Parishad at village Manpur in Satna district was arbitrarily declared illegal by the Subdivisional Magistrate, who went with a posse of policemen and beat up the activists and people who had congregated there. Then, he had some of them arrested and sent to jail.

Subhadra and her fellow activists, too, got a taste of police highhandedness. One day, a policeman came to their office in Dahi and called Subhadra and her co-worker Shraddha to the police station, where they were told in no uncertain terms to stop "inciting the adivasis". They were also ordered to leave Dahi. Subhadra and Shraddha contacted another activist they knew and complained about the sub-inspector's highhandedness to the Inspector General of Police in Indore. In typical contempt for their complaint, the IG refused to take any action against the sub-inspector and warned that he was not going to be responsible for the safety of the young girls in Dahi.

Subhadra and Shraddha however came back to Dahi after Bhargavji intervened and got an assurance from the woman Chief Secretary at that time, who promised an enquiry into the matter. But within a couple of days, a police constable came to their office and summoned them to the police station again. The sub-inspector told them that even if they thought they were smart, actually the reverse was true. He said that an enquiry had been ordered into the incidents of the other day when he had packed them off from Dahi and that he had been asked to conduct it. So if they had anything to say in complaint against him, they should say it to him and he only would take down their statement. This sounded absurd to the two women, so they came back without recording any statement. This is par for such departmental enquiries. An earlier enquiry into the Kakrana incidents, instituted by authorities in Delhi, saw the SDO Police, who had beaten up Khemla, noting complaints against himself!

The great hopes of posing a viable challenge to the established order that had been generated over the past few years began falling apart within the space of just a year or so of repressive actions by the state. All the mass organisations found themselves fighting rearguard actions. Instead of increasing, the mass bases kept on shrinking continuously. The tragedy of this turnaround is even more poignant than the instances of things falling apart in the colonial era because now these systemic collapses are taking place in a sovereign democratic republic whose Constitution declares inter alia that social, economic and political justice will be provided to all its citizens.

On September 28, 1992, the first anniversary of Niyogi's assassination, a massive rally was organised by all mass organisations to protest against police repression, which, however continued unabated after President's rule was clamped following the demolition of the Babri Masjid on December 6th 1992. The net result of all this was that all over Madhya Pradesh, the groundswell of opposition these movements had generated against destructive development and callous governance began to ebb.

Personally speaking, the silver lining to these dark clouds was that Subhadra and I came closer during those days. Once when a journalist from Delhi had asked me a question about "relationships" with adivasi women, I had dismissed it saying that it was politically unsafe to nurture any romantic liaisons with them. Both Subhadra and I, in our own ways, had kept aloof from romantic overtures, focussing on our work. Even though some of the other activists who had come with her to Dahi had paired up during the course of their work, Subhadra had remained aloof from such equations.

The offensive launched by the BJP government upset our political apple carts altogether and made us more amenable to the proverbial apple of romantic predilections. As fate would have it, we came back together from a meeting in Bhopal to protest against the murder of the CMM workers in Bhilai in 1992 and got twelve hours to talk to each other in the bus. We never knew how this journey drew us close to each other; very soon we were making excuses to meet more often than we would have in the normal course of work. One thing led to another, and we began thinking of tying the knot. That is how we took the plunge in Bhopal in 1993 and later found ourselves in Machla, physically ill, politically uncertain and economically poor but romantically rich and with our zest for life undiminished!

14 Love is all you need

The Bhil adivasis are among the most romantic of people; they start falling in love early in life. The Bhils' primary claim to cultural fame is their colourful Bhagoria festival, which takes place just before the Hindu festival of Holi in spring. The Bhil festival is celebrated by turns in the market villages or towns on the market day of that particular village or town. The festival has been filmed a number of times. A celebration of the kharif harvests, it is also associated with the custom of teenaged boys and girls eloping from the festival to lead a married life.

Marriage for the Bhils remains a loose arrangement to bring up progeny, and countless pre-marital affairs between boys and girls and extra marital affairs between men and women add spice to the humdrum of family life. As long as people don't get caught in the act, everyone winks an eye at this side current of free sex that laces Bhili marital life. But once such liaisons become known, the Bhili society takes it upon itself to keep some semblance of order. What they do provides them with great entertainment. Apart from this, there are instances of forcible capture of girls and even married women by boys or men for marriage; cases of rape are rare because there is so much opportunity for free sex. Finally, there are the inevitable divorces. One of the enduring aspects of Bhili society that has survived the ravages of modern development is the role of the traditional community panchayat in resolving all kinds of disputes involving man-woman relationships.

All the parties involved, two, if it is just a matter of resolving the elopement of a couple and three, if it is a case of an extra marital affair or the carrying off of a betrothed or married woman or the desertion of one man by a woman for another or vice versa, get together to sort out the matter. They usually sit at a distance from each other, communicating through messengers who are called "vataars". This is a safety device to prevent direct confrontation between the opposing parties, which could become murderous considering that people often come armed with bows and arrows and guns to these panchayats. But this means that the vataars have to bear the brunt of the abuses and taunts when they go from one side to the other with proposals for a solution, which are wild at the start with, before they reach more realistic levels through bargaining. That is why there is a saying in Bhilali that the behinds of buffaloes and vataars regularly get taken!

The Bhils also have a system of arranged marriages to keep the youth under control and prevent the onset of unbridled sexual and marital anarchy. So even though the custom of a girl running away with a boy to get married is quite common and has social sanction, in such instances the boy's family has to pay a premium over the prevailing rate of bride price. The bride prices are negotiable and keep increasing with time. In case of extra and pre-marital affairs, the boy or man has to pay a fine, which again is negotiable, depending on the seriousness of the offence and the prestige of the offended family. So the whole business of settling romantic disputes is a highly entertaining affair, what with all the people hearing the colourful evidence, the hyperbolic demands for money and the choice epithets that are traded back and forth. There are times when the settling of these disputes requires quite a few sittings. A kind of "politics of honour" is also involved in these matters, which sometimes makes these disputes take on major political overtones between sets of villages.

People not owing allegiance to the KMCS would often use these disputes to try and put one over the villagers who were members of the KMCS. We activists had to frequently sit through these panchayats to ensure that the KMCS villagers did not lose face. Nevertheless, I used to enjoy the proceedings to the hilt, irrespective of whether our villagers came up tops or not.

For a while these panchayats assumed an overt political character in the early 1990s, when the KMCS decided to do something to limit the ever increasing bride price levels. A massive meeting was held, and after putting the whole process of fixing the bride price under the scanner, the amount of the bride price and the accompanying gifts were decided on. The more difficult task was to get people to agree to this reduced bride price. The villagers outside the ambit of the KMCS naturally refused to see the logic behind this move and tried their best to sabotage this initiative. There were many instances in which we would come away from the panchayats refusing to pay anything more than the bride price. This inevitably led to the matter going into the hands of the police and the dalals. These agencies, led by the MLA were only too happy to put a spanner in the works. So despite a sustained effort, eventually this campaign fell through after a few years. The bride prices that are paid have now reached proportions in some areas where marrying has become an extremely expensive proposition for the boys and sometimes leads to them having to mortgage their land and become migrant labourers.

In one village near our headquarters in Attha, extra-marital affairs were the rule rather than the exception. Almost every week, the people of the village could be seen sitting down to resolve these disputes, which invariably ended in someone or the other being made to pay a nominal fine. Now the person who had been cuckolded was not satisfied with just this paltry fine; so he would look for an opportunity to have an affair with the offending person's wife or unmarried sister. He would usually succeed, once again prompting the need for a panchayat in which it would be his turn to be fined. It would carry on like this in a form of sexual vendetta. Appetite whetted, these fellows would try to have affairs with the wives or unmarried sisters of other men. In this way the entire village would remain involved in a sleazy game of "cuckold my neighbour." Old age was no bar. There was a man in his fifties who continuously had affairs with other women in the village and was regularly fined, but his wife always remained true to him, not even once falling prey to the numerous advances that must have been made to her. When his Sati Savitri wife died, this man married a second time. His second wife was young and an easy prey for the other men who had been on the lookout to take their revenge. Despite all the old fellow did to prevent it, one enterprising man soon cuckolded him. To ensure that the old fellow was well and truly floored, this man nicked his own neck with a dharia, a kind of machete and then lodged a false complaint in the police station along with a hefty bribe that the old man had attempted to murder him and got him into jail.

There was an air of celebration in the village as at last the old man had been castled in style; no one went to bail the old fox out. I happened to go to jail following a mass action at that time, and the old man narrated to me his tale of woes, pleading with me to bail him out. Nearly two decades later, when I happened to be in Attha on a visit, I enquired after him and found that he was no more. I was, however, assured that the tradition of sexual vendetta in his village continues to flourish, and the new generation had continued where the older people had left off. The weekly panchayats over extra-marital affairs were still the order of the day. Habits die hard they say. Other villages were not as bad, but that such affairs were a frequent phenomenon can be gauged from the fact that the wives of all those men who had been forcibly sterilised during the emergency period later had more children in spite of this. This is why Bhil men do not like to undergo the vasectomy operation, fearing that their wives will have more children anyway from other men!

There have to be some bad guys to spoil this picture of romantic bliss and entertainment and these are the old villains - the dalals and the police. Like in the case of other disputes, the police have put their dirty fingers into the adivasis' romantic pie also. According to the provisions of the IPC, a boy running away with a girl can be indicted for abduction and rape in case the girl lodges a complaint to that effect with the police. The dalals and the police have used this with vengeance to spoil the pretty picture. Sometimes, the girl's family, instead of agreeing to settle the dispute at a panchayat, listens to the dalals and lodges a complaint with the police. The police then arrest the boy and terrorise the girl into saying that she has been abducted and raped. Since the increasing incidence of rape cases has become a cause for serious concern in India, the courts are extremely strict in these cases, and the boy does not get bail until the case is disposed of. Eventually, of course, in most cases the girl's and boy's families come to an understanding, leading the girl and all other witnesses to become hostile. The boy is acquitted and they get married. But in the process, the dalals, police and lawyers earn hefty packets.

The most dangerous thing about such cases is that all those who even remotely offer any help to the eloping couple are liable to be prosecuted for abetment once the girl turns round and lodges a complaint that she has been abducted and raped. I remember, once in Alirajpur, a young adivasi couple eloped and landed at our office in Attha since the girl's parents were opposed to the match. Luckily both the boy and girl were educated and of legal marriageable age, which was rare among the Bhils in those days. So I advised them to go to Alirajpur and prepare a marriage affidavit in front of a notary. The girl's parents, along with a dalal, had in the meantime gone to the police in Bakhathgarh and demanded that a complaint of abduction and rape be lodged against the boy and some members of the sangathan and that I also be charged with abetment of this crime.

Fortunately, knowing the law well in this regard, I had told our activist to meet the SDO Police with the boy and the girl and submit a memorandum to him, along with the copy of the marriage affidavit. This saved the day for us as the SDO Police sent a wireless message to the officer of the Bakhatgarh Police Station to the effect that he had listened to the boy and girl and was satisfied this was a genuine case of love marriage between two adults, and so no complaint should be registered against the boy. I thus just missed, by the skin of my teeth, being falsely charged of abetting rape in addition to the numerous false charges of murder and attempted murder that were already hanging round my neck!

On another occasion, two members of a street theatre troupe associated with the Vadodara Kamdar Union eloped and got married in an Arya Samaj temple in Vadodara in Gujarat. One of our younger activists from Alirajpur invited them to spend their honeymoon in our office guestroom. In those disappointing times, when the battle against the dam was in the doldrums, the KMCS was well on its way to transforming itself into a marriage bureau for eloping couples!

Aghast at this development, I made the legal consequences of our young friend's gallantry clear to the entire group—that in such circumstances, an Arya Samaj marriage held no legal value without a parallel court marriage. The Gujarat government would say that frustrated in our attempt at throttling their "jeeva dori" we Ravans had now begun abducting their Sitas! We packed off the couple to a remote village and were much relieved when the girl's parents came around to accept the fait accompli. I, for one, breathed one of the most satisfying sighs of relief I ever had. A charge of murder or attempted murder is one thing, but one of abduction and rape is something I can live without.

Another festival that is a happy hunting ground for eloping adivasi couples is the Indal. Indal is in fact the quintessential expression of pristine pre-modern Bhili anarchism. The small traditional Bhili village communities were bound together by close cooperation in almost all aspects of life, starting from their agricultural operations to their social celebrations. This cooperation could be maintained only if there was near total equality between the families. One way of ensuring this was to distribute the individual surpluses generated by families from their agricultural, pastoral and gathering activities among the community. The Indal was traditionally the means of doing this. This is a celebration in which the family thanks the Gods for having been bountiful. Every five years or so a family distributes the surpluses it has accumulated among the community by treating the latter to a feast. Songs in praise of the Gods are sung during this time over three days and nights; on the final night, people, especially young boys and girls, congregate to dance through the night to the beat of drums. In the morning, they partake of the feast. The songs sung during the Indal vary from place to place, but they all give a sense of the vastness of nature and the strength of natural processes and inculcate a respect in the listener for these.

Sitting in a dark room with the singer Gayan and his chorus seated in front of the diya or lamp, singing in a lilting cadence that slowly builds up its tempo to the tune of the dhak or small drum, the listener cannot but feel transported into a different world where all the petty rivalries and desires of the mundane do not matter anymore. In that atmosphere, one can immediately understand why the Bhils have remained averse to development based on greed and profit that we in the modern world crave so much after. There is a great sense of peace in those hills adjacent to the river. Even though the life is very hard, the great advantage is that it is simple. The people think nothing of climbing up the high hills to reach some of their farms every day during the farming season and later to bring down heavy bundles of reaped harvest upon their heads. What unsettles them is the inevitable contact with the "modern" world, which is often through some rapacious local government official or the equally extortionate sahukar. That is why, in a fit of rage, Bava of Jalsindhi once held forth at length in a meeting that forests and rivers and lands belonged to the Gods, and the government had no right to usurp this treasure that had been bequeathed to him and his people for safe keeping. One of the activists of KMCS took down this outburst, translated it into Hindi and sent it off to the chief minister and the press as an open letter. It remains to this day the most authentic and eloquent deep ecological statement to come out of the struggle against the dam.

Young Bhils, however, have little time for the gayna going on inside and are more interested in enjoying the pleasures of loving, singing and dancing. The Indal is a rare event these days as families do not earn surpluses any more; they suffer from chronic debts instead. So in place of the earlier five-year period, these days a particular family does only one Indal in the lifetime of its household's head. Shankar, for instance, has not been able to celebrate an Indal of his own, and the last one was celebrated when his father was alive. Khemla only recently managed to celebrate his own Indal. This is why the people of Anjanbara were so incensed when the survey team disrupted the Indal that was in progress in their village after a gap of nine years. But when it does take place, the Indal is the grandest of celebrations. There is the custom of sacrificing goats on the final night. Apart from the household celebrating the Indal, close relatives or family friends bring their own goats for beheading. They also bring their drums. Thus, the final night is a great show of dancing, singing and feasting, which is so entertaining that thousands of people gather from far and near to join the revelry.

In the early years of the KMCS, we would be concerned with the fact that the adivasis were so ignorant of the modern economic and political systems that they had to depend heavily on us for all kinds of interactions with the modern world. So we would conduct two-day workshops for the youth, where the various aspects of modern political economy would be explained to them. Once, a ten-day workshop was planned for the youth in Attha, as we found that two days were not enough for training them properly. It so happened that an Indal celebration was going on in one of the nearby villages, and the final night celebration coincided with the fourth day of the workshop. During the night, all the participants left the workshop venue to go to the Indal; they never came back. So much for our attempts at modernising a set of people who had pristine anarchistic tendencies coursing through their blood! We, of course, did not give up and began organising the week-long training workshops at the ashram at Machla from where there was no escape!

One of the important paeans of praise that is sung during the Indal is to the Goddess Kansari. She symbolises the Bhils' staple cereal of sorghum or jowar as they call it and so happens to be their life giver so to speak. The felicitation of Kansari is extremely important to ensure that future harvests are equally bountiful as the ones in the past. The importance of this Goddess can be gauged from the fact that traditionally oaths among Bhils are administered in the name of Kansari Mata or Jowar Mata as she is sometimes referred to. The oath taker has to take some grains of jowar in his hand and take the oath. The belief is that an oath taken in Kansari's name has to be fulfilled; otherwise it will boomerang on the oath taker with mishap befalling him.

Historically, the Bhils had fought bravely to maintain their habitats and traditional lifestyles, but with time, they had become subdued. Towards the end of the 20th century, they had resigned themselves to being thrown around from place to place like counterfeit coins, when the struggle against the dam started. Initially, they rose gloriously in revolt, but after a few years they realised that the old story of displacement was going to repeat itself. So except for a few people like Bava, most others opted for whatever they could get, which was in any case much more than they would have got had they not fought as they had done. However, even at the peak of the struggle, they knew in their heart of hearts that the dam would not be stopped. One of the practices in the NBA was to stand together and take oaths that no one would leave their homes and land, come what may - "Doobenge par hatenge nahin." As long as these oaths were taken empty handed, most people were ready to take them, but they would never take these oaths in the name of Kansari mata with jowar in their hands.

The Bhils' worldview is thus a materialist one, woven around their agri-pastoral livelihoods. Their gods are animistic representations of the forces that govern their habitats and livelihoods. They are practical people governed by material needs. The Bhils did not take the spiritual pole vault taken by the early Hindu Upanishadic philosophers from a more or less similar material base. The subordination of the material world to that of the spiritual by the ancient Hindu sages is most vividly portrayed in the Katha Upanishad, which narrates the story of a young prince Nachiketa, who is appalled when his father distributes old cows to Brahmins as presents, and offers himself for sacrifice to Yama, the god of death. Yama is not at home when Nachiketa reaches his doorsteps, and the young boy has to wait for three days for his return. As penitence for having kept a Brahmin waiting at his door without food or water, Yama grants him three boons, one for each day.

As the first boon, Nachiketa asks for his father to recognise and accept him on his return to earth; Yama readily grants this boon. He then asks to be told of the fire that leads to heaven, which is beyond all sorrow, hunger and thirst and, this boon, too, is granted to him. But Yama is perplexed when Nachiketa wants to know the secret of immortality. He offers the boy the whole wealth of the universe instead. Nachiketa remains adamant and Yama then reveals the path to immortality, which according to him is as sharp as a razor's edge, and consists of doing the preferable as opposed to the pleasurable. In a beautiful metaphor set out in exquisite Sanskrit verse Yama says that a person's soul is the master of the chariot that is his body and is seated within it. His intellect is the charioteer and his mind is the rein with which he controls the horses, which are the senses running on the roads, which in turn are sense objects. The person who unites his soul, intellect, mind and body in reining in the senses from galloping down the road of sense objects attains true knowledge!

This is the kind of high spiritualism of complete renunciation of material desires that forms the philosophical foundation of Gandhian political theory and action. It requires little imagination to see that there is a vast difference between the anarcho-environmentalism of the Bhils and that of Gandhians. In the former case, love and respect for nature has made the Bhils evolve cultural and livelihood paradigms that prevent its exploitation by limiting growth and development beyond a certain point while allowing them to satisfy their material desires as much as they want to. In the latter case, material desires and consumption are sought to be reined in obviating the need for development and growth and consequent depredation of nature altogether. Naturally, being materialists, the Bhils have tended to militantly defend against intruders, the material bases of their culture—primitive agriculture, pastoralism and hunting and gathering. Gandhians on the other hand, being of spiritual dispositions, have relied on non-violent passive resistance to win over the hearts of the oppressors. We shall see a little later how this variance in preferred modes of action against modern industrial development has been one of the important factors in the NBA losing its influence over the adivasis in the valley.

Despite this crucial difference, the one common thing between the anarchism of the Bhils and that of Gandhians is their village and agriculture-oriented and eco-centred worldview, based on the principle of "vasudhaiva kutumbakam" – treating the entire world as family. The Norwegian philosopher Arne Naess who acknowledges his debt to Gandhi coined the term "deep ecology" for this worldview in 1972 to emphasise the deeper ecological foundations on which it was based and later went on to call it "ecosophy". All over the world, this principle has been gradually marginalised since the Columbian encounter by the devouring greed of aggrandisement that propels modern industrial development. The creed now is to produce and consume ever more, in the process laying waste both nature and the people who believe in living in harmony with it. In order to sell the ever increasing products, the homogenising culture of western consumerism is being popularised worldwide through television soap operas, sports broadcasts and commercials. The village youth in Chhattisgarh prefer playing cricket on dry beds rather than desilting the tanks. During the telecast of the Cricket World Cup in 2003, an old Bhil woman from a village in Dewas lamented to me that India had lost the final match to Australia. Indeed, how catastrophic as compared to the loss of the ecological paradise that her village had been a few years back!

So when Subhadra and I arrived in Indore in the autumn of 1994, we might have been steeped in our love for each other, our love of nature and our love of our fellow human beings, but we were also confused as to the course of action that we would take to try and spread these feelings of love to the ruling elite of the world who were bent on making war. But like the immortal John Lennon who sang in the "Our World" concert in 1967, the first ever to be telecast simultaneously worldwide, we still believed in our heart of hearts that

There's nothing you can do that can't be done.

Nothing you can sing that can't be sung.

There's nothing you can make that can't be made.

No one you can save that can't be saved.

Nothing you can do but you can learn how to be in time

It's easy all you need is love, all you need is love.

Bava's speech (transcribed in a Letter to the Chief Minister)

We, the people of Jalsindhi village are writing this letter to you, the Chief Minister of Madhya Pradesh.

We are people of the river bank. We live on the banks of the great Narmada. This year, our village Jalsindhi will be the first village in Madhya Pradesh to be submerged by the Sardar Sarovar dam. We will give up our lives, but we will not move from our village. When the water comes into our village, when our homes and fields are flooded, we will also drown; this is our firm resolve.

We are writing this letter to let you know why the adivasi peasants of Jalsindhi are preparing to drown themselves.

You, and all those who live in cities, think that we who live in the hills are poor and backward, like apes. "Go to the plains of Gujarat. Your condition will improve. You will develop" - this is what you advise us. If it is true that our situation will improve in Gujarat, then why aren't all of us ready to go there?

We have lived in the forest for generations. The forest is our moneylender and banker. In hard times we go to the forest. We build our houses from its wood. From its rushes and splints we weave screens. From the forests we make baskets and cots, ploughs and hoes, and many other useful things... We get various kinds of grasses; and when the grasses become dry in summer, we still get leaves... If there is a famine, we survive by eating roots and tubers. When we fall sick, our medicine men bring us back to health by giving us leaves, roots, bark from the forest. We collect and sell gum, tendu leaves, bahera, chironji and mahua. The forest is like our mother; we have grown up in its lap. We know how to live by suckling at her breast. We know the name of each and every tree, shrub and herb; we know their uses. If we were made to live in a land without forests, then all this knowledge that we have cherished for generations will be useless, and slowly we will forget it all.

The river, too, is our sustenance. The Narmada has many kinds of fish in her belly. Fish is our standby when we have unexpected guests. The river brings us silt from upstream, which is deposited on the banks so that we can grow maize and sorghum in the winter, as well as many kinds of melons. Our children play on the river's banks, swim and bathe there. Our cattle drink there throughout the year, for the river never dries up. In the belly of the river, we live contented lives. We have lived here for many generations; do we have a right to the mighty river and to our forests or don't we?

After the forests and the river, how can we live in the plains or in cities? You city people live in separate houses. You ignore each other's joys and sadness. We live with our clan, our relatives, our kin. All of us pool together our labour and build a house in a single day, weed our fields, and do any small task as it comes along. Who will come to lend a hand and make our work lighter in Gujarat? Will the big Patidars come to weed our fields or to construct our houses? ... In Gujarat, if any sorrow or evil befalls us, to whom can we go to tell of our troubles? You are not going to give us the bus fare and send us back, are you?

... You tell us to take land in Gujarat. You say that our leaders are inciting us, that we should not be swayed by them...We are not being swayed by them. We are being swayed by our land, our forest, our river and our livestock. They are the ones leading us astray.

You tell us to take land in Gujarat. You tell us to take compensation. For losing our lands, our fields, for the trees along our fields... But how are you going to compensate us for our forest? ... How will you compensate us for our river - for her fish, her water, for the vegetables that grow along her banks, for the joy of living beside her? What is the price for this? ... Our gods, and the support of our kin - what price do you put on that? Our adivasi life - what price do you put on that?

The land in Gujarat is not acceptable to us. Your compensation is not acceptable to us. We were born from the belly of the Narmada, and we are not afraid to die in her lap. In the summer before the monsoons, our village will be filled with water, and we will drown.

We will drown, but we will not move.

Bava Maharia

15 The Neglected of the Earth

On a biting cold morning in the winter of 1996, a Bhil woman lay naked, shivering on the floor of her ramshackle hut in village Rajna. Beside her, lay a shriveled new born baby, also shivering. The woman had lain like that for the whole night, and her ordeal wasn't over yet. A pair of twins waited within her to be born; but for the past three hours, there had been no movement inside, so the baby was stuck inside the womb. The earth beneath the woman was wet with blood and placental fluid, but neither she nor the dai seemed to be the least bothered. Just then, the mobile dispensary of the Kasturba Trust happened to pass by and was stopped by the people in the village. Although five nurses were present in the dispensary, they expressed their inability to help owing to lack of instruments. When the villagers beseeched them to take the woman and the baby to the Primary Health Centre at Barwah, they pleaded their inability saying they were on their way to different villages to administer vaccines under the Pulse Polio immunisation programme.

A doctor in another jeep whom the villagers stopped and pleaded for help even went to the extent of saying that the lives of thousands of children were at stake, and he could not put them at risk for the sake of one woman and child. Eventually, the husband of the woman had to borrow money from a moneylender at an exorbitant interest rate and hire a jeep to take her to Barwah. The woman just about survived, but her twin babies died. Tests revealed that the woman had a haemoglobin count of just 4 grams per decilitre, dangerously below the ideal level of 12 or above. Clearly, the achievement of health, which, according to the World Health Organisation, means a state of complete mental, physical and social well being and especially reproductive health for poor adivasi women, is a daunting task in adivasi areas.

In the summer of 1995, while I was recuperating from my illness and writing reports, Subhadra, not one to sit back and twiddle her thumbs, volunteered to work for the Kasturba Gandhi National Memorial Trust at its field area in the Barwah tehsil of Khargone district and Bagli tehsil of Dewas district, about fifty kilometres from Indore. The Trust used to run a mobile health clinic staffed with a qualified doctor and a rudimentary dispensary visited the villages in the area three days a week. In addition, it had provided training from time to time to thirteen dais or traditional birth attendants of the area in better delivery practices and basic medicine. The trust gave them a monthly stipend of a hundred rupees. Subhadra began to work with the two female supervisors who were based in one of the villages there. Thus, she was already familiar with the area and the people when we decided to start our own mass organisational work with women in the autumn of 1996.

The failure of the Sangharsh Yatra and the subsequent repression let loose by the government, which had reversed the rising tide of environmental mass movements in Madhya Pradesh, had troubled me for quite some time in Alirajpur. I used the free time I got in Machla to undertake a serious review of the modus operandi we had adopted thus far. We activists of environmental movements were mixing the understanding of the deep ecologists that the preservation of nature could only be possible by abandoning modern industrial development, with the concerns of the affected people about the serious threat this development posed to their livelihoods. Thus the environmental mass movements we were taking part in constituted an "environmentalism of the poor", distinct from that of the rich in India and the West, which was concerned with only sequestering environmental niches like national parks and wildlife sanctuaries and were not genuinely bothered about the people who lived in proximity to them.

As I looked back and tried to theorise our past struggles, I realised that besides the fact that we had demonstrated a lack of appreciation of the coercive power of the state- in that the Marxists certainly had a better idea about the nature of state power and therefore of counter- mobilisation strategies, we had also neglected the question of women's rights and needs.

Modern feminism can be said to have started with the publication of Mary Wollstonecraft's classic Vindication of the Rights of Women in 1792. The effects of the European Enlightenment were nowhere more pronounced than in the emancipation of women from centuries of bondage decreed by religious obscurantism. In the West, there has been a tangible improvement in the condition of women since then. The new wave of feminism since the 1960s has been both divided and enhanced by different streams within it—liberal, Marxist, socialist and radical. The last school has made the significant contribution of the concept of patriarchy or the deep-rooted structural oppression of women by men that has now become universally accepted.

Black and coloured women hailing from poorer backgrounds provided a new dimension, complementing and also opposing this Euro-American feminism. Simultaneously, third world women considerably widened the scope of feminism by analysing their experiences in the historical context of colonial and neo-colonial exploitation. Earlier, the mid-1970s had seen the emergence of eco-feminism with the publication of Rosemary Ruether's seminal work New Woman, New Earth. This last challenges—the male domination of nature and women and their depiction by men as passive objects, submitting meekly to reason and force. They argue that the tendency to control others and the aggression arising from this are patriarchal attitudes that enslave both men and women. This school has emerged from the ecology and peace movements that are underway across the world and is currently the only feminist movement that rejects the dominant mode of development and governance, just like the deep ecologists do.

This theoretical and empirical work done over the years to establish the identity of women bore fruit in the form of universal recognition of the rights of women as embodied in the United Nations Convention on Elimination of Discrimination against Women. In 1995, the reproductive rights of women were recognised and population control policies, which targeted women as objects without any decision-making powers of their own, were rejected. The importance of women enjoying their sexuality for the achievement of complete reproductive and sexual health got recognition for the first time at the International Women's Conference held at Beijing in 1995. Under the impact of these, the Indian government too jettisoned its earlier sterilisation target based population control programme in favour of a reproductive health and rights approach. Male-dominated ruling establishments of various countries have since then stymied the holding of the next decadal UN Women's Conference, which is now overdue.

The women's movement in independent India started in a conscious manner in the mid-1970s with mobilisations against male violence. Later, the movement extended to the violence of the government's policies. To address the economic marginalisation of women, attention was directed at development policies. The women's movement has succeeded in getting the government to enact protective laws and frame favourable policies. Like in the West, here too, there are a lot of differences within the movement, but thankfully these tend to get blurred when strategic choices have to be made. There have been struggles against the government's population policies and especially against the introduction of harmful contraceptives like depo provera and norplant and the testing of anti-fertility vaccines. Issues such as the sati, the burning of a widow on her husband's pyre in Deorala in the state of Rajasthan, the rape of the women's development programme worker Bhanvri Devi (also in Rajasthan) and reservation of seats for women in Parliament and legislatures too have been important rallying points. From 1996 onwards there has been a lot of activity around the implementation of the new target-free approach to population control, based on the paradigm shift in the thinking on women's health, following the population conference at Cairo. A particular problem of serious proportions that has vexed feminists of late is that of "the missing Indian females", the declining sex ratio, which has gone down to as low as 861 females to 1,000 males in the state of Haryana and 933 for the entire country, according to the 2001 census.

Patriarchy not only forces most women to stay at home, but its internalisation makes it difficult to organise them. In rural areas, the problem is compounded by illiteracy and lack of medical infrastructure in general and the occurrence of these problems with respect to reproductive health in particular. Health being an issue that affects everyone, makes it easier to mobilise adivasi women around it and helping them create a space of their own within their society.

Women's health, however, is a much more complex issue than ensuring the provision of adequate healthcare services. It requires a multi-pronged approach to combat poverty, through the creation of labour intensive work opportunities, removal of social inequalities of all kinds, a campaign against traditional and modern myths, and a comprehensive community healthcare system with primary and referral services. That mere service delivery without accompanying mass organisational work is ineffective is amply illustrated by the experience of the Kasturba Trust, which, despite a fifty-year record in providing exemplary health and education services for rural women in the Malwa and Nimar regions of Western Madhya Pradesh, has not made any substantial dent in the patriarchal structures, which stifle the lives of the area's rural women.

The primary cause of ill health in women is their low status in society, wherein they are relegated to a position of subordination from the moment of birth. Girls eat last and the least, are over-worked and under-educated, and have to bear children from an early age. They receive inadequate medical treatment when ill and are often passed over for immunisation. Despite the biologically proven fact that women have a longer lifespan than men, in India, the reverse is true in rural areas where more girls are likely to die than boys, leading to a sex ratio skewed against women in the population. Lack of property rights contributes to the general preference for a male offspring as insurance in old age. Women often go through the rigours of repeated pregnancies and childbirths to produce sufficient male children that can survive through to adulthood. Malnutrition, lack of sexual hygiene, repeated pregnancies, and overwork lead to most rural women being anaemic and therefore prone to other diseases in general.

The prevailing pattern of development has been particularly harsh on women. Destruction of resource bases has led to increasing workload with a decrease in nutritional levels of the food intake. The introduction of artificial input based, mechanised agriculture has deprived women of the little control that they had over the production processes in traditional agriculture. This practice has further reinforced patriarchal power relations. Forced migration, whether temporary or permanent, has exposed women to sexual violence in unfamiliar surroundings. The loss of traditional livelihoods has been accompanied by the induction of women into low-paid jobs in the informal sector where the work environment is unhealthy and the workload high. The general level of violence in society has gone up, to further sequester women in their homes, thus reducing employment opportunities.

Primary healthcare has received short shrift both in terms of financial outlays and the introduction of participative healthcare systems. Apart from foreign-funded immunisation campaigns such as the Pulse Polio programme, rural populations rarely ever receive any effective healthcare from government health services. Consequently, for the poor, infant mortality levels are still dangerously high as are maternal mortality and morbidity levels. Spurred on by the neo-Malthusian myth that population growth is responsible for poverty, the government had launched an aggressive population control programme in the 1970s that targeted women for sterilisations and the use of various unsafe and unhealthy contraception measures. With the introduction of the sterilisation target-free reproductive health approach from 1996 onwards, there had ostensibly been a so called paradigm shift at the policy level in population control and maternal and child healthcare. However, the ground reality in rural areas remained much the same as before.

When we started work in this area, we realised that not only were the adivasi women burdened too much by multiple oppressions, but specifically in the sphere of reproductive health, there existed an intimidating culture of silence that we had to contend with. Weeks were spent in visiting the villages and going from house to house to talk to the women.

The first meeting in Chainpura drew just five women and initially met with a subdued response. Only when specific problems like white discharge from the vagina, leucorrhoea, were mentioned, did one woman say that she was suffering from it as well as from back pain. Another revealed that she had a slight prolapse of the uterus whenever she did hard work.

The picturesquely set village of Golanpati unfortunately doesn't have any electricity. Most of the men and young unmarried women were away, labouring on the fields of rich farmers atop the Malwa plateau, in order to earn the money to buy diesel for running their engine-driven pumps with which to irrigate their winter crops. After a short, polite conversation, some of the women decided to go fishing in the Kanar river with small nets called dahwalia. The people of the area are able to supplement their normal simple diet with such occasional infusions of rich fish protein.

The village Akya too was at that time without electricity. Situated on the banks of the Sukhri stream, the people here had already got diesel and were busy in the fields irrigating the standing crop of wheat and gram. Once again, we spent the day visiting the women in their houses and fields. The houses here, being on the farms, are scattered over a distance of some three kilometres. Over thirty women attended the meeting. Of them twenty-three not only reported various kinds of reproductive health problems, but demanded remedies. The women complained that local quacks only gave them ineffective injections or suggested that they get their uteruses removed. The government health worker rarely visited the village.

Typical bureaucratic apathy has led the twin villages of Okhla and Chandupura to lie in two different panchayat clusters, but they have a Hanuman temple which has seen the epic Ramayan being recited continuously for the past twenty-five years. Okhla village also has electricity. Even though the adivasis and their deities hold no value for the government, the same is obviously not true when it comes to Hindu gods and their devotees! These villages, home to dalits as well as adivasis, have been enterprising enough to draw water over great lengths from the river Kanad, using electric pumps and PVC pipes. During the initial house visits, one woman in Chandupura said she could get all the women together in a jiffy if she was given a share of the pickings from the project being planned for them! Here, for the first time, we encountered women who candidly said that the lust and violence of their men, fuelled by alcoholism, was the primary deterrent to good health. They underlined the need for a health clinic in which specialist doctors could diagnose their problems.

Limbi is a village of Jat farmers. Originally from the state of Rajasthan, they own most of the land in the village on which the dalits and adivasis work as labourers. The Jat women were prepared to talk individually, but none of them came to the meeting, even though a separate one had been organised for them, keeping in mind the caste equations. One Jat woman had lost her mental balance because she could not bear the mounting pressure on her to produce a male child after repeated births of girls; another had been tricked into marrying a doddering old Jat in his seventies who had later died, leaving the young widow with a five-year-old daughter and some land.

In Mundla, where the Dangis hold a position similar to the Jats, we found that the adivasis and dalits worked for wages as low as twenty rupees a day, which was then less than half the statutory minimum wage. Here, the men, not the women, attended the evening meeting. The men listened and went on saying "Ha bahenji, Sach Bahenji" - *yes sister, true sister*, but did not make any comments of their own when they were told that they should be more considerate of the health of their women. Even though they promised to send their women to the repeat meeting to be held in the morning, no one came to attend that.

The village of Palsud is situated between these two villages and the villagers there, a mix of dalits and adivasis, are continually troubled by the Jats and Dangis. There have been murderous fights, and two dalits from Palsud are serving a life sentence in Indore jail for having murdered a Jat from Limbi. The women in this village enthusiastically took part in the meeting and talked candidly about their reproductive health problems. There are two other villages, Bargana and Barkhera nearby, but in both of these, the meetings drew only four or five women each. One Jat woman went around wearing a cloth belt around her loins to prevent her uterus from coming out. She would have liked to have a hysterectomy, but did not trust the private doctors in Sanawad where most of the other women had got themselves operated. In the local dialect this is referred to as the "burra operation" to distinguish it from the sterilisation operation which is called just "operation" and is done free by the government doctors as part of the family planning programme.

The last set of villages is in a cluster on the banks of the Choral river. The villages of Aronda and Kundia lie to the west of the river, while the villages of Sendhwa and Karondia lie to the east. In Sendhwa village, the high caste Brahmins and Patidars do not let the dalits draw water from the public hand pump; the latter have to drink water from the Choral river. Every monsoon season an annual epidemic of waterborne diseases attacks these people. In 1995, there were three deaths due to gastro-enteritis. Here too, the meetings were sparsely attended, but the women who did come complained of reproductive health problems and of the insensitivity of their men. The upsarpanch belonged to the Muslim community, where patriarchal attitudes dominate. The upsarpanch's wife herself suffered from anaemia with a haemoglobin count as low as 6 grams per decilitre, despite the family being well off economically. She spoke about her problems individually, but did not come to the meeting.

Katkut village is located roughly at the geographical centre of this area. By virtue of being the weekly marketplace and also for having a civil dispensary, banks, the forest range office and a police outpost, it happens to be the commercial and administrative centre.

Being the local market village, it is home to a lot of traders and moneylenders and, at that time, five quacks. There is an ayurvedic dispensary of the government with a doctor and a compounder. Little or no medicines are available in this dispensary, and mostly the doctor spends his time reading a newspaper or treating patients with allopathic medicines for a fee. The other government health functionaries—the para medics, too, are engaged in the same clandestine allopathic practice. All the local government servants working in various departments stay in rented apartments. Satellite television and liquor shops—one licensed and many unlicensed ones make the ambience of the village more urban than rural. The hybrid, half Western, half Indian pop culture of television soap operas and their commercials, furthers the urban aspirations of the youth, although the people still retain their traditional abhorrence for constructing latrines in their houses and prefer to defecate on the sides of roads and fields! Thus, the approach roads to Katkut would all stink in the morning with the stench of stools and urine until pigs polished them off. The Kasturba Trust in true Gandhian fashion offered to supply the material for the construction of latrines and soak pits for the people if they would only contribute their labour. The people treated this with suspicion and went on defecating on the sides of the roads. We took up residence in this village in a rented accommodation at the beginning of our work, as we still had to make friends with the people and earn their confidence before settling into one of their villages. Needless to say, we too had to get up early while it was still dark to defecate on the roadside!

Dominated by the Jats, the defacto sarpanch of the village was, in fact, the husband of the woman sarpanch at that time (1996). The Jats of Katkut are held in low esteem by their caste men from other villages because of their arrogant and boorish behaviour, and the men find it difficult to get brides. One young Jat woman, the only daughter-in-law in a family of four sons, complained that she repeatedly aborted. She approached us for a remedy. Her mother-in-law, Karmabai, was an assertive woman who had fought a long legal battle with her brothers to gain the rightful possession of her share of her father's land. A village panch or elected ward member of the village government, Karmabai cautioned us that given the entrenched patriarchy in this village, hardly 50 kilometers outside Indore, there was little hope of us achieving anything worthwhile. The women here, regardless of whether they are from relatively well off households or from the extremely poor adivasi and dalit ones, are under patriarchal oppression. Despite all the rhetoric and policies of women's empowerment in the women's policy document of the government of Madhya Pradesh, the stark reality that came through from our initial forays was that the women of this area suffered from severe neglect, both from their families and from the society and government.

Truly, these women are the neglected of the earth.

16 Gynaecology in the Wilderness

Introducing ourselves as activists among the adivasis would have invited suspicion among the non-adivasi government servants in Katkut, so we introduced ourselves as workers of the Kasturba Trust. The forested areas of Nimar and Malwa, where Katkut lay, had been opened up by the British who had implanted Jats and "lower" caste menials from Rajasthan, thus creating a caste hierarchy with the Jats at the top, the menials in the middle, and the adivasis at the bottom. Thus there was a powerful exploitative non-adivasi presence in the villages, apart from the traders and government servants. They had become edgy with the rising tide of adivasi mobilisation in the state and would have strongly resisted our activities.

Our initial plan to mobilise women in the area by organising health care camps bit the dust early on. The women were reluctant to talk about their problems at the meetings. Finally, one of them shared the reason behind the silence: most families bore grudges against each other, and the women were afraid to make their diseases public knowledge as this would provide ammunition for further backbiting.

Subhadra, too, got a feel of the pulse in the form of a verbal whip lashing when a woman from Okhla mistook her for an auxiliary nurse-medic (ANM) for not doing her job properly. This woman from Okhla had had a baby at the Primary Health Centre in Barwah, and during the delivery the vaginal opening had been ruptured and had had to be stitched. The ANM was not competent to do the later stitch cutting, and this woman had to go all the way to Barwah for getting the stitches removed.

Similarly, Bansi of Akya village asked "How will it help if I understand my problem if I do not have the technical expertise to solve it?" She had been ill ever since she had given birth to her fourth child under complicated conditions some three years ago. Everywhere, the women insistently demanded that arrangements be made for proper medical attention, instead of holding reproductive health workshops. The demand of the women was for checkups by women gynaecologists from Indore. The gynaecologist in the PHC in Barwah had never set foot in these remote adivasi areas.

The governmental health services were in a sorry state. There was a perennial shortage of commonly needed medicines and staff. For example, iron and folic acid tablets were not available in the PHC Barwah for six months in 1996. In Bagli tehsil, these were available, but there was no staff to distribute them. There was no ante-natal care to speak of. However, everything was hunky-dory as far as the records were concerned; our investigations revealed that the government village-level workers were submitting false reports; in some cases they did not even travel to the remote areas which they would have to reach on foot.

The provision of reproductive health services is difficult to monitor as compared to the completion of sterilisation targets. So for years, the health records of the Barwah PHC and possibly most other rural PHCs in Madhya Pradesh have had no relation to the reality prevailing on the ground. Yet, when it comes to one-shot affairs like the polio eradication or sterilisation campaigns, there is no dearth of enthusiasm or resources.

The Kasturba Trust had been running a minimal community health programme under which the community organisers, along with the dais, motivated the people of the village to improve their health awareness. They were also supposed to keep track of the diseases in the villages and bring the sick to the mobile clinic when it visited these villages. This plan had not worked partly because of the formidable social obstacles in its path and partly because of a lack of motivation among the workers who were, to be fair to them, often burdened with excessive paper work and reporting responsibilities. It came as a surprise to them that there was a target-free plan in place for the last two years and that there had been a paradigm shift in maternal and child health care. They even felt that not having targets is a very rash step on the part of the government!

We soon had to trash our preconceived plans in the face of shocking lack of infrastructure and the mindset that women's healthcare was a marginal problem compared to the more pressing livelihood problems. We scouted for local resources for the infrastructure, sensing that to be a better approach rather than setting it up ourselves.

Three reproductive health clinics were held one each month in the winter of 1996-97. Organising the first one at Palsud village required a lot of preparatory work. Inspection tables had to be constructed. The mobile clinic of the Kasturba Trust did not have any obstetric instruments so these and gloves had to be acquired. The gynaecologists from Indore had to be contacted. The PHC in Barwah had to be informed to requisition the services of a pathologist. The school building in Palsud had to be cleaned and temporary inspection rooms needed to be readied with sufficient lighting provisions. Everything turned out very well in the end. Three gynaecologists, one physician, and one paediatrician attended to more than eighty patients. Thereafter, the other two camps at Okhla and Kundia did not pose too many problems as we had got the hang of the process. The camp at Okhla was immensely successful with more than a hundred patients turning up. The camp at Kundia had only about forty patients because some influential but dubious non-adivasis in the nearby villages objected to our not involving them.

Even when sufficient women turned up for the preparatory checkups, they usually went missing at the time of physical examination. Some even ran away to their farms rather than getting dragged to the examination table! The reason for the confusion turned out to be a rumour that free medicines were being supplied, since we had given away a few doctor's samples.

More revelations lay in store for us. Vaginal tablets given to some women for cure of leucorrhoea were taken orally, while one woman, who was subtly told by the doctor to keep it "inside," without a mention of the vagina, thought this was some totemic item and kept it inside a box! Indeed, the idea of miraculous injections that would cure them of their problems immediately was widespread. One woman, when we went to her for weekly follow ups, fumed at us: "Mujhe aise lafde nahin chahiye, mere naam tumhari chopdi se kat do"(*I do not want to get into such trouble. Please remove my name from your register*).

The quacks were playing an extremely dangerous role as far as the reproductive health of women was concerned. Initially, they gave antibiotic injections and pain-killers to the women who approached them for treatment. When this did not succeed, they advised the women to undertake hysterectomies. These quacks acted as touts for gynaecologists in Sanawad and Indore who have private clinics. Kusma of Akya related how, on one occasion, she was taken along with five other women who were complaining of various kinds of pains to a gynaecologist in Sanawad by a quack in Katkut. All five of them were told to get hysterectomies done. Kusma was extremely relieved when the doctor at the Okhla clinic told her that she suffered from hyperacidity and high blood pressure, and there was no need for her to take the burra operation. These quacks also provided unsafe abortion services, which had led to the death of a woman from Katkut the year before.

Invariably, the women continue to suffer from pains and leucorrhea even after undergoing this burra operation, although a few reported improvement after taking the vaginal tablets. Since leucorrhoea required more analysis and treatment than was possible in the clinics, we tried alternative treatments like homoeopathic and ayurvedic, and these proved to be more effective in many cases. Another phenomenon was that of women's vaginal opening having become so extended and loose from repeated childbirths that when they got up from a squatting position, air was sucked into the vagina, which was then ejected with an embarrassingly loud sound when they sat down again. Many women had complained of stomach pains and dizziness. Their problems were diagnosed as acidity and hypertension. We found that often their diet was heavy in salt and hot chillies and lacked sufficient water intake. Combined with low nutritional levels, this was a sure-fire recipe for hyperacidity and high blood pressure. Subhadra suggested to one woman to drink a litre of water first thing in the morning every day. She retorted, "Why should I drink so much water when I do not feel thirsty?" Why indeed!

In another incident, we recommended to a boy affected with scabies, a medicine his parents would have to procure from Katkut. In the meantime, we advised them to apply a paste of neem leaves on the boy's affected body parts so as to give him temporary relief. Five days later when we went back the dalit basti to verify, we found that not only was he in a worse condition, but he had also passed it on to a few other children. The medicine was not available in Katkut, and we had to procure it from Indore. Among adivasis, scabies assumes epidemic proportions because they do not clean themselves properly and rarely apply appropriate medicines.

There were some serious cases, ranging from piles, stones in the bladder, suspected cervical cancer and the like which required detailed examination and treatment in Indore, but the patients were too poor for this. The camps threw up three advanced cases of tuberculosis. These people were getting themselves treated by private practitioners at a great expense, unaware that the government had a TB eradication programme, which provided free treatment. One of these patients was from Katkut, yet even he did not get wind of a TB camp held by the PHC in his village in October 1996, which had drawn a blank. When he finally came to know from us, he took the trouble of walking twelve kilometres to the Kundia camp for registration and treatment. Thus, just medication alone is not a solution to the health problems that women face. The culture of instant treatment through injected medication and intravenous drips introduced by irrational allopathic practice over the years has destroyed the people's capacity to seek their own solutions. Consequently, patients want immediate medical solutions and are impatient about sitting and understanding the cause of their problems.

By reviewing our interactions with the people and the experience of the clinics we realised the very tangible fallouts of patriarchy on women, especially after marriage. We decided to conduct a reproductive health survey to determine the extent of women's health problems and their relationship to patriarchy. However, we had to first contend with the phenomenon of "survey fatigue". Numerous surveys conducted by government agencies and the Kasturba Trust had made the people unresponsive. Health workers at the ground level were just fudging the data. Moreover, rarely are the respondents of a survey involved in the design of its structure or in the policy decisions adopted on the basis of such surveys.

When, however, surveys are done in a small local population, with the intention of providing immediate relief to the respondents based on the information gathered from them about a specific problem, the question of ethics does not arise. This is illustrated by a landmark study carried out by the Search project in Garhchiroli district in Maharashtra. Our survey fell into this category, too. Nevertheless, we took no chances and had detailed discussions with the women to decide on the best possible design of the questionnaires so as to ensure their full cooperation. The survey was conducted in the first week of April 1997 by adolescent girls in the 15-18 years age group, studying in the high school run by the Kasturba Trust in Indore. Before this, a three-day orientation workshop was held for these girls. The first day was spent in making the girls aware of the extent to which women are oppressed by patriarchy. This was done not in a pedagogical manner, but by inducing the girls to analyse various kinds of injustice being suffered by women in their own surroundings. The second day was devoted to explaining the workings of the reproductive system in particular and the human body in general. The third day was utilised to give the girls an idea of the kind of reproductive health problems being faced by women in the survey area and to explain the survey design and schedules to them.

The workshop revealed that even young girls have internalised patriarchy and are not at all sensitive to the ways in which women are continually downgraded in their society. There was stiff resistance on the second day to an open discussion conducted by Subhadra to describe the reproductive system with the aid of overheads. The girls just did not want to discuss sex and the ways in which lack of knowledge about sexual matters could lead to serious reproductive health problems. These girls mostly came from middle and upper middle-class backgrounds, and they all had misconceptions about the menstrual discharges. These misconceptions were reinforced by the various taboos that accompany the onset of menses in Hindu society. There is an urgent need for sensitising adolescent girls, not only to reproductive health issues, but also to the societal factors that contribute to widespread morbidity among women.

The aim of the survey was to get a comprehensive idea of the extent of reproductive health morbidity among women in the reproductive age group. We also used the survey as a means to test our hypotheses regarding the influence of patriarchy. The hypotheses were that the high levels of morbidity had a close relationship with the poor general health status as reflected in the anaemic condition of most women; that this morbidity had more to do with the pernicious effects of patriarchy, which were so evident and was not just the result of poverty; and finally, that the influence of patriarchy was more pronounced among married women. The survey questionnaire addressed parameters like the number of childbirths and deaths and the age at marriage for women in the 15-45 years age group. The haemoglobin percentage of the women in the 15-45 years age group also tested using haemometers.

Although a census survey of all women was sought to be conducted in thirteen villages, only a few women responded. The villages of Limbi and Aronda, with their higher well-off upper caste population, were chosen as the control population to test the hypothesis that reproductive health problems were related to patriarchy and not to poverty alone. The other control group was that of unmarried menstruating girls older than 15 years of age. They were surveyed to test the hypothesis that the effects of patriarchy were more pronounced on married women than on unmarried women.

Subhadra, I, and a doctor of the Kasturba Trust handled the logistics of organising the survey. This was a difficult task because the area is a hilly terrain without proper roads, and the haemometers and nurses had to be ferried around on time.

Both the villagers and the team members enjoyed the whole exercise immensely. With just three functioning haemometers, the haemolglobin levels of only 168 women in eleven villages could be determined, in addition to twenty-eight unmarried girls above 15 years of age.

The results presented a shocking picture. As many as 84.7% of the women suffered from some reproductive health problem or other, 49.1% suffered from vaginal discharges and 45.4% from dizziness arising possibly out of high blood pressure. 65% of the women complained of waist pains. 6.8% of the women suffered from STDs, which was quite a high figure for such a remote rural area with no prostitution. On an average, the number of diseases being suffered simultaneously by a respondent, called the morbidity index, was as high as 3.1. For adivasi women, it was highest at 3.5 while that of the dalit women stood at 2.6 and that of other caste women at 2.1. Thus even though the other caste women who are economically well off as compared to the adivasis and the dalits, the level of morbidity among them, too, is rather high. Muslim women, too, showed a high morbidity level of 3.2, almost at par with the adivasi women.

The survey convinced us that poverty is not the only cause of poor reproductive health. Significantly, none of the 28 unmarried girls surveyed reported as suffering from any problems.

The average haemoglobin level of the women was only 7.36 grams per decilitre of blood, which was about 46% of the desired value. The close relationship between the anaemic condition of the women and their poor reproductive health status was amply evident. Unmarried girls showed an average of 11.1

grams per decilitre, which was much higher than those for married women, confirming that it was the latter who were more subject to the pressures of patriarchy. Other results were also equally disturbing: 73.6% of the women had been married before completing 18 years of age, 41.7% had lost at least one child, 17.3% of women had more than five children and only 10.4% of the women had been sterilised.

These discouraging statistics pointed towards the pervasiveness of patriarchal values. The survey also revealed that there was no statistically significant difference in the literacy levels of boys and girls, and the nutritional levels of girls was slightly better. Expectedly enough, these levels were far below that of the upper socio-economic strata in urban areas. Thus, these data, too, confirmed that the effects of patriarchy begin affecting women only after marriage and that gynaecological solutions alone were not enough to solve the reproductive health problems of women. For this, the problem of patriarchal oppression had to be dealt with simultaneously, in order to ensure the women's reproductive rights.

17 Voodoo and its Cure

The Bhil adivasis have traditionally relied on 'burwas' or traditional medicine men for the solution of their health problems. Traditional adivasi aetiology has it that a variety of evil spirits are responsible for various diseases, and hence it is necessary to exorcise them by chanting mantras. The burwas know these mantras and other ways in which evil spirits can be exorcised. Herbs, too, are prescribed as a supplement to these mantras. Even today, this view of disease persists among the adivasis. Since its administration is cheap, it is usually the first option for them. There is little understanding of the fact that disease is caused by germs and bacteria of various kinds. The only difference is that now, in addition to the burwa, the people also approach doctors who give them injections and pills or intravenous drips. These things are as arcane to illiterate adivasis as the mantras chanted by the burwa, but appear at times to be more effective. The adivasis do not take any chances, however, and go to both quacks and burwas either simultaneously or alternately when seriously ill.

The doctors, quacks, nurses and health workers all take advantage of this mindset of the adivasis to indiscriminately inject antibiotics and apply intravenous glucose drips for even such diseases as colds and dysentery. There is never any serious attempt to diagnose the problem being faced by the patient. These are also supplemented by inadequate doses of oral antibiotics. Consequently, the patient has to come again and again to the doctor for treatment. The doctors consider the monsoon to be their earning season, since at this time of the year they take advantage of the natural increase in the prevalence of diseases to fleece patients.

There is not much difference between a mechanic who repairs a bicycle and these doctors. In the case of the bicycle, at least the owner can see the working of its parts and form an idea of how it works. In the case of the human body, however, the working of its inner parts is not visible, and so the patient normally does not know what is happening. This ignorance about the working of the human body extends to the general public and is not restricted to just adivasis. A modern voodoo of the irrational use of injections, drips and drugs has grown up around this ignorance. This suits the interests of the drug industry, which spares no effort to promote this irrationality among both medical practitioners and policy makers. Thus, the market has been flooded with formulations sold at exorbitant prices through unethical promotional means. With the cessation of the process patent regime in India, which allowed the production of a drug through a process different from the one for which the original licence exists, the cost of medicines is bound to increase even further, adding to the miseries of the people.

This state of affairs is even more critical in the case of reproductive health because the working of the reproductive system is not just more difficult to understand, but there are also all kinds of taboos and superstitions associated with it. In such cases, the doctors go a step further and advocate hysterectomies as the final solution for persistent problems such as vaginal discharges, waist pains and blood pressure. The government health system is woefully inadequate in this respect. This sordid situation with regard to the lack of quality service providers and the miserable state of health awareness among adivasis is surely on the extreme side in this area, but it is more or less the case all over the third world.

Invariably, the suggested solution to this problem is to step up the resources devoted to the public health system as well as to increase the number and training of grassroots workers of the public health system. Given the resource crunch faced by the government and the total lack of motivation in its staff, there is no possibility of this strategy succeeding, as is evident from the little progress that has been made in the implementation of the target-free approach. If anything, over the past few years, the rural public health system has deteriorated and is on the verge of collapse as allocations have not kept pace with demand. A fact that is sought to be camouflaged by launching such eye-catching programmes as the National Rural Health Mission which is high on publicity but low on performance.

NGOs can definitely provide better service, but they can touch only a miniscule section of the populace and have to constantly depend on external sources for funds. Apart from this, such funds are more readily available for high-profile work such as AIDS prevention rather than for the basic work of primary reproductive health services. The vast majority of poor rural women are doomed to suffer in silence. Even when they do seek solutions, they mostly go to inadequately trained and extortionate private practitioners. The challenge is to build up health awareness in the rural populace so that they can make better utilisation of the resources, which are at present being siphoned off by quacks.

A locally self-sustaining community health system is not impossible to achieve; it only requires a lot of hard work. Community health programmes for adivasis cannot succeed without bringing about a drastic change in their mindset with regard to health. This will involve their understanding of the way in which the human body works, the causes of various kinds of illnesses, and a rudimentary knowledge of the way in which the various drugs operate. Identification and prescription of locally available herbs, too, can go a long way towards reducing the costs of health care. The close link between patriarchy and ill health has to be understood and acted upon as well. The NGO, CEHAT, has made some practical contributions in this area by collaborating with the many adivasi mass organisations of Western Madhya Pradesh to set up such community-run health systems.

The more serious problem, of course, was that of patriarchal oppression. A recurrent theme in the meetings we had with the women and even in our conversations with individual women was that of the behaviour and attitudes of their men. The women complained that they had no control over either their bodies or family decisions. So there was no question of their being able to improve their health. Ramanbai of Chandupura was suffering from piles, and the doctor at Sanawad had told her that she would have to get herself operated. The doctor at the Okhla clinic also said the same thing. Yet, her husband, who was capable of spending the money, was refusing to do so. She said that while talking about such matters, women have to be afraid of their children also lest they go and tell their father. Kesarbai of Okhla had already had three daughters and did not want any more children, but her husband was not agreeing. She had thought of getting a copper T inserted, but another woman's bad experience in this regard had discouraged her. When Subhadra advised the use of condoms, she refused, saying that her husband would not listen to anything; if she resisted intercourse when he was drunk, he would charge her of being involved with some other man.

Another woman, let's call her Sumati, was particularly troubled. Her husband was involved in an affair with another woman. On some days, her husband's penis was swollen and full of pus, indicating that possibly he was suffering from a sexually transferred disease, which he would transmit to her. This was a classical helpless situation in which so many women find themselves. In Kundia, there was a woman who was beaten up by her husband and forced to spend the night out in the cold because her brothers did not entertain him properly when he went to their village. Reshma of Chandupura said that her husband was angry that she got herself treated at the camp at Okhla, which had brought her closer to Subhadra, to whom she confided many secrets. Echoing Reshma, several young women complained that their mothers-in-law did not look favourably on this new process.

A social custom of the Bhils that is detrimental to women is the importance associated with alcohol as a holy spirit. Children are given alcohol even when they are just babes in arms. The Gods have to be propitiated every now and then with alcohol. This gives the men and sometimes even women the licence to drink. Alcoholism brings to the fore the worst manifestations of patriarchy in men. As mentioned earlier by Kesarbai, under the influence of alcohol, men make sexual demands of their wives and resort to violence if these are not met. Men frequently go on drinking sprees, doing no work at all for days together. This increases the burden on women, who then have to work harder. These alcoholics invariably object to their women taking part in organisational activities and quite a few of them are active as informers and collaborators of the police.

Having been a martial race, the Bhils have a clear gender division of labour, which is not easily broken. The men, even if they want to, find it difficult to help out with domestic work. Interestingly, the need to migrate in search of employment has resulted in the loosening of these social taboos, and men have begun to do domestic chores. This taboo against men doing household work is widespread across Indian society. Being free from such hang-ups myself, I often cook food and wash clothes for my family. Water came only once a day in the morning in Katkut, and the tap from the public line was at the front of our rented house. So the washing had to be done on a stone on the road front. One day, the landlord, an irascible old man, told me that I should not wash Subhadra's clothes. A debate ensued with the old man saying that he hated the very idea of a man washing his wife's clothes. He went on to say that the sacred scriptures of the Hindus forbade men from doing housework. Instead of challenging this patently false statement, I asked him why he went to the police station to report disputes when the ancient scriptures mention that they should be resolved within the community. He retorted that the domestic world was governed by the scriptures, but not the outside world of work, where modern ideas had to be accepted for progress! Indeed, in Indore word has spread in the neighbourhood where we now reside that since I cook and wash clothes, I do not qualify to be called a proper man! And it is the maids who come to work in our house who have spread this message around. Talk of patriarchy being internalised!

Initially, my landlord refused to believe that the British, who had introduced the police system as well as the sewing machine with which he earned his livelihood, had also accepted the equality between men and women. He finally relented, saying that he would concede that men should wash their wives' clothes only if I could show him a book written by an Englishman that explicitly said so. The landlord's wife related to Subhadra, how on one occasion, when she had overstayed at her father's house well beyond the time that her husband had told her to come back, she had a nightmare that her husband was chasing her with a stick. She had packed her bags and returned the very next day! Thus patriarchy too is a kind of voodoo that has stifled women for thousands of years.

All this pointed again and again to the fact that conducting programmes to remedy reproductive health problems would be inadequate without addressing the thorny issue of reproductive and gender rights. Things took a dramatic turn when circumstances forced us to take up rights issues in an unanticipated manner.

Hundreds of adivasi women dressed in their multicolour sarees, ghagras, lugras and doglis were seated under the shade of the two big mahua trees in Akya village one sunny afternoon. It was the first week of May 1997 and the peak of marriage season. An adivasi coming from outside would have wondered why only women were congregated and why there was no drum beating. But this was not a marriage party. It was the meeting called to review the results of the reproductive health survey. Subhadra painstakingly explained, with the help of coloured charts, what all the data collected meant. Then she let the bombshell drop—the data had revealed that all women, irrespective of whether they were rich or poor suffered from reproductive health problems because of patriarchal pressures and that medication alone could not provide lasting solutions to them. There was a dam burst after this. Woman after woman got up and said that they could do nothing as the men would not listen and would impose themselves on them, especially when in an inebriated condition. Previously, the Bhils had had to brew their own liquor from the flowers of the mahua tree, which is a laborious and time-consuming task and so could be undertaken only occasionally. With the easy availability of illicit liquor from the two distilleries in the area, this constraint had been removed. In the end, the meeting remained inconclusive, as there seemed to be no solution in sight to tame the chauvinistic men and their alcohol addiction.

It was clear to us that the twin problems of alcoholism and bootlegging and the larger issue of patriarchal oppression could not be tackled without involving the men in the organisation process. However, this meant that we would once again have to stray into the area of general organisation against the poverty arising from exploitation by non-adivasis and the wrong policies of the state that had been underway in the whole western Madhya Pradesh region for a decade and a half. This would then pose the problem of women's issues being sidelined in the heat of struggle, something that we were running away from. Our hands were forced in a way because some of the adivasis of the area who had relatives in the Western Nimar region, where the adivasi mobilisation was in full flow at that time, came back after a visit there with the news that a husband and wife couple had gone east to their area to help them organise themselves. These people put two and two together, sought us out and asked us to get things moving in Barwah too.

We were very cautious about not sidetracking women's issues in the heat of struggle, something that was the case with the other mass organisations of the region right from the word go. To ensure that women remained at the forefront of all activities of the organisation process, we made it mandatory for women to be present in large numbers. After an initial reluctance from the men, the women started coming in because we would simply refuse to continue with the meeting in the absence of a sufficient number of women. Once the initial barrier was overcome, we conducted separate meetings for the women to inspire them to get out of the daily rut of household work and involve themselves in organisational activities instead. My role henceforth was only that of a trainer and the adivasis—men and women—were trained to negotiate with the government officials—starting from the lowly forest guard to officials higher up the ladder.

We had just one preparatory workshop in which Khemla came from Jhabua, and the two organisations, Adivasi Shakti Sangathan in Barwah tehsil and Adivasi Morcha Sangathan in Bagli tehsil were formed. After that a domino effect began, with people walking in the footsteps of others in the western Madhya Pradesh region who had been fighting for their rights for more than fifteen years, attacking the bastions of oppression and demolishing them. The first casualty was the forest department, which was totally marginalised within the space of just a month. The forest guards initially tried to intimidate some of the people in Akya village and confiscated a cassette and some literature from them. A protest meeting was called in Okhla, and the Divisional Forest Officer in Barwah was given a notice to attend and explain why his subordinate staff had behaved in such an illegal manner. Hundreds of men and women gathered on the appointed day at Okhla, but no forest department official showed up. Even the forest guard and deputy ranger who manned the barrier had fled. Then, something unexpected happened that changed the course of events completely.

A week before this, I had conducted a workshop exclusively with men on the issue of patriarchal oppression of women. The group discussions had ended with the conclusion that alcoholism was the severest problem for the women. The men also said that it was proving to be a financial drain, and something had to be done about it.,The workshop ended without any decision on the action to be taken, but with the agreement to hold another meeting. On that fateful day in Okhla, when people were discussing what to do next since the forest officials were absent, Rajaan, a teetotaller, got up and said that the illegal liquor shop should be shut down. The bootlegger who ran this shop was a notorious goon as is usually the case all over India. He used to abuse and beat up the adivasis. Thus, the wrath of the people, which had been reserved for the forest officials, now turned on the bootlegger. They raided his shop, confiscated his liquor, smashed the bottles and warned him to close shop immediately.

The nature of their trade demands that goons and bootleggers be made of stern stuff. So that night, he and his cohorts went to Okhla village to raid the house of a leading member of the sangathan, Shivlal, and beat him up. Word spread immediately, and by early morning, hundreds of men and women had gathered in Katkut in front of the police outpost and were demanding the arrest of the goon who was an upper caste trader. For so many years the non-adivasis of Katkut were the ones who used to get cases lodged against the adivasis to keep them cowed down. The tables were turned and the massive demonstration resulted in the goon being booked under the Prevention of Atrocities against Scheduled Tribes and Scheduled Castes Act. The adivasis then took out a rally in Katkut, and the village reverberated for the first time to the slogans, which had become so popular elsewhere – "Lootnewala Jayega, Kamanewala Khayega, Naya Jamana Aayega" - *the exploiters will go, the labourers will eat, a new era will dawn* and "Jal, Jangal, Jameen Kunin Chhe, Aamri Chhe, Aamri Chhe" - *to whom do the water, forest and land belong, to us, to us*. Sometime later, some forest officials in Sulgaon village impounded some buffaloes from the jungle in which they were grazing. A posse of women forcibly freed the buffaloes from the forest check post. Later, in a massive mass meeting held in Sulgaon in support of this action, one man came drunk and began creating a ruckus on the podium. Since this man was a notorious troublemaker, the other men hesitated to take action against him. Two women, armed with bows and arrows, climbed onto the podium, took hold of this man by the scruff of his neck, and dragged him off the stage and away from the meeting—to a rousing applause from the audience.

This set in motion a powerful movement against alcoholism and bootlegging on a scale not seen before in western Madhya Pradesh. At that time, the Madhya Pradesh government had a system of selling liquor licenses through annual auctions, wherein a contractor would bid for the right to sell liquor through licensed outlets in a tehsil for a year. To maximise his profits, this contractor sold more liquor than he had the license for, by encouraging franchisees to set up illegal shops in addition to the licensed outlets. This required bribing the police and the excise department staff and also maintaining of a gang of goons to ensure that all the illegal liquor being sold in his area was sourced from him and not from some other contractor or directly from a distillery. Incidentally, distilleries in Madhya Pradesh, too, produce more liquor than they reveal to the excise department and offload it clandestinely onto the market. So even remote villages have illegal liquor outlets. After the successful action against the bootlegger in Okhla, the people of Bagli tehsil just across the border in Dewas district began demanding a similar action in their area.

The situation in the Udainagar sub tehsil of Bagli was slightly different from that in Barwah. While in the latter, there were a lot of non-adivasi farmers in the villages, in the former, this was not so as most villages were populated by overwhelming adivasi majorities. However, Udainagar, the market village, was dominated by non-adivasi sahukars who had lorded it over the adivasis for the better part of a century. Such was their power that when a debtor failed to pay his due on time, an employee of the sahukar would visit him and take away any moveable property that he may have had and also extract a fee of rupees 100 for the trouble of having to come to recover the dues. The first rumblings of change were heard when the Indore Diocesan Social Service Society (IDSSS) began to form grain banks and thrift and credit groups in adivasi villages of the area from 1990 onwards. This NGO not only formed and consistently ran self-help groups (SHG), but also pioneered their linkage with the branches of the regional rural bank and the commercial banks operating in the area for supply of cheap credit, a practice that has now become standard all over the country. Such is the quality of its work that this NGO has been chosen under the World Bank funded Madhya Pradesh District Poverty Initiatives Programme for the promotion of women's SHGs in Madhya Pradesh, the Swashakti Yojana. The organisation is currently supervising over a hundred SHGs in Bagli Tehsil.

The SHGs begun by the IDSSS not only disbursed credit, but even arranged for the supply of agricultural inputs. In some places, they also organised the adivasi farmers into collectively selling their produce in the wholesale market in Indore. Thus, a comprehensive dent was being made into the power base of the sahukars. Things came to a head when these groups also began to act cohesively in the political sphere. The Bagli legislative assembly constituency had traditionally been a BJP stronghold and had, since the formation of Madhya Pradesh, been represented continuously by Kailash Joshi who had once served briefly as

Chief Minister of the state. This influence was being maintained in the Udainagar region through the sahukars, and they had their henchmen among the adivasis in the villages. The SHGs decided to field their own candidates for the elections to the Panchayat bodies in 1994 against the candidates of the BJP. This angered the sahukars, so they hired goons to beat up some of the SHG members and simultaneously had the latter arrested by the police.

On learning of the arrest of members of the SHGs, Sister Rani Maria of the IDSSS went to the police station in Udainagar to enquire about their offence. This prevented the police from beating up the adivasis. Instead they had to be produced before the magistrate in Bagli, where they got bail. This intervention upset the sahukars so much that they secretly began plotting the murder of Sister Maria. One day in the spring of 1995, when she was travelling by bus to Indore from Udainagar, she was accosted midway in an area where the road passes through a forest, by hired assassins and murdered in broad daylight in front of other passengers by repeated stabbing. This incident created a furore all over the state and brought out the hollowness of the rule of law at the grassroots level. This was the state of affairs when we kicked off a more overt political process in 1997. The whole area was literally flowing in alcohol at this time, and there was an illegal liquor godown in Pandutalav village from where all the liquor was supplied.

Naturally, a murderous goon had been hired by the contractor to oversee the operations. He was a ruthless fellow. On one occasion, he had caught a man selling the liquor of another contractor and as punishment had taken him from his village to Udainagar, beat him up publicly on the way and then got him arrested by the police on a false charge. A mass meeting of the sangathan was scheduled in Pandutalav village. The contractor got word of this and came down on the appointed day with a jeep loaded with his henchmen. However, on seeing men and women in thousands, he turned tail and ran away. The liquor store, worth some two lakh rupees, was sealed and the keys handed over to the police. There is no parallel to this action in the history of mass actions against bootleggers in Madhya Pradesh. On that day, as the skies above Pandutalav reverberated with the sound of vociferous slogan shouting by thousands of people, the prospect of a revolution, which I had long given up hope on, seemed to become a distinct possibility once again, even for a cynic like me. Such was the power of the anti-liquor movement that even men who had not given up drinking participated wholeheartedly in the actions against the sale of illicit liquor. The sale of liquor during festivals and marriages was stopped completely.

There was a fundamental difference in this mobilisation from what we had undertaken earlier. In Alirajpur, we non-adivasi activists played a frontal role in the organisation and the net result had been that the adivasis themselves, apart from Shankar and Khemla, had not been able to blossom into leaders in their own right. This lack of a wider base of indigenous activists later led to the KMCS losing its influence after we non-adivasi activists left, despite all that Shankar and Khemla could do. So a new technique evolved, which let the adivasis play a more prominent role in the organisation process. While Subhadra had to take a pro-active role, given the fact that she was working with women and in a sensitive area like reproductive and gender rights, I restricted myself to just conducting training workshops with the people. Khemla, Shankar, Vaharu and other adivasi leaders were called in to train and lead people in the initial stages, but later, as a local leadership developed, both among the men and the women, they were able to carry all the organisational work on their shoulders.

Such was the impact of this process that a leading Hindi daily of Indore did a front-page feature on the Sangathan underlining the fact that its main leaders were all adivasi women. The transition from addressing reproductive health issues to mobilising people around reproductive rights proved to be a successful one. Some of the iron that had crept into my soul due to the setback to our earlier struggles got banished at the sight of these poor illiterate women portraying such powerful leadership roles.

18 Demand And Thou Shalt Be Crucified!

In the mid-1990s, the Adivasi Mukti Sangathan waged a long-drawn and moderately successful struggle in Sendhwa town, against the malpractices of the agricultural produce marketing committees or the Krishi Upaj Mandi Samitis as they are called in Madhya Pradesh. These committees control the auction of agricultural produce at the tehsil level and have a mandatory adivasi representation. Despite that, local power lords, including politicians and traders, often rig these auctions. The many ways in which the farmers are duped in these Mandis are a fit subject for a separate book altogether.

Sendhwa is situated near the border of Madhya Pradesh with Maharashtra, and its hinterland is a rich cotton-producing belt. Thus, adivasi farmers from both the states come to the Mandi in Sendhwa to sell their cotton. The cotton season is a windfall for the traders as there is a large influx of adivasi farmers to the market, and in collusion with the Mandi officials, they seize the opportunity to fleece the farmers by paying lower prices and under-weighing the produce. The profits thus made are so huge that cotton is locally termed as white gold, or "safed sona." The Sangathan's persistence in demanding the use of automatic weighing machines, transparent auctioning process, and payment by cheque in lieu of cash led to an agreement, but as usual, there wasn't any implementation of the agreement. On the contrary, this invited the traders to send their goons to beat up the adivasi activists.

The Sangathan responded with mass action, and in February 1997, the Agra-Bombay National Highway passing through Sendhwa was blocked by around ten thousand people who had come in from as far as Dewas and Jhabua districts to show solidarity. The ghat section of the highway, just south of Sendhwa as it crosses the Satpuras, has been a troublesome area since British times, when the Bhils would often waylay caravans and armies. During the Great Bhil Rebellion of 1857-60, the famous battle of Ambapani, in which the British finally defeated the forces of the rebel leader Khajya Naik took place near Sendhwa on this road. As in the past, the Bhils had once again blocked this road, demanding justice. This galvanised the administration into action and the roadblock was lifted only after the goons were arrested. Subsequently, all the demands were fulfilled and the Mandi in Sendhwa has since been running according to rules.

The functioning of the agricultural credit cooperative societies and banks, too, is bedevilled with problems similar to those that beset the Mandis. Even though the adivasi farmer members are in theory the shareholders and through their elected representatives the governors of these banks, in reality, their relationship with the officials of the societies is no better than the one they have with their sahukars. In remoter areas, where the adivasis are largely illiterate, the officials even cheat them of the loans that are advanced to them on paper. These societies are weighed down by non-performing assets (NPA) arising from large loans that have been doled out on political rather than sound financial considerations to strengthen the big farmer-trader nexus.

The pressure on the finances of these banks created by such malpractices is sought to be relieved by putting the screws on minor adivasi debtors to pay up the small consumption loans they take, even when they are unable to do so due to crop failure. In May 1997, officials of the district cooperative bank murdered Gyan Singh, a twenty-six-year-old Barela adivasi of Savriyapani village in Barwani tehsil. Gyan Singh's father, Rabba, had taken a loan of rupees 3,500. Four bank officials went to collect the interest on this loan in a jeep. Not finding Rabba they instead caught his son Gyan Singh and thrashed him so badly inside the jeep that he died of injuries by the time they reached Barwani. The news spread like wildfire, and within no time, thousands of adivasis of the Adivasi Mukti Sangathan gheraoed the police station in Pati demanding the registration of a case of murder against the culprits and their arrest. Following this, the Adivasi Mukti Sangathan held a massive rally and public meeting in Barwani on the May 9 in which the president of the district panchayat paid a cheque of rupees 1,00,000 to the widow of Gyan Singh as compensation.

This incident and the uproar created by it due to the massive public action undertaken by the Adivasi Mukti Sangathan started a debate regarding the state of the cooperative banks in the adivasi areas and the way in which they had become institutions for the exploitation, not emancipation of the adivasis. Incidentally, the arraigned officials were not only non-adivasis; two of them were, in fact, from the trader caste. The main point to come out of this debate was that even after fifty years of independence, adivasis in the western Madhya Pradesh region had not yet been accorded an equal status with the non-adivasis and there were blatant violations of their rights. To the extent that even officials of a cooperative bank could assume unto themselves arbitrary powers of arrest and torture with impunity.

The burgeoning mobilisation of the adivasis was perceived as a serious threat by the leaders of the ruling Congress party. Several cabinet ministers, including the two deputy chief ministers, hailed from this region, and they perceived this increasing expression of people's power as a death knell for the kind of corrupt cronyism that they practised in the name of democratic politics. The bureaucracy, being of colonial lineage, has always been inimical to people's mobilisation. In the initial stages, mainstream politicians could not go against the people for fear of alienating their voting blocks. But gradually, as movements grew to challenge their hegemony and their political bases, they became apprehensive and harked back to colonial repression in time-dishonoured fashion. The last straw was the action against the cooperative bank officials.

This was followed by a massive police crackdown on the Sangathan in August 1997, for which a murderous skirmish was instigated around a private dispute between the block president of the Congress party and some Sangathan activists. False charges were registered against many members and activists. In many areas, adivasis had to flee to the jungles to avoid getting arrested or beaten up by the police. Fraternal organisations from nearby areas and human rights organisations from all over the country jumped to the Sangathan's assistance. On September 18, 1997, the adivasi organisations of western Madhya Pradesh took out a massive rally in Indore to protest the atrocities being perpetrated by the administration all over Khargone district. Thousands of men and women came to that rally disregarding dire threats. This drew the attention of the world at large and the press in particular to the blatant violation of the rule of law by those entrusted with securing it. This flare up received attention in the press, with the focus being on the antipathy of the government and the bureaucracy towards the legitimate demands voiced by the mass adivasi organisations.

The Adivasi Shakti Sangathan (ASS) was targeted, too. Innumerable false cases were lodged against scores of its members, and they were prevented by the administration from taking out rallies and holding public meetings to vent their grievances. When massive rallies were planned to be taken out in the towns of Sendhwa and Barwah on November 24 and 25, 1997, the administration clamped Section 144 of the Criminal Procedure Code, preventing the assembly of five or more persons, on the entire Khargone district. A massive force of some 3,000 police personnel was brought in from other districts to enforce the ban. Since such mass public rallies invariably show the administration in a bad light, it always tries to prevent them and thereby stifle the voices of dissent.

All the adivasi organisations of western Madhya Pradesh took up the challenge and decided to take out rallies and hold public meetings, come what may. A jeep full of men and women going to take part in the rally in Sendhwa were stopped at the dead of night at 2.30 a.m. on November 24, 1997 by the police in Katkut and arrested along with the driver. Their jeep was confiscated in a blatantly illegal misuse of the provisions of section 144 of the CrPC. The women of the Sangathan then staged a sit-in in front of the police outpost in Katkut to agitate for the release of those arrested and to protest against the highhandedness of the administration. This was a first for Nimar—the act of women in their hundreds sitting in front of the police outpost for 24 hours, braving the cold and the rain. Immediately, the police personnel and the non-adivasis began misbehaving with the women and calling them all sorts of names. The police outpost is situated in the panchayat of the non-adivasis and has two gates. The women then sat in dharna in front of one the gates in protest against the misbehaviour of the police and the non-adivasis. The executive magistrate who came to Katkut refused to intervene against the non-adivasis saying that the women should lift their sit-in or face the wrath of the latter. Two false police cases were registered against Subhadra for publicly berating the magistrate for taking the side of the non-adivasis.

A revolt of sorts took place after this on the morning of January 8, 1998, in Katkut as a group of women arrived in a rally at the police outpost to be arrested and sent to jail in connection with the various false cases that had been registered against them. They shouted slogans, the main one being, "sarkar ni jail mein katri jagah baki chhe, dekhne chhe dekhne chhe" - *we want to see how much space is left in the government's jails.* Instead of meekly bailing themselves out, these women had decided to launch a struggle against governmental apathy and repression by going to jail instead. The first victory in this struggle was won at the police outpost itself, when the police refused to arrest all the twenty women who had cases against them and took only eight into custody despite repeated attempts on the part of the women to be arrested.

By frightening the police into not arresting all the women, an authoritative statement was made by the Sangathan in defence of the right of the area's downtrodden people to organise themselves. The arrested women subsequently shouted slogans even in court and argued with the magistrate that they had a right to do so when the latter objected.

The Sangathan members were used to being implicated under false cases whenever they protested; even the judicial magistrates increasingly used their discretion to send them to jail instead of releasing them on bail. Usually the Sangathan members would resist arrest, forcing the police to conduct raids that led to confrontation. Eventually, this reduced the authority of the local police. This time, however, they decided not to resist and instead go to jail and fight their battles from there.

The ASS members took the decision to court arrest voluntarily and launch a "jail bharo" or *fill the jails* agitation to show the administration that they were not afraid of going to jail. Subhadra subsequently went on a hunger strike in jail from January 11, 1998, as a last resort, stating that as a dalit woman she did not find any substance in the guarantees to life and liberty enshrined in the Constitution and so preferred death in jail instead. Her demand was that the arrested members of the ASS be released on personal bonds from jail, all the eleven false cases lodged against the members of the ASS be withdrawn, and the right of the adivasis to stage peaceful demonstrations be restored.

The rest of the members of the ASS who were outside remained active during this period by taking out a massive rally in support of the struggle of those inside jail in Barwah and by enlisting the members of a sister organisation, the Adivasi Mukti Sangathan, in a sit-in in front of the Divisional Commissioner's office in Indore to demand the transfer of the District Magistrate and Superintendent of Police of Khargone district. The administration had on that occasion given an assurance that the false cases would be withdrawn, and no further victimisation of adivasis would take place. The Superintendent and District Magistrate were also transferred at the behest of the election commission, and Subhadra broke her fast after eleven days.

Repression, however, continued unabated, with two more false cases registered against the members of the ASS. It all started with a seemingly innocuous problem of proper hostel facilities for adivasi girls studying in Katkut. The non-adivasi headmistress of the government adivasi girl's hostel in Katkut had been defalcating funds meant for the running of the hostel for over a decade, resulting in poor living conditions for the girl students, which affected their academics. Some of the Sangathan's members whose daughters were studying in the school got together and submitted a detailed report about the irregularities to the Joint Director of the Adivasi Department in Khargone. The department conducted a perfunctory enquiry and went to the extent of warning the students not to complain! The headmistress not only berated the girls, but also started depriving them of food.

The Sangathan proceeded cautiously and first asked the girls to give a written complaint to the Sangathan with a copy to the police officer in Katkut. The general body meeting of the village gram sabha then passed a formal resolution for an enquiry into the running of the hostel. An enquiry committee was set up that then held discussions with the girls as well as the headmistress. It submitted a formal report to the headmistress with a copy to the Joint Director of the Adivasi Department in Khargone, recommending that he take steps to improve the sorry state of the hostel.

Following this, the girls decided to take over the hostel's management themselves with the help of some adivasi teachers. The money for running the hostel was deposited in a bank account, which was jointly operated by two of the senior students. The headmistress used to draw out all the money by forcing the students to sign on the cheque every month. The girls now began withdrawing the money themselves and managed the hostel activities with this money by keeping records.

All these years the headmistress had been getting away with her corrupt practices by bribing the higher authorities in

Khargone and also the local political leaders. Now, in her hour of distress, she turned to them. They got her to register a false case of abuse against the Sangathan activists who had investigated the running of the hostel. Five members of the Sangathan were charged and arrested for having abused and threatening to kill the headmistress.

The women once again intervened. When the third person was arrested and beaten up, the women staged yet another sit-in in front of the police outpost and prevented the police from taking the arrested person to court. Even though the Tehsildar and the Sub-divisional Police Officer assured the women that such illegal actions would not take place in the future and that no case would be registered against them for the sit-in, another case was framed against fifteen members of the Sangathan including Subhadra and I of threatening to kill policemen.

All the accused immediately went underground in preparation for a long struggle. A press conference was called, followed by a rally in Indore where hundreds of women participated and a memorandum was submitted to the Divisional Commissioner listing the demands: administration to provide proper reproductive health facilities, prevent the sale of illicit liquor and stop its repressive policies. Significantly, this was the first mass rally of women in support of reproductive health and rights in Madhya Pradesh since the introduction of the target-free approach. The Commissioner was typically uppity. He initially refused to believe that policemen could misbehave with adivasi women and then chided the activists on the loss to nation that was being caused by the bonded labourers striking work in the cotton fields for non-payment of the minimum wages. In other words, the adivasis may not have bread, but that did not mean that they could spoil the cake of their masters!

The problem of agricultural wages is a deep-rooted one. Modern artificial input-based green revolution agriculture has become unprofitable due to increasing input costs, decreasing yields, and rising prices of output and decreasing state subsidies. Big farmers are consequently unable to pay the stipulated minimum wage to the agricultural labourers as this would squeeze their margins. The priority of the ruling class, echoed in the response of the Commissioner, is to maximise output regardless of the agricultural labourers being deprived of the statutory minimum wage.

It has been suggested that the great dynamism of capitalist growth in the Information Technology and other high-tech industrial and service sectors of India in recent times are an indication that its hidden potential has been "unbound" and so it should be given further unrestricted flight. Characteristically, the problems confronting agriculture are ignored on the presumption I suppose, that they will wish themselves away. However, the serious crisis in the agricultural sector and the consequent impoverishment of the vast majority of people who are dependent on it cannot be solved through capitalist growth, which as we shall see, has actually created these problems. Capitalist growth in the cities that has been so eulogised has only resulted in the elite becoming unbound enough to be able to take off to greener pastures abroad while the likes of the adivasi women of Katkut are cynically bound by the policies of the state to continue living their abject rural lives.

The continual rejection by the administration of their demands and pleas forced the women to launch a hunger strike. In June 1998, eighteen Bhil women went on an indefinite hunger strike to demand an end to police repression and the withdrawal of false cases, provision of adequate health services, and action against the exploitative practices of the non-adivasi people of the area. The police administration was particularly obstinate in refusing to change its repressive ways, especially since the ASS had effectively put a spanner into their corrupt and repressive works. The previous Superintendent of Police of Khargone district had categorically stated that he could not tolerate his staff being scared of the organised power of the adivasi masses. The strike was eventually called off on June 10, after an assurance from the National Human Rights Commission that an independent enquiry would be conducted into the complaints of human rights violations made to it by the ASS.

In the face of unrelenting state oppression, the women made a last-ditch effort by forming the organisation Kansari nu Vadavno, or *Felicitation of Kansari* in honour of Kansari, the goddess symbolising the life-giving power of the cereal jowar (sorghum), the staple of the Bhils. In this way, the women were stressing both the importance of women power and also the need to conserve traditional Bhili agriculture, of which sorghum used to be the mainstay, but which was gradually declining due to the spread of environmentally unsustainable, nutritionally undesirable yet commercially more profitable soybean cultivation.

It is interesting to note that these adivasi struggles were happening at the same time as the Chiapas movement of the Mexican indigenous people was taking place. Both faced repression from centralized states and could not live up to their initial promise of turning the tide against the greed and destruction of modern industrial development.

State repression, even though it was not able to crush the organisation process altogether, nevertheless achieved its immediate objective of putting a brake on the revolutionary advances being made by the adivasis. In Katkut, the women were no longer able to take action against the sale of illegal liquor, which resumed. This in turn resulted in the men reverting to alcoholism. The social control that had been established over the consumption and sale of liquor, and therefore on the patriarchal oppression of women, was thus undone. Women, the worst sufferers of alcoholism, have been at the forefront of the innumerable prohibition movements in India, right from the time of Gandhi. On occasions, these campaigns have succeeded. The anti-liquor campaign in Andhra Pradesh took off from the Total Literacy Campaign that was being conducted by the government there. Despite the government's best efforts to curb it, this snowballed into a mass movement of such proportions that mainstream political parties had to espouse the cause and prohibition had to be imposed. However, this wasn't to last, and prohibition had to be later withdrawn in Andhra Pradesh. In Gujarat, where prohibition is still in place, liquor remains freely available.

The state encourages drinking because it is an important source of revenue, and the police condone the illegal sale of liquor because they profit from it individually. The more important reason for the rampant sale of illegal liquor is that it is in the interests of the powerful classes in society that the poor and oppressed douse their frustrations in alcohol rather than give vent to them through organised mass action to improve their condition. There is a beautiful medieval English ballad, one version of which has been sung in modern times by the British rock group Traffic, which ends with these words:

Sir John Barley-Corn fought in a Bowl,

who won the Victory,
Which made them all to chafe and swear,
that Barley-Corn must die.

John Barleycorn is symbolical of alcohol, which has been cursed by alcoholics and women throughout the ages for the miseries that excessive alcohol dinking has brought on, and yet he refuses to die. The swashbuckling novelist, Jack London, has, in a moving autobiographical novel of this name, described his own lost battle against the bottle. He begins by saying that he voted for the amendment allowing women the right to vote in elections in the early 20th century because, "When the women get the ballot, they will vote for prohibition...It is the wives, and sisters, and mothers, and they only, who will drive the nails into the coffin of John Barleycorn."

Ultimately, there seem to be no easy solutions to the problems faced by poor adivasi women. Women's empowerment has become a buzzword among feminists and also within the more sedate establishment. There is, of course, a difference in perspective between the two. While the more radical feminists urge for the fulfilment of what have been called strategic gender needs, those within the establishment and the less revolutionary among the feminists generally content themselves with meeting practical gender needs. The former question the gender division of labour and the male control of women's sexuality that lie at the root of patriarchal oppression. The latter accept these for the time being and try to alleviate women's troubles without challenging patriarchal structures and with the hope that education and increased employment opportunities will gradually improve matters. Distinct from these two is the grassroots perspective, which stresses that empowerment should be a process from within the oppressed community rather than being imposed from above. Thus, the women should themselves decide on the needs, whether strategic or practical, that they would like to fulfil.

This dilemma at the grassroots—of choosing between practical and strategic gender needs—cropped up in the struggle of the Bhil women of Nimar, too, where even such a minor issue as adivasi girl students demanding that they be given proper food in their hostels, brought the wrath of the state on them. Not even women are spared if they begin rubbing the state the wrong way, as they must if they have to free themselves from patriarchal oppression. The sad reality is that poor women everywhere are the end sufferers of a vicious combination of globalised capitalist industrial development and patriarchal oppression.

In the initial stages of our work, we were actually encouraged by the local Block Development Officer to help him meet the development fund disbursement target for the year. Such was the distrust against the government in their minds that despite repeated enticing announcements, not even a single woman came to the tent set up for the purpose, even though it was a market day, and the village was crowded with people. Subhadra went round and convinced some twenty odd adivasi women she knew to come to the camp and register their names for financial assistance. However, things changed dramatically when the women began demanding development services as a right in an organised manner. That was when the state came out in its true colours. Beg and thou shalt be tolerated if not humoured, but demand and thou shalt be crucified! Things haven't changed much since the time of Jesus Christ, even though there have been quite a few more social revolutions in the two intervening millennia.

Meanwhile, the Panchayat Provisions Extension to Scheduled Areas Act (PESA) had been passed in 1996 as a consequence of the sustained campaign in this regard that had been carried out under the aegis of the Bharat Jan Andolan led by Dr. B D Sharma. The Madhya Pradesh Panchayati Raj Act was amended in 1997 to accord with the PESA. Later in 1998, the rules for the implementation of the Act were also framed and published in the gazette.

For the first time, this provided grassroots mass organisations in adivasi areas with a powerful legal instrument for viable village self-rule. Faced with the intransigence of the local administration, the provisions of this new Act were used to set in motion a robust process of rural mobilisation that immediately began to bear fruit. Even though Subhadra and I left the Katkut area after 1998 to move back to Indore, the mobilisation for the establishment of village self-rule in accordance with PESA continued in this region for three more years. Both men and women took the struggle to a peak, until eventually, the state struck back with illegal vengeance to crush the movement at high noon on April 2, 2001, in Mehendikhera village.

19 Reliving the Myth of Sisyphus

Greek legend has it that the king of Corinth, Sisyphus, was cursed to continually roll a heavy rock up a mountain in hell, only to see it roll down again because of his scornful attitude towards the Gods. When Pluto abducted the daughter of Esopus, the latter came to Sisyphus for help. Sisyphus agreed to help Esopus recover his daughter if the latter promised to give water to the citadel at Corinth. Thus, in exchange for water for his people, Sisyphus bore the wrath of the Gods and was banished to the nether regions. Much in the same way, the environmental mass movements have borne the wrath of the false Gods of modern development in trying to ensure a more sustainable and decentralised water resource plan for the country.

Following the failure of the Sangharsh Yatra in 1991 and the repression by the BJP government that led to an erosion of its mass base in the valley, the NBA went about cultivating a wide base among urbanites the world over. As a result of its lobbying, the independent review commissioned by the World Bank expressed dissatisfaction over the design and execution of the SSP and recommended that it be stopped. Under pressure of the World Bank, the Indian Government had to decline the remaining tranches of the loan for the SSP. The Japanese government, too, withdrew the loan it was going to offer for the purchase of electricity-generating turbines from Japan.

The euphoria created by the withdrawal of the World Bank was short lived because the Gujarat government proceeded with the work on the dam with its own resources and those garnered from the public issue of a debt bond. With the height of the dam continuously rising, the villages behind it gradually began to be submerged. As a result, land in the first village in Maharashtra, Manibeli, was to be submerged in the monsoon season of 1991. So Medha led a motley crew of adivasis, Nimari peasants and urbanites from across the country and the world into staging a satyagraha in a hut called "Narmadai", specially built for the purpose in Manibeli, waiting for the waters of the Narmada to come and engulf them. Despite heavy police presence, the satyagraha was conducted well with people coming and going in batches from the entire valley to keep Narmadai inhabited at all times. The whole operation was a grand success in publicity terms, the waters in the monsoons came only upto fifteen feet of the hut, and so the actual test of drowning did not occur. This later became well known as the "Manibeli Satyagraha".

After the monsoons the construction work of the dam resumed, and by the time of the next monsoons in 1992 it was clear that the Narmadai hut would be drowned. Not every Manibeli villager was with the NBA. Some of the people had resettled in Gujarat earlier. The government used heavy police presence to move out their houses and belongings to their resettlement site in March 1992. The police capitalised on this as a pretext to attack the supporters of the NBA sitting in the Narmadai hut, and a series of skirmishes ensued in which upwards of two hundred people were jailed, and the hut itself was demolished. This repression continued throughout the monsoons; a police picket was posted in Manibeli to ensure that the hut was not rebuilt at the same place. So it had to be built higher up. People, even children from Anjanbara village who had gone to hold a vigil at the newly constructed hut, were arrested by the police and sent to jail. Many supporters from outside the valley also bore imprisonment in solidarity with the valley people.

All this, however, had no impact on the government, and after the monsoons the work on the dam resumed. Medha, along with an oustee from Nimar, Devarambhai, launched a hunger strike in June 1993 in Mumbai. They were armed with the moral authority of the critical report of the Morse Committee, which demanded that the work on the dam be stopped and a full review of the SSP be undertaken. After fourteen days, the Union Water Resources minister agreed to a comprehensive review of the dam by an independent committee of experts, but didn't assure stoppage of work on the dam. The hunger strike was withdrawn on this agreement. With the onset of the monsoons in July 1993, the houses in Manibeli began to be submerged, but the villagers remained inside their huts in a valiant demonstration of resilience, braving the rising waters and not fleeing like rats as the government had thought they would. Subhadra's parents and the oustees of the many other dams that had been built earlier had done the same thing. The police then forcibly removed the

Manibeli residents to tin sheds that had been built higher up for the purpose. The swirling waters of the Narmada engulfed the huts and all their belongings. Vitthalbhai of Manibeli declared that he did not consider this to be a loss at all. He said he would think that he had given alms to the government as he would to a beggar.

The intransigence of the Gujarat government and the bureaucracy in the Union Water Resources ministry meant that no concrete steps had been taken to begin work on the promised review of the SSP. This and the submergence of the villages of Manibeli and Bamni forced the NBA to announce that Medha along with other activists and villagers would commit "Jal Samarpan" or drown themselves in the Narmada if the review was not undertaken. A cult figure by then, Medha was at the peak of her popularity. I realized this when once travelling in a local train, my co-passengers began talking about the state of governance in our country, lamenting the lack of integrity and sensitivity on the part of the leaders of the mainstream political parties and the bureaucracy to the needs of the masses. Everyone concurred when one of them declared that what the country needed was more Medha Patkars, observing that here was a lady who had courageously taken on the corrupt politicians and bureaucrats, and if only she had more people to support her, things would change for the better in India. Throughout the country and abroad, there were many people who felt the same. So there was a general concern about her well-being, given her professed resolve to drown herself in the Narmada. Police were deployed in large numbers along the Maharashtra and Gujarat sides of the river to ensure that Medha did not commit Jal Samarpan.

Medha Patkar went underground and declared that unless construction was stopped she would jump into the river at any location that proved suitable. A furore in Parliament, then in session, forced the government in August 1993 to finally constitute a team of five independent experts to review the SSP. Still, no firm assurances on stopping the work were forthcoming. Medha withdrew her Jal Samarpan threat on the announcement of the constitution of the review committee and came out into the open in Gujarat where she was arrested. The Gujarat government refused to cooperate with this review committee and after the monsoons once again resumed construction of the dam, even while the review process was under way. In November 1994, a dharna was organised in Bhopal to pressurise the Madhya Pradesh government to withdraw from the SSP and demand that it be scrapped. Here, too, Medha went on a hunger strike along with some other oustees when there were no signs of this demand being met. When Medha's condition began to get serious after three weeks, the police, in a pre-dawn swoop, arrested all the hunger strikers and took them to a hospital where they were forcibly put on intravenous drips.

Seeing little possibility of the dam being stopped through symbolic mass actions and lobbying alone, the NBA took recourse to legal action and approached the National Human Rights Commission (NHRC) and the Supreme Court of India in May 1994. Both of them took cognisance of the issues raised by the NBA and issued notices to the governments concerned. Since it was not legally possible to continue proceedings in both forums simultaneously, the petition to the NHRC was later withdrawn. The Supreme Court, after hearing out all the parties, decided to review the facts and arguments on the basis of which the SSP was being constructed on December 13, 1994, the day on which Medha and her co-hunger strikers were arrested in Bhopal. Taking a cue from the Supreme Court, the Chief Minister of Madhya Pradesh announced on December 16 that his government would also review its support to the SSP. On this assurance, Medha and her colleagues withdrew their hunger strike. Later the Supreme Court ordered a stay on the construction of the dam in May 1995, pending the disposal of the case. This brought some relief to the NBA as far as the battle against the SSP was concerned. This was the highest point that the NBA scaled in its struggle to save the Narmada valley.

The tenacious struggle against the SSP succeeded in igniting many more such struggles all along the valley. In 1992, things began simmering upstream near Jabalpur, where the Bargi dam had been completed and the gates closed in 1990, submerging one hundred and sixty odd villages. Once again, no adequate provisions had been made for the rehabilitation of the displaced people. A lot of the poor oustees had to migrate to Jabalpur and pull rickshaws for a livelihood. Soon, an agitation started there as well. The immediate fallout of this was that the Bargi Baandh Visthapit evam Prabhavit Sangh, an organisation of the oustees, was given the fishing rights to the reservoir, which had been appropriated by the government and the contractors. Later, the adivasi oustees of the Tawa dam constructed in the 1980s on the river Tawa, a tributary of the Narmada, also began agitating under the aegis of the Kisan Adivasi Sangathan and got this right after undergoing the usual police beatings and stints in jail. These federations of oustees have managed fishing activities in these reservoirs so well that they have earned profits for both themselves and for the government. Fish from these reservoirs is now supplied to far off places such as Kolkata. This has been achieved despite opposition from vested interests among the erstwhile fishing contractors and the bureaucracy.

However, the more important demand of land in place of the land lost due to submergence was not acceded to by the government, despite a few long hunger strikes and Jal Samarpan campaigns. As always, the government would give some assurances and then take recourse to repressive measures to break the agitation and renege on the assurances made. Similarly, movements against the construction of the dams on the tributaries of Man and Veda, too, have met with repression and false assurances. Hunger strikes by the oustees have been broken and the displaced people deprived of the right of rehabilitation with land in place of the land lost to submergence.

The Supreme Court finally disposed of the case against the SSP in 1998 saying that the dam should go on, but adequate steps should be taken for the proper rehabilitation of the oustees according to the NWDT provisions. The apex court lifted the stay on the dam's construction. This put things back to square one and completely deflated the NBA's balloon of unrealistic expectations regarding the possibility of a complete cancellation of the dam by the court. Not only were the political forces in support of the dam much stronger than the NBA, but there were very few takers for the NBA plea that the dam would prove a disaster in the future and hence should be scrapped. The NBA was forced to fall back on the less effective Jal Samarpan actions to try and stop the dam. This was the time when Arundhati Roy jumped into the fray and pumped some adrenalin into the NBA's veins for this renewed battle. However, this was not enough, and the SSP has continued to be built, submerging an ever-increasing number of villages by the year.

Due to the Supreme Court's stipulation on rehabilitation of those displaced, the NBA got an opportunity to delay the construction of the dam by repeatedly bringing up the matter of non-rehabilitation in the form of contempt petitions. However, the basic problem was that there was no cheap agricultural land of good quality available any more—either in Gujarat, Maharashtra, or Madhya Pradesh. If the oustees were to be given good agricultural land in accordance with the NWDT provision, the costs of the project would shoot up astronomically. So the Madhya Pradesh government, which had to provide for most of the oustees, tried to palm them off with monetary compensation. Despite the NBA's protest, the Narmada Control Authority gave the go ahead for further construction of the dam in 2006. Medha went on a hunger strike in Delhi along with a few other oustees and supporters. Once again, with her health deteriorating, she was arrested and hospitalised. The NBA approached the Supreme Court, and Medha broke her hunger strike. However, this time, the Supreme Court refused to stay the construction and and threw the hot ball back into the government's frying pan by reiterating its earlier judgment that further disputes in the matter be referred to the Prime Minister. Given the tremendous pressure created in Gujarat with the Chief Minister on a hunger strike and massive mass rallies organised by all political parties in support of the dam, the NBA finally lost out.

The numbers game is just not in favour of the NBA. Most of the oustees in Madhya Pradesh are taking what they can get in cash compensation from the government and clearing out. Only a few hundred diehard NBA members from the valley are still continuing the fight with the support of a section of the urban intelligentsia across the country and around the world. That is why the Narmada valley has been dammed with impunity. Other dams also have either been completed or work is progressing apace on them. The work on the Indira Sagar dam near Punasa began in 2000 with the formation of a company, Narmada Hydroelectric Development Corporation (NHDC). Later, the NHDC also began work on the Omkareshwar dam downstream of the ISP. The contract for the actual construction of these dams went to the same Jayaprakash Associates that has been building the SSP. The state adopted a vigorous policy of distribution of cash compensation to the influential landed people. So the initial mobilisation that had been there at the time of the Harsud rally in 1989, dissipated, and the dam was completed in 2004. This has led to the submergence of the very town where fifteen years before we had gathered in large numbers and pledged in right earnest to stop destructive development. This is a telling reminder of the

weakness of mass environmental movements in this country—
even when it is one with such a wide national and international
support base as the NBA—in the face of the intransigence of the
state. "Proper rehabilitation" never happened, and the people were
forced to tear down their houses and leave literally at gunpoint.
The NBA has tried to salvage something for the oustees to get
them at least decent cash compensation of which the government
has tried to cheat them.

Temporarily, the movement to stop the construction of the
Maheshwar dam on the river Narmada in between the dams at
Omkareshwar and Navagam had been successful for some time.
This was primarily because this dam is being built by a private
company, which has neither enough finances nor technical
competency of its own. Initially, the government sought to crush
the movement against the dam into submission through repressive
measures, and for a time it did succeed. However, the tremendous
international support base the NBA has built up is so powerful that
it has succeeded in stalling international funding and technical
support for the dam. But now, the work on the dam has resumed as
the company has managed to tie up fund agreements with Indian
financial institutions. The NBA has begun agitating against this,
but there is every likelihood of the government resorting to
repression to bulldoze its way through to building the dam. The
movement against the Omkareshwar dam has been able with the
help of the High Court of Madhya Pradesh been able to ensure
some rehabilitation for the oustees but has not been able to stop
the dam.

What price satyagraha then as an action strategy for
bringing the modern state to heel?

Satyagraha has some chance of succeeding in crunch
situations, only when those practising it are in very large numbers
and are so convinced about their cause and the philosophy of
Gandhism that they are able to exert moral pressure and bring
about a change of heart in the oppressor. Heavy reliance on Hindu
asceticism and mysticism means it is far removed from the lives of
common everyday people and even more so from that of the Bhil
adivasis. Arundhati Roy, who has pitched in lyrically in support of
hedonism in her Booker Prize winning novel "The God of Small
Things", has admitted in the monograph 'Greater Common Good'
that the theory and practice of Gandhism requires a very strong
moral fibre, especially when it comes to renouncing sex and

shopping, which most ordinary mortals cannot do without. Significantly, Gandhi himself wrote in the course of the freedom struggle that, whatever his personal anarchistic beliefs, at the societal level he was not trying to establish the kind of village self rule he had advocated in Hind Swaraj but was fighting for the more practical goal of establishing parliamentary self rule only.

So even during India's freedom movement, when there was such a groundswell of mass protest against the British, Gandhians could rarely achieve their immediate demands, let alone win the jackpot of freedom through satyagraha in general and the hunger strike in particular. A prime example of the failure of these methods of protest was the hunger strike by Bhagat Singh and his associates. One of the strikers, Jatindranath Das, died during the course of the fast.

The only time that Gandhi himself did succeed to some extent with a fast came in rather controversial circumstances in 1932 over his standoff with Dr. Bhimrao Ambedkar against the proposal for separate electorates for the untouchable dalit castes. The satyagraha worked only with Ambedkar, whose heart was amenable to change. Gandhian hunger strikes didn't move the hearts of the British or the Muslims. The saga of dalits not voting continues to this day as there are sections of dalits in some parts of this country who are still not allowed to cast votes by the upper castes.

Immediately after independence, Telegu sub-nationalist aspirations were very strong, and a mass movement began for a separate state of Andhra Pradesh to be carved out from the erstwhile princely state of Hyderabad and the Madras Presidency area. One of the movement's leaders, Poti Sri Ramulu, began a fast unto death in November 1952. Jawaharlal Nehru, following the practice of the British, ignored this and allowed Sri Ramulu to fast to death on December 15, 1952. All hell broke loose after this in the Telugu speaking areas as the masses came onto the streets. Eventually, Nehru had to backtrack, and the state of Andhra Pradesh was formed in 1953. This is one rare instance in which the determination of the hunger striker to bear death and the tremendous mass support for his demand was able to bend the obduracy of the state apparatus.

In stark contrast, however, was the hunger strike of Master Tara Singh, the venerable Sikh leader and one of the founders of the Sikh political party, Akali Dal. He began a fast in 1961 to press for the formation of the separate Sikh majority state of Punjab, only to withdraw it after some vague assurances by the Central Government. This not only cost him his premier position within the Dal, but also led to a delay in the formation of the state. Thus, the success of a hunger strike in securing an important and radical demand hinges crucially on the striker going on to bear death and the demand being supported by a substantial and organised mass base. Such a mass base was never possible in the Narmada valley, given the serpent like geographical spread of the affected people and the worldview of most of them, which is vastly different from that of Gandhi. The NBA has not met the conditions for success of Gandhian political action in the numerous hunger strikes and jal samarpan andolans it has staged.

The biggest mass upheaval against the state in independent India was started by Jayaprakash Narayan in the state of Gujarat in 1974, in the form of the Navnirman Andolan, which later spread to the state of Bihar and became the Sampoorna Kranti Andolan. This too, however, failed in the face of state oppression. Soon, Emergency was declared, heralding nineteen months of dictatorial rule.

As the mobilisation of the NBA or all the other environmental mass movements has not achieved even a small percentage of this historic level of mobilisation, it is not surprising that these movements have not been able to withstand state repression and impact upon state policies in any significant manner. In recent years, mass mobilisations in Manipur against the Armed Forces Special Powers Act 1958 (AFSPA) have taken place. Enacted to deal with the armed secessionist militancy in the North Eastern states, the AFSPA gives draconian powers to the armed forces to detain and even kill people that they arrest without any due process of law. These mobilisations, owing to their strength, have achieved some success, and a review of the AFSPA is in progress by a committee headed by a retired Supreme Court Judge. However, there is little likelihood of the act being scrapped altogether. Here, too, a young lady, Sharmila Irom, went on a hunger strike from November 2, 2000, demanding the repeal of the AFSPA. She was arrested under the charge of attempting to commit suicide and is being kept alive since in solitary confinement through intravenous drips. Once again, the character of the state that emerges is that of a soulless entity, not amenable to the change of heart that is proposed to be brought about by satyagraha.

Ironically, the most successful application of mass satyagraha in the post-Gandhian era has not been in India but in the United States of America under the charismatic leadership of Martin Luther King. His famous dream of removing poverty and exploitation of the blacks has proved a more difficult proposition and today the blacks, despite constituting thirteen per cent of the population, have only eight per cent representation in the United States Congress while comprising a whopping fifty percent of prison inmates.

In this context, one can't help wondering in awe at the tremendous achievement of Babasaheb Ambedkar in his battle over a more or less similar issue in which he almost single-handedly achieved much more for the dalits in this country, even in the absence of the kind of mass support that King or Gandhi enjoyed. He was steeped in the liberal democratic tradition, but was at the same time aware that in reality, parliamentary democracy in India is only a top dressing over the main course, which is essentially undemocratic. So his exhortation to the dalits was to "educate, organise and agitate." Unfortunately, the dalits have not been able to build on this inspiring legacy and pose a concerted united challenge to the domination of the upper castes in independent India. Some hopes were raised in the 1980s when the Bahujan Samaj Party (BSP) was formed. Calling the casteist Hindu society "Manuvadi" because it followed the discriminatory prescriptions of the ancient Indian lawgiver Manu, the BSP called for a total rejection of the domination by the miniscule upper castes. However, the corrupt dynamics of electoral politics in India soon overwhelmed them, and they have now lost their radical cutting edge.

Another serious problem in the practice of mass satyagraha is that it frequently gets caught in a pincers between the violence of the state and the spontaneous retaliatory violence of the agitating masses. The difficult Gandhian tenets are rarely followed by the masses in such situations, and in the absence of a well thought out alternative practice, the energy of the masses gets dissipated by state repression.

The most famous example is that of the Chauri Chaura incident of 1922 during Gandhi's Non-Cooperation Movement, following which Gandhi called off the movement.

The history of the NBA, too, corroborates this. Even though the NBA has worked within the Gandhian framework, time and again the adivasis, who have an enviable martial tradition, have broken out in spontaneous violence in response to the illegal violence of the state. Whether it was the violence of the villagers of Anjanbara in 1993 or later that of the villagers of Nimgavan, Sikka and Surung in Maharashtra in the same year, which resulted in the death of the only martyr of the NBA, Rehmal Punia Vasava, in police firing, these were all instances of the people fighting in their own idiom, disregarding the directions of their leaders. In such cases, the state responds with even greater repression and crushes the movement altogether. Gandhians and Marxists approach the problem of state violence from two opposing standpoints, but despite these debates, the question of whether to counter violence with violence remains a tricky one.

When we started political mobilisations in the Katkut area, we tried to prepare the people for this inevitability—the use of illegal violence by the state. Thus, the people there were much more consciously resilient to this violence and not given to responding with counter violence. However, since the mobilisation was spread over only about twenty villages, it did not have even a miniscule amount of the huge mass mobilisation needed to challenge the state in any significant way. In the end we found ourselves in a similar cul-de-dac as the NBA, despite our conscious appreciation of the might of the modern Indian state and the inadequacies of satyagraha as a means of countering it. Indeed, this has been the fate of almost all environmental mass movements in India, beginning with the Chipko movement of the 1970s, they have been agitating in isolation around issues that concern only a very small number of people directly affected by some project or environmental disaster and are thus incapable of building up substantial mass bases that can challenge the destructive development policies at a national or global level.

Sisyphus was such a daredevil that on one occasion he even kidnapped the God of Death and kept him chained in his palace. Pluto had to send the God of War to free him. Eventually, he was doomed to eternally rolling a rock up a hill, only to see it roll down again. We in the environmental mass movements in

India, too, have been trying to chain the God of Ecological Death, and like Pluto, the high priests of the God of Modern Development have continually sent their dogs of war in the form of the police to stymie us. It looks as if we are similarly doomed to eternally rolling the rock of mass mobilisation up against the mountain of state obduracy, only to see it go crashing down time and again. What can be more punishing than such futile and hopeless labour?

According to the French author Albert Camus, Sisyphus is at his glorious best when he is back at the foot of the mountain because at that point he doesn't bemoan his fate, but ponders over its inevitability, given his rebelliousness against the Gods. He accepts his fate and decides to defeat the Gods by enjoying the struggle as he endlessly rolls the rock up the mountain regardless of the failure to keep it up there permanently. Thus, seemingly intractable ideological and practical problems notwithstanding, Medha Patkar and the NBA deserve laurels for having led from the front in the mission to keep the rock of environmental mass movements rolling in this country and thereby inspiring many people to spurn the God of Modern Development and continue to relive the myth of Sisyphus.

20 The Exasperated Anarchist

The only viable way in which the centralised forces of the state apparatus can be fought and overthrown, whether violently or non-violently, is through the formation of a massive centralised organisation of the masses prepared to adopt underhand means to counter the illegality of the state. But by definition, anarchists are against all forms of centralisation and stress on the maintenance of the purity of means to achieve desired ends. So they cannot posit a viable mass challenge to the state that they would so much like to get rid of. This results in a classic Catch-22 situation. Faced with this seemingly impossible scenario, some individual armchair anarchists such as Thoreau have contented themselves with holding forth from their isolated ivory towers against the iniquities of the state, while others of a more practical bent like our own Shaheed Bhagat Singh (before he gave up anarchism and became a Marxist during his incarceration prior to execution) have laid their faith in individual acts of violence against the state. Both these strategies have naturally proved ineffective.

There have been many ways in which anarchists, who have actually tried to change the world on a mass scale, have tried to get around this dilemma. One common way has been to form a skeletal anarchist organisation and then latch it on to a larger centralised mass organisation that is at work against the state. Gandhi followed this course during the freedom struggle. The problem with this is that the purity of anarchist theory and action often has to be compromised to a greater or lesser extent. Additionally, there is always the danger that when power is eventually won from the oppressors, the centralised organisation tends to shrug off the anarchists and pursue a course directly in opposition to all that the latter hold dear. This is what happened in the case of the Gandhians after independence, and this is also what happened to the Russian anarchists in the aftermath of the Bolshevik Revolution of 1917. Gandhi postponed his anarchist programme of village self-rule for parliamentary self-rule during the freedom struggle in the naive hope that the former could be achieved after the latter was in place, thereby contradicting his own pet dictum of not divorcing means from ends. The Congress led by Nehru, cashed in on this ideological confusion and rode piggyback on the tremendous charismatic influence of Gandhi to attain state power.

The establishment of a parliamentary system with the first past the post in elections being declared the representatives, instead of a distribution of seats on the basis of votes polled, resulted in a scenario that gave undue advantage to the ruling Indian National Congress. Even though it got less than the majority of votes, it nevertheless got a majority of the seats. Moreover, the Congress used a combination of engineered defections and sops to wean away elected representatives and their supporters, leading to a continuous exodus of workers and leaders from among the socialists and communists.

Nowadays, all political parties—and there are many to accord with the varied diversity of the people across the spectrum from the left to the right and from the bottom of the social order to the top—that take part in elections, have recourse to unfair electoral practices prior to winning and dubious parliamentary practices after that. Indeed, the Bahujan Samaj Party of the dalits, which had given a clarion call for cleansing the dirty politics of the "Manuvadi" upper castes when it first began participating in elections, too, has gone the corrupt way of the other parties. All parties have also duplicated the Congress model. No wonder then that hardened criminals who have both power and pelf in the local settings have begun winning elections in embarrassingly large numbers and dictating what little is left of party policy. Since winning elections and staying in power have become ends in themselves, rather than being the means for social transformation and people-oriented governance, both electoral and legislative practice have been reduced to being a theatre of the absurd.

The decade of the 1990s saw this theatre of the absurd enacted even at the grassroots level, with the 73rd and 74th Constitutional Amendments introducing a third tier of governance at the community level in urban and rural areas all over the country. In the initial years of the republic, Panchayati Raj was given a complete go by. However, the failure of the Community Development Programme initiated in the early 1950s led to the appointment of the Balwantrai Mehta Committee to review this in 1957. The Committee found that in the absence of people's planning and participation, the programme had fallen prey to bureaucratic malfeasance. The Committee suggested the setting up of a three-tier Panchayati Raj system. Thus, a rudimentary local government system was begun in many parts of the country. But it soon perished. The main reason was that the state governments did not want to devolve powers to the panchayats. Given the strong concentration of resources and power with the Union Government, the state governments had little room for manoeuvre, and they did not want to lose what little they had. Apart from this, the district level bureaucracy was obviously dead against handing over the control of rural development schemes to the panchayats.

The Naxalite upsurge of the late 1960s, followed by the mass movement of Jayaprakash Narayan in 1974-75, had made it abundantly clear that mass aspirations at the grassroots were seeking new vistas. After the elections in 1977, the Union Government set up the Ashok Mehta Committee, and it too made wide-ranging recommendations for the establishment of Panchayati Raj. Following on this, the Left Front government in West Bengal and the Janata Party government in Karnataka began on a new note with institutionalised rural local self governance. These experiments were immensely successful as they provided greater participation of people earlier excluded from electoral politics, in governance and development. The dominance of Congress in Indian politics began to decline, and strong regional parties began to emerge. The states thus began to increase their share of power and resources at the cost of the Centre and gained more independence in their own spheres of action. This made them more amenable to the idea of devolving resources to the grassroots. So with time, the pressure building up at the grassroots has resulted in the countrywide adoption of Panchayati Raj.

However, the malpractices of the parliamentary elections have extended to the village level, leading my friend and colleague Shankar to aver that the rule of the sarpanch or the elected head of the Panchayat is in reality a "parpanch" or hoax perpetrated on the people.

Theoretically, it should be possible to counter the corrupt political practices at the level of the panchayats if there is a fairly good local mass organisation. This is what prompted the KMCS to actively participate in the panchayat elections when they were first held on a direct voting basis in Madhya Pradesh in 1989. The KMCS was in a clear majority in four panchayats. In two of them, prior meetings held to decide on the candidates for the posts of panches or ward members and the sarpanch ended amicably with unanimous choices. Hence there were no contests as only one candidate filed nomination papers per seat. In the two other panchayats, things were not so smooth. The Congress saw to it that candidates filed nominations to oppose the KMCS for the post of sarpanch and panch. Despite this opposition, the KMCS coasted through with handsome margins in one of these panchayats. However, shockingly for us, the KMCS lost the post of sarpanch in the Attha panchayat, where we were headquartered. To add to that, the KMCS candidate for panch from our ward lost by one vote. It was clear that KMCS members had voted against the official candidates that had been decided on in the meetings prior to the elections.

A post-mortem revealed that the Congress candidate, a former KMCS activist who believed that a softer approach should be taken with the administration after the rights to cultivation of newar land had been secured by the KMCS, was supported by the ordinary voter who was in no mood for a long confrontation. In the case of the panch it appeared that the KMCS candidate had, in the early years, when the logging contractors had begun operating, acted as their agent and cheated the rest of the people of their wage dues. He even used to beat up the people when they protested. Despite the fact that he had later reformed himself and played a stellar role in setting up the Sangath, the people decided to pay him back for their earlier insults and torture at his hands.

What shook me most was that we activists did not get an inkling of this massive undercurrent of secret "resistance" among the people to the radical anti-state direction that we were giving to the Sangath's politics. Instead of coming out and stating their preferences openly in the meetings, they decided to use the secret ballot against us! I learnt an important lesson at that early stage of my activism—that the peasant masses offer covert resistance not only to their oppressors, but also to their liberators when the latter begin to go too fast for their comfort.

This, of course, is an old problem that has confronted activists fighting for radical socio-political change. The vast majority of people just want a decent life and with even a little bit of improvement are content to desist from active political struggle. Alternately, in the face of repression they opt for a compromise rather than confrontation with the state. Due to the patron-client system of electoral politics, the state in independent India, however oppressive it might be, still has to be responsive to a certain extent to the demands of the people in order to retain legitimacy. Following this episode, the politics of the KMCS became diluted to accord with the preferences of the people rather than that of the activists!

There is an anecdote about a king once asking his people to contribute a glass of milk each for the purpose of a feast. The people had to secretly pour the milk into a big cauldron through a hole in its lid. When finally the lid of the cauldron was taken out it was found that it was filled with water. Everyone had contributed a glass of water, thinking it would go unnoticed amidst the contributions of milk by the others! Similarly, for anarchists like us who rarely have anything tangible to offer to the people in the short run other than stints in jail, secret first past the post secret ballots result in a watery gravy for our anarchist dreams.

That panchayat election of 1989 marked the only time in my life when I've ever voted. Previously I had considered the whole system of elections a sham and never voted. The hectic campaigning and managing that I had to do in the run up to those elections enthused me enough to go and vote. A number of women, it later emerged, had not even stamped the ballot papers owing to ignorance! Over the past decade and a half, the women have surely become more proficient what with electronic voting machines and regular training in the technicalities of voting. But disillusioned totally with the electoral process after that debacle, I have since busied myself with stamping cockroaches rather than ballot papers.

The corruption in panchayats is made possible because of the first past the post electoral system that has been adopted at this level too, overriding the traditional method used by the villagers where the decisions are taken by the monthly gram sabhas, generally small in size. The elected executive of the panchayats, the sarpanch and panches do not have any salaries. They perforce resort to graft to compensate themselves for the time that they give to the panchayat. This problem came up in the three panchayats in which the KMCS came to power in 1989. We tried to circumvent this problem by having a team of people working by rotation in support of the sarpanches and we activists too did a lot of running around. Soon we found that it was a herculean task getting any work done because of the opposition of the "local state," constituted by the rural development bureaucracy, to our plans.

Nevertheless, we did some good work in watershed development for the first time in Jhabua district and used most of the development funds for income generation at the village level. This arrangement was not a sustainable one as it depended for its success on us activists monitoring it closely. The moment we withdrew from the process to get involved in wider issues, the system we had put in place collapsed. People tended to leave the sarpanches to their own devices and only expected them to deliver the goods. Eventually, all the three sarpanches were forced to resort to graft in collaboration with the bureaucracy who were only too willing. Things became even weirder in later elections, with members of the Sangath fighting against each other. The KMCS finally took the position that it would not actively participate in the panchayat elections as an organisation even though its members were free to do so.

The Mazdoor Kisan Shakti Sangathan (MKSS) in Rajasthan, which later took up the same issue of corruption within the panchayats and elevated it into a successful national campaign for the right to information, has also not been able to overcome this basic problem of the apathy of the people towards higher political goals and support for the sarpanches who have to give their time for panchayat work. The two MKSS sarpanches who had won in the 2000 panchayat elections had to be compensated with funds garnered by the organisation from outside sources for the time that they had spent in managing the panchayat affairs. Despite having worked well in the interests of the panchayat with this external support, the MKSS was unable to retain these seats in the 2005 elections. One of these seats includes the village that is the headquarters of the organisation. The MKSS fought these elections on an anarchist plank with a people's manifesto and a declaration that no candidate for sarpanch would spend more than Rs. 2,000 on election expenses and the promise that the elected sarpanches would be supported with external funds for the time that they give to the panchayat. Yet, only two of the twelve candidates for sarpanch managed to scrape through against the other candidates who spent tens of thousands of rupees on their election campaigns. The people demand immediate fixes to their problems, without fighting long drawn battles to change the skewed over-centralised distribution of political power and the resulting corruption. Thus, between the devil of the state and the deep blue sea of the inscrutable masses, the true blue anarchist stands alone, thoroughly and exasperatingly checkmated.

This inability to make its presence felt in Parliament and the legislatures and even at the panchayat level has severely handicapped the environmentalist movement in India. It has perforce had to rely on lobbying and advocacy. However, these modes of applying political pressure have their limitations when fundamental issues of development and governance are involved. The NBA has taken the lead in forming a coalition of all the major environmentalist mass movements in the country under the umbrella of the National Alliance of People's Movements (NAPM). But since all these movements separately do not have a mass presence capable of winning elections, they have not been able to do much better together either. Like in mathematics, small fractions multiplied with each other have resulted in a smaller negligible fraction at the national level! Despite arguing factually against the now defunct Enron Corporation promoted Dabhol Power Company project in Maharashtra and predicting that the Maharashtra State Electricity Board would not be able to buy the expensive electricity produced by it, the NAPM could not prevent its construction. Today the NAPM can turn round and say "I told you so," given the fact that its prediction has come true and the project is bogged down in legal wrangles, but that is little consolation. In a similar kind of bull headedness, governments of all hues are going ahead with the grandiose plan to link rivers through inter-basin transfer of water resources, disregarding the impeccable logic being given against this foolhardy venture by the NAPM.

Yossarian in Joseph Heller's novel Catch- 22 is asked which he prefers more, staying alive or winning the war. He replies that he wants both, because winning the war is of no use to a dead man. He is castigated for such a view, which, it is alleged, would only help the enemy. He cynically replies that the enemy is the person who gets one killed, regardless of the side he is on. Present day anarcho-environmentalists find themselves forced to be part of a highly centralised human civilisation at war with nature. The crazy warriors who control the affairs of this global civilisation are constantly berating them for not wanting to win this war, which is both futile and fatal. When the anarchists are castigated for being enemies of progress, they can only reply forlornly that such progress would, in the long run, emerge as the enemy of both nature and humans. Of what use is progress if billions of deprived people all over the world have to continually pay with their lives and livelihoods for it?

Like Yossarian, anarcho-environmentalists too can find no escape from a crazy predicament brought about by the warmongers incorporated.

21 Casting Pearls Before Swine

The greatest tragedy for the Indian masses has been the replacement of British colonialism with an internal colonialism at the time of independence. In this internal colonisation, rightist politicians, landlords, princes, industrialists and bureaucrats were to benefit at the expense of the masses. Such is the spirit of brotherhood between these exploitative groups that over time there has been an increasing flow of landlords, princes, industrialists and bureaucrats into electoral politics, with film stars and hardened criminals being the latest entrants in the Punch and Judy show that is Indian politics. The Indian Constitution, which was finally adopted in 1951 to provide a legal framework for this to be possible, had as many as 250 out of a total of 395 articles copied almost verbatim from the colonial Government of India Act of 1935. The basic thrust was that of a strong centralised state apparatus that could easily quell organised protest by ordinary citizens. For this purpose, all the draconian colonial laws like the IPC, CrPC, Police Act, Preventive Detention Laws, Indian Forest Act, and Land Acquisition Act were allowed to continue. The bureaucrats who drafted the Constitution were also clever enough to retain the provisions that protected them from prosecution by the citizens. The citizens of the country were given some fundamental rights, which were not there during British rule. These related to various basic freedoms and social and economic justice. However, since violations of these by the state and the bureaucrats could only be remedied by expensive litigation in the High and Supreme Courts, this effectively put paid to the hopes of the poor for civil, social and economic justice.

The utter failure of the Indian state in bettering the lot of the millions of its poor citizens due to this unholy nexus between the ruling politicians, industrialists, feudal lords and the bureaucracy and its devious attempts to camouflage this became apparent towards the end of the Nehru era itself, when the maverick Socialist party leader, Dr. Ram Manohar Lohia, moved the famous first no-confidence motion against the Congress government in 1963. He alleged that whereas a whopping amount of Rs. 25,000 was being spent daily on Nehru, the poor person was earning barely three annas or about 20 paise a day. The government's response was that according to the estimates of the Planning Commission, the average daily earning of a person were 15 annas or 95 paise and not three annas. In one of the most moving and well-researched of rebuttals in the history of Indian parliamentary debates, Dr. Lohia showed how the Planning Commission had arrived at its estimate by averaging the earnings of the richest people in the country with that of the poorest, while his own estimate was based on a sample of only the poorest people of the country who constituted seventy percent of its population. Member after member from the opposition who had been listed to speak on the motion gave up their time to allow Dr. Lohia to put forth his case, which ruthlessly unmasked the reality of mis-governance and mal-development that Nehru's penchant for temple building had led to. The "three anna - fifteen anna debate" as it came to be called, shook the complacency of the Nehruvian establishment for the first time in Parliament and was to be a precursor of the eventual decline of the Congress party later.

A fair idea of the hierarchical attitude of the Indian Civil Service (ICS) officers of the British era who were to set the trend for civil administration in independent India can be had from the reminiscences of K. P. S. Menon, one of the foremost Indian civil servants, "A Collector could shake hands with a Deputy Collector or Superintendent of Police, even though he belonged to the Provincial Service. He could be offered a seat. He could even be called by his first name without prefixing, 'Rao Sahib' or 'Khan Sahib'. But to a Tehsildar or Inspector of Police, no such courtesies could be extended, except on the first arrival or departure from the station. It was by such taboos that the British officer maintained his prestige. The Indian officer of the ICS also conformed to this tradition". Given this milieu, it is not surprising that one of the early IAS officers of the country, B. P. R. Vitthal, who used to spin khadi yarn on the charkha as a student enamoured with Gandhism, had to precipitately give it up after becoming a civil servant in 1950 because "For a young IAS officer to be seen spinning would have been taken as self-serving hypocrisy, like the young taking up causes like secularism and gender justice." Gandhi, of course, had, mercifully for him, gone to heaven by that time.

Another early doyen of the IAS, T S R Subramaniam, who later rose to adorn the top bureaucratic post of the country, that of Cabinet Secretary, has in his memoirs paid homage to the British Viceroy Cornwallis as being the epitome of a good administrator for having instituted the first systematic (and highly retrogressive) land settlement system in India. Subramaniam's first posting as Collector was in 1965 in Ghazipur district in eastern Uttar Pradesh, which had witnessed a massive peasant uprising against the British in 1942. The skewed land distribution and the hobbled agriculture of this district is so disastrous for the poor peasants that even today a large section of them have to migrate to the cities of Mumbai, Delhi and Kolkata in search of livelihoods. Given his reverence for Cornwallis, this IAS officer could hardly have been expected to set about suo moto, setting things right for the peasants as he could have done under the various land reform and control of usury laws that had been enacted by that time. He instead preferred to busy himself with setting up 'nets' in the garden of his official residence for providing coaching and practice to a cricket team that he built there. He proudly declares that it had begun winning matches with other districts before he left for greener pastures.

Closer to home, in 1994, Alirajpur had a freshly inducted IAS officer as Subdivisional Magistrate (SDM). He wanted a cable TV connection immediately in his bungalow. The only cable TV provider had run out of cable and said it would take him a day or two to get fresh supplies from Indore. The SDM would have none of it and had him arrested under section 151 of CrPC, which provides for preventive detention of people who may cause breach of peace. The SDM must have felt that his being deprived of television viewing in a godforsaken place such as Alirajpur was a breach of his peace of mind. The poor cable TV provider stayed in jail until his staff went to Indore, got the cable, returned and established the connection. When I advised the cable operator to go to the Collector and complain about this high handedness, he clasped his hands with fear, saying that he had had enough, and I should keep my advice to myself!

This section, along with some other such sections in the CrPC, all provided for ensuring public order and preventing breach of peace by criminal elements, are handy tools with which the administration can easily snuff out any democratic mass protest whatsoever. Theoretically, there is a division between the police who actually arrest people under these sections and the executive magistrates before whom they are produced before being sent to jail. However, when it comes to controlling democratic mass protests, the magistrates themselves take the decision for arresting the protests' leaders. The police carry out these orders and bring the arrested persons before the very same magistrates who have ordered their arrest. The person arraigned has to bail himself out and after that regularly attend the court. In the end, the arraigned person is made to sign a bond to the effect that in future he will maintain peace. Once a person signs this bond, he automatically acknowledges that he has broken the peace in the case in question. This amounts to him admitting to his guilt, and he is then considered to have been convicted. Once a person is convicted in this kangaroo court manner a few times, he becomes a hardened criminal in the eyes of the administration who can then start a process under another draconian law, once again enacted for the control of criminal activity, for externment from the district in which he lives as well as from all the adjoining districts. Often people in mass movements have other similar false criminal cases against them, and so it is easy for the administration to pass an order of externment against a mass movement activist.

I have lost count of the number of times I have been jailed under section 151 of CrPC. But I have never ever signed on the dotted line saying that I am going to keep the peace in the future. When it was slapped on me for the first time, the police had to release me after the High Court reprimanded it for not following the procedures. That was the first time anyone in Jhabua had moved the High Court against the arbitrary and illegal use of preventive detention by the administration, and it created a minor flutter within the local administration. On later occasions, sometimes I have gone on hunger strike and on some others, the administration, knowing that I would not sign on any paper, has released me on its own. On one occasion, the Superintendent of Police of Dewas had me arrested from a bus in which I was travelling, just to show me who was the boss. He then sent wireless messages all around over the five districts of western Madhya Pradesh to see if there were any arrest warrants pending against me. There were none; so eventually after having kept me in custody for eight hours, he ordered his henchmen to prepare a false chargesheet against me under section 151 of CrPC. I had, in the meantime, been continually pestering these lower level policemen to make out an arrest memorandum stating the reasons for my arrest as per the rulings of the Supreme Court. So when they finally asked me to sign on the arrest memo under section 151 CrPC after eight hours, I refused to do so. This created a problem for the police, and eventually the SDM before whom I was produced declared that the chargesheet against me was false and so discharged me unconditionally!

The same kind of toughness cannot be expected from adivasis. These people invariably sign a bond stating that they will keep the peace in future and so convict themselves. One such adivasi activist, a veteran of many battles, including the one against the hostel warden in Katkut mentioned earlier is Chhotelal Bamnia of Katkut village. The Superintendent of Police of Khargone district put in a proposal to the District Collector, listing all the cases pending against him and demanding that Chhotelal be externed from the district. This, despite not been convicted in any of the cases, apart from the ones under section 151 CrPC.

When he was served the externment order, we prepared an application against the order, and I accompanied Chhotelal to Bhopal to file it with the Home Secretary. This followed the massive repression carried out in Mehendikhera to snuff out the Adivasi Morcha Sangathan, wherein I had been labelled a dangerous subversive. I thought that if I were to reveal my identity to the Home Secretary, whatever little chance Chhotelal had of getting relief, would be scotched. So I asked Pushpendra, who had by this time become the editor of an evening daily in Bhopal, to set up an appointment; I would tag along as his assistant.

The three of us went off to the Secretariat, and after some preliminary exchange of pleasantries, Pushpendra handed the Home Secretary the application on behalf of Chhotelal. When he read that Chottelal was a member of the Adivasi Shakti Sangathan, he warned Pushpendra that this was a dangerous organisation out to destabilise the state, and if Pushpendra did not watch his step, he might get into serious trouble. He went on to state that Chhotelal and other adivasis like him were simple people, and the real culprit was Rahul Banerjee who was instigating them from behind the scenes. He also suggested that I was a cunning fellow, secretly preparing the base for the spread of Naxalism in western Madhya Pradesh. He regretted that despite the crushing action taken by the state in Mehendikhera, it had not been able to wipe out the seeds of extremism from the region precisely because of my presence.

Warming up to his theme, the Home Secretary asked Pushpendra to do a story on the way in which I was vitiating the atmosphere in the region by using the press and the international human rights agencies to counter the efforts of the state to root out extremism. The Secretary began reading out from a confidential file about my activities. Pushpendra "commanded" me to take the notes! I felt flattered while I wrote down all the exaggerated insurgent activity that had been falsely imputed to me. Among other things, it stated that Subhadra and I were not married and that we were only living together. What a sin. Subhadra had not changed her surname after marriage. This led the police to arrive at this deduction. Indeed, Subhadra's decision to retain her maiden surname has led to many bizarre encounters with the bureaucracy. On one occasion when I had gone to register our names in the electoral rolls after shifting to Indore, the SDM refused to put down Subhadra's surname as Khaperde. When I told him that Subhadra is an independent person and free to use whatever surname she liked, he told me that I had got a golden opportunity to put such an uppity wife in her place and should jump at it and put her surname down in the electoral rolls as Banerjee! We had to go to the Collector after that to get Subhadra's surname properly registered in the electoral rolls. Even then the published electoral rolls show only Subhadra's father's first name and not her surname!

At the end of the meeting with the Home Secretary, Chhotelal asked him to sign on the copy as proof of receipt of the application. Once again, the Secretary flared up, saying that he could not imagine a simple adivasi not trusting him and plucking up the courage to ask him, the Home Secretary, for a receipt. All this was my handiwork, he fumed. We came out of the office, and once safely out of hearing range, we burst out in laughter that rang through the corridors of the Secretariat. Pushpendra finally recovered and clapped me on my back and said, "Rahul all your years of struggle have not gone in vain." Needless to say that after dillydallying for about two months on various pretexts, the Home Secretary finally rejected the appeal. We then went in further appeal to the High Court, and after another seven months or so, we had the order quashed. The High Court held that the order of externment was illegal and had violated the provisions of the externment law and also the basic principles of natural justice. We then sent a demand of justice notice to the Superintendent of Police and District Collector, saying that the High Court order clearly stated that they had illegally harassed Chhotelal, and so they should give a written apology and pay compensation. There was obviously no response from the culprits. We have subsequently sent applications to various authorities, right up to the President of India demanding permission to prosecute the two in the courts as is mandatory under the law. These applications are still pending, as the sanction order for prosecution from the state has not yet materialised. We are biding our time before going to the High Court once again.

An idealistic young IAS officer once tried to provide the minimum statutory wages to the agricultural workers in Barwani, only to be transferred immediately to Alirajpur, where he began to investigate the local police's practice of passing off murders as suicides. Once again, he earned the ire of the local political bigwigs who got a non-bailable arrest warrant issued against him. He desperately appealed to us to use our contacts in the press to help him. He even told me once that the police are "A gang of criminals who had sanction of the law."

By the time we encountered him again in 1993 as the District Collector in Jhabua, this young man had morphed into a cynical bureaucrat. Choosing to forget our cordial relations of the days when he was on the run, he decided to break the back of the KMCS and the NBA, whose activities were then in full swing. The result of all this was an inevitable confrontation at Kakrana village, where he slapped Khemla. Khemla and others were then beaten up by the SDM in Alirajpur, another IAS officer, and the police. Then they were all paraded in handcuffs on the streets of Alirajpur. He came into his own after the Anjanbara confrontation, letting lose his legal gang of criminals on us, beating us up and packing us all into jail. He even engineered a rally against us in Alirajpur with government money. Madhya Pradesh was under President's rule at the time, which basically translates into the bureaucracy taking over the state's rule when a state assembly is dissolved and there is no elected government. Since his actions were backed to the hilt by the administration, one can safely assume that the whole bureaucracy of the state connived in this illegal repression of our organisation. It was only with the intervention of the Supreme Court where we filed a petition challenging the human rights violations he had ordered, that we could finally get this officer transferred.

One IAS officer has made an anonymous assessment of his colleagues, which speaks volumes for their irrelevance, nay evilness, for a largely rural developing country like India, "A critical lack of concern for the poor is reflected in the way IAS officers grade their jobs...Posts in the Industrial and Commercial Departments and the corporations occupy a very high rank. These enable the IAS officer an entry into the Government of India, his Mecca, as also afford an opportunity to hobnob with industrialists and businessmen with whom he has class affinity. Next in the list would be posts, which carry a lot of patronage and influence like a district charge, the departments of Home, Establishment, Finance, etc. The lowest rank goes to jobs where excellent performance would directly benefit the poorest, such as Harijan and Social Welfare, Revenue Administration, Land Reforms, Land Settlement, Rural Development, etc". He goes on to say, "An officer in the late 1960s went to a backward district in Central India, but his only recollection of the two year stay was that the district was full of ancient statues and how excitedly he used to look forward to unearthing and obtaining such antiquities. Not only did the illegality of his action not bother him, but he did not notice the poverty of the people, social indebtedness and intense exploitation in the district".

Some IAS officers did help us in the early stages of our work in Alirajpur. Some of these officer sympathisers later helped Subhadra fight an important personal battle of hers. One of the biggest tragedies of the Indian society is the lack of property inheritance rights for women in almost all communities, barring some matrilineal ones in the Northeast. This is even more of a problem in the rural areas, where land is sometimes the sole economic resource, leading to severe patriarchal oppression of women. As the first law minister of independent India, Babasaheb Ambedkar tried to pilot a law to give equal inheritance rights to women and came up against stiff opposition. After four years of fruitless effort, he resigned in disgust in 1951. However, later such laws did get enacted in some states. In Madhya Pradesh, the law regarding inheritance of agricultural land clearly states that daughters as well as sons will have to be given an equal share of their parent's ancestral plot. However, in practice, this is never implemented. Subhadra decided to claim her share when her father passed away in 1993. Her brothers obviously demurred. So she decided to move the administration to get her share.

Luckily, the District Collector of Bastar at that time happened to be an IAS officer whom we had known in Alirajpur. He got things moving, and the Tehsildar registered a case which went in favour of Subhadra. However, the implementation was stalled as the District Collector was subsequently transferred. Once again, the Secretary to the Chief Minister whom we knew intervened and in no time the Tehsildar went to Jepra with a posse of policemen and measured Subhadra's share of land. The bureaucracy has its uses, after all, when your side of the toast has to be buttered. A central Act has now been enacted to give women this right all over India. The moot point is how many poor rural women will be able to muster the same kind of contacts within the IAS as Subhadra to be able to get this law implemented.

These officers who had helped us out earlier in our battles against the local state, which were not fundamentally challenging to the system, distanced themselves from us, preferring to go with the system rather than against it when we took on the larger state apparatus. In the preparations for and the aftermath of the grossly illegal oppression by the government in Mehendikhera, not a single of our IAS friends spoke up for us. The more sensitive souls in the IAS have sooner or later been forced to resign, given the basic anti-people nature of the system. Dr. B. D. Sharma was the first to do so in Madhya Pradesh. Many years later, he was followed by Harsh Mander, who resigned after the Gujarat pogrom in 2002. He had taken leave from government duty much before that to work in the NGO sector after his early experiences as an administrator had shown him how difficult it was to do something for the poor from within the system. The most shining example of an IAS officer who has resigned and then devoted her life to the emancipation of the oppressed is that of my one time colleague and mentor Aruna Roy.

When I met her for the first time in 1985, she told me that as an IAS officer she was not able to sit cross-legged on the ground and talk freely with the common people. How could you understand their problems if you did not do that she asked? She had resigned from the IAS in 1974 and joined SWRC to be able to do something with the people. But after a decade of rural development work, she too, like Khemraj had felt that the rhetoric of participatory development would remain hollow unless the structures of oppression were smashed to enable the people to think and act freely. She had encouraged Khemraj to go to Jhabua and had gone and spent some time helping him with his work there in the early stages. Later, she decided to move out of Tilonia and go and work in the Bhim tehsil of Udaipur district in southern Rajasthan in the late 1980s. This was an area from where most of the peasants had to migrate for work, as the produce from their fields was not sufficient to sustain them even in years of normal monsoons. Moreover, since 1986 the area had been in the grip of drought, which resulted in further dwindling of the agricultural production. This made Aruna and the organisation of the peasants and agricultural workers in the region, Mazdoor Kisan Shakti Sangathan (MKSS), search for alternative ways in which to improve employment opportunities in the area.

Their investigations revealed that there were rampant irregularities in the implementation of the rural development works being carried out through the panchayats. Thus began a campaign to root out the corruption resulting from the nexus between the local state and the elected panchayat representatives. "Hamara paisa hamara hisaab" or *our funds our audit* became the slogan of the MKSS. It was clear that funds were being defalcated by various means such as fraudulent muster rolls and nonexistent construction that was evaluated and certified to be up to the mark. But to get documentary proof, it was necessary to scrutinise the records of the work done and payments made. Here, the MKSS came up against the obdurate refusal of the bureaucracy to open its records for inspection, with the latter claiming that they had been certified to be in order by the government auditors. Attempts to get the higher-level bureaucracy and the politicians to intervene did not bring any tangible results because this demand was a potentially dangerous one that could prove to be the thin end of the wedge for public access to records at higher levels. The MKSS then took recourse to the traditional Gandhian means of satyagraha to try and force the government to make these records available. Initially the organisation met with the same kind of police repression that is the fate of such agitations. Eventually, however, the Rajasthan Government made some concessions in this regard.

This is when the MKSS hit upon a new strategy in the year 1995 that has brought about a sea change in the field of public action in India. Faced with the stalemate of the state regularly using repression to crush "jan karyavahi" or militant mass action by mass organisations, the MKSS hit upon the idea of holding a "jan sunwai" or public hearing. This involved mobilising the press and influential people in society, including government and bureaucracy representatives to be present in specially organised meetings in villages. People would congregate in these meetings and give details of how they had been cheated of their wages or other developmental benefits. The intention was to build up moral pressure on the government and the administration and make them accede to just demands. This soon became a movement that spread its wings across the whole nation. Jan sunwais began to be held in every nook and cranny around all kinds of instances of denial of rights to the deprived sections. The movement took the shape of the National Campaign for the Right to Information. The jan sunwai perfected and formalised the tactic of synthesising both people's mobilisation at the grassroots and the mobilisation of sympathetic people in civil society at large, along with the press that the NBA had begun utilising earlier. Not only has this led to the enactment of a Right to Information Act in 2005, but it has also inspired the launch of many other national campaigns such as those for adivasis, housing, child, employment and the rights of specially-abled people. The jan sunwais have come in particularly handy for directing the spotlight on human rights violations by agencies of the state. Aruna was awarded the prestigious Ramon Magsaysay Award for community leadership in the year 2000 as had been Jayaprakash Narayan and Baba Amte earlier.

Jan Sunwais, however, cannot be a substitute for jan karyavahis or militant mass actions involving vast numbers of oppressed people for bringing about lasting radical changes in society. Although the jan sunwais are a means of focussing attention on rights violations, they cannot by themselves ensure that these violations will be remedied. In the absence of massive mass mobilisation in support of the decisions taken at the jan sunwais, this form of political action suffers from the same impotency in the face of state obduracy as other forms of Gandhian struggle. In one well publicised example of jan sunwai conducted by the MKSS in Umarwaas Panchayat of Rajsamand district in Rajasthan in the year 1999, things backfired embarrassingly. The sarpanch of the panchayat who was a dalit had been sponsored by the powerful upper castes in the 1995 elections since the seat had been reserved for scheduled castes. He was a pawn in the hands of these upper caste leaders who had got themselves elected as ward members. They then engaged in various malpractices. When the unaccounted withdrawals in his name grew to huge amounts, the sarpanch got worried and contacted the MKSS. This infuriated the upper caste leaders and they connived with the rural development bureaucracy to indict him for having defalcated funds, had him suspended and had a recovery notice for the amounts due slapped on him. The jan sunwai that was organised after this was a high profile one with Arundhati Roy presiding and the Collector and Superintendent of Police of the District attending. The villagers spoke out in favour of the sarpanch despite attempts by the upper castes to intimidate them. Detailed statements were recorded of how the upper castes had defalcated the funds in collusion with the bureaucracy. Surprisingly, despite the passage of a resolution at the jan sunwai that a criminal case should be filed against the corrupt ward panches and bureaucrats, the police registered a case against the sarpanch for defalcating the panchayat's funds!

Eventually, Aruna had to use her contacts in the high-level bureaucracy to salvage something from this effort by getting the FIR against the dalit sarpanch withdrawn. Even then, no criminal case could be instituted against the powerful upper caste ward panches who had actually embezzled the funds. The success of the MKSS has not been replicated so easily elsewhere by other mass organisations and NGOs that have held jan sunwais because they have not been able to garner the same kind of contacts in the bureaucracy and the mainstream political parties as the MKSS. It is indeed unlikely that the ruling elite will go beyond supporting such one off successes as those of the MKSS and welcome any widespread movement for transparency at the grassroots, which will cut into its hegemony of power. After all, the gap between demanding transparency and demanding greater allocations of resources for local development or like in the case of the adivasis of the Narmada valley, demanding the scrapping of mega development, is a small one. Unlike Medha, who has directly challenged the state to repeal unjust laws and policies and implement fully its just laws, Aruna has remained content with coaxing it to just formulating good laws and implementing them in fits and starts and so has tasted a little more success. When the National Advisory Council was formed under the chairpersonship of the Congress President, Sonia Gandhi, to act as a super think tank for the Congress-led coalition government at the centre in 2004, Aruna was chosen to be a member of this powerful body. She used this opportunity to make two very good interventions that resulted in the passage of the Right to Information Act, 2005 and the National Rural Employment Guarantee Act, 2005.

Advocacy and lobbying, however, have serious limitations. These are political strategies that have been developed in the United States of America where the rules for state funding of political parties make it near impossible for small groups to even participate in elections, let alone win them; so the radical political formations there have even more of a "bin pende ka lota" image than the ones in India. However, civil society in India is much less developed than it is in the USA, and so lobbying and advocacy or a mixture of this with weak grassroots mobilisation as in the conduct of jan sunwais, has even lesser chance of bringing about the major people-oriented changes in development and governance that the environmentalists envisage.

The Right to Information Act was finally passed by Parliament in 2005 after some high drama behind the scenes. Aruna used her membership of the National Advisory Council to impress upon Sonia Gandhi the need to get the draft formulated by the National Campaign on RTI passed, instead of the toothless one drafted by the bureaucrats. Both these ladies carried the day in the face of stiff opposition from the bureaucrats, and the most radical Act yet in independent India became a reality. It is treated with derision by bureaucrats who thwart access to information on one pretext or the other. With the result that the Information Commissions at the Centre and in the States have become overloaded with appeals, which they cannot dispose of expeditiously because of lack of staff.

Later, the government was all set to amend the Act to prevent the revelation of the notes made by the bureaucrats on the files regarding the decisions taken by the Cabinet of Ministers on major economic and political matters. Media criticism and lobbying has managed to stall this for the time being, but this is the thin end of the wedge. The day is not far when the humdinger of a provision making the Public Information Officers responsible for delays or refusals in providing information and penalising them for this will be sought to be removed through an amendment, rendering the Act toothless like the many others that adorn our statute books.

One of the more sensitive IAS officers from the Madhya Pradesh cadre, who was at that time the Director of the Lal Bahadur Shastri National Academy of Administration in Mussoorie where the IAS cadres are trained, once related an interesting anecdote. He said that he had introduced a course in which the IAS probationers had to stage street plays and write, compose and sing songs around some theme of importance for village development. He had introduced this to inculcate a feel for modes of people-friendly communication among the probationers. The probationers, on the other hand, reacted by saying that they had come to learn how to rule over people so why were they being taught how to sing and dance? When the vast majority of the bureaucrats in this country still suffer from such a hangover of colonial power intoxication, appealing to them to heed the sane logic of transparent, people-centred governance and environment-friendly development is akin to casting pearls before swine.

22 Jailhouse Rock

The memory of the crippling fear I saw on the face of my cable TV provider friend in Alirajpur after his arbitrary incarceration in jail reminds me continually that the power of the state over its citizens is maintained through the latter's fear of police lockups and jails. These two modern institutions are an integral part of all forms of states—from the right to the left of the political spectrum. Without these, no state can continue in existence in the face of challenges posed by rebels of all kinds. Thus, any mass movement for political change has to have a practical strategy to counter the debilitating effects of these institutions, instead of just singing along with the American folk singer Joan Baez and making the militant anarchist demand for prisons to be razed to the ground. Dr. Ram Manohar Lohia had stressed that jails were the best finishing schools for the people and activists of social movements, and so they should be filled up to bursting in the course of civil disobedience actions. "Civil disobedience is armed reason" and "Jail Bharo" or filling up jails is its main weapon. While ridding the masses of the fear of incarceration, this form of mass action simultaneously stretches the state's disciplining power to its limits. That is why the radical mass social movements have always tried to push the people into conflict situations with the state that results in them landing up in jail. Vaharu of the Shramik Sangathan in Shahada has composed a very nice song that goes like this -

Aana jana police thana (To and fro to the police station)

Jail hamara ghar   (Jail is our home)

Court hamari anganbari (Court is our play school)

Kahe ke liye dar   (What is there to be afraid of)

Mat chhero police wale (Police, please do not bother us)

Mat chhero bhai   (Please do not bother us brother)

During our work in Katkut, where women were at the forefront of the struggle, Subhadra went to jail along with seven other women. This was the first time they had done so.

Confrontation started at the jail gate itself where the jailer asked them to take off their ornaments and deposit them with the gate warden. Subhadra and the women refused to do so as they said they were activists and not criminals. An altercation ensued, which the women won. This set the tone for the rest of their fourteen-day stay in jail as they had established their superiority before even entering its premises. They fought for and got food in accordance with the provisions of the jail manual, and they were even provided with sanitary napkins, which was probably a first in jails for women. Later, Subhadra went on a hunger strike in jail, and she had to be evacuated to a hospital before finally being released on her personal bond without having to furnish bail as she had demanded. Thus, during their stay they got royal treatment because of the tough stand they took in establishing their status as political prisoners, despite being arraigned on false criminal charges.

The closest we have ever come to a sustained jail bharo situation was during the Anjanwara incident in Alirajpur. On that occasion, a broad section of the KMCS was incarcerated and beaten up in police lockups and then sent to jail. The members of the KMCS kept the jail populated for one whole month. The first person to be arrested in the Anjanwara incident was an adivasi activist, who had been severely beaten up before being sent to jail where he was again persecuted by the jail inmates. Amit, who had tried to hold a press conference back then, was arrested along with his companions. The husband of one of the activists, then teaching in Delhi University, who came down to reinforce our dwindling team was immediately arrested too, falsely charged of attempting to murder policemen.

While he was in the police lockup, yet another person, a friend of the activist whose husband had been arrested also came down from the USA. By this time, enough noise had been made nationally and internationally against the high handedness of the police and the administration for things to cool down somewhat. The police did not dare to arrest this person, but he was summoned to the police station for enquiries. When he was brought to the police station, the university teacher in the lockup, fearing the worst, thought of some way to warn him of trouble. Incidentally, this university teacher is also an accomplished musician, and so to warn the other guy outside, he began desperately whistling Pink Floyd's classic number "Wish you were here" missing the irony!

The guy outside started and wondered how someone was whistling Pink Floyd in the police station. He put two and two together and began insisting that he be allowed to meet the activist in custody, as that was one of his basic rights. The police did not allow this and shooed him away.

Avalsingh of Attha who had gone to the Chhaktala for the Sunday weekly market was picked up from there, given customary lashings, and then sent to jail. He did not even know at that time that some major incident had taken place at Anjanwara. On seeing this, another of his fellow villagers, Guthia, slunk off through a back alley; after returning home, he took off into the hills to camp there until things cooled down. People associated with the KMCS were being arrested left, right and centre, beaten up in police lockups and sent to jail. While being taken to the court or sent to jail they were all paraded in handcuffs along the main streets of the town. There was terror everywhere. So we, who had not been arrested, gathered some people, and then, under Medha's leadership, took out a rally in Alirajpur. It was only after this that the situation pacified somewhat. A meeting was held, where people from outside came and addressed the audience. This put the administration on the backfoot for some time. Anticipatory bail applications were filed for the women activists, and once these were granted by the court, they could operate freely to have those inside the jail released.

By this time, there were some twenty people including Amit in jail. They were given a spare barrack all to themselves, and with some demanding, they also got a dholak or drum. So they spent their time singing songs and cracking jokes and composing new ones about adivasis and activists. One new joke they composed was really hilarious. An illiterate adivasi had heard an activist saying in a meeting that according to the Constitution, which was the "kanoon ki chopri" or main book of law in this country, he had the right to shout slogans against the police for their misdeeds, and the police could not do anything about it, not even beat him up. Elated and enthused by such a liberating exhortation, he went to the thana, stood outside it and began shouting slogans against the police. He was promptly arrested and beaten up. The adivasi hotly protested that the kanoon ki chopri said that he had the right to do what he had done. The police then took out the IPC and asked him to point out to show them this right. The adivasi put his finger randomly on one page. The police arraigned him under the section he had pointed to, concocted a false charge sheet and sent him to jail. After coming out on bail he accosted the activist with his experience, which had been contrary to what the activist had said. The activist went with the adivasi and indignantly asked the police why they had acted in contravention of the Constitution, the supreme law of the land. The latter replied that the only law they knew was the IPC and booked both of them for preventing the police from doing their duty by unnecessarily bringing in the impediment of the Constitution, beat them up and sent them back to jail. On the way to the jail, the adivasi patted the back of the disconsolate activist and said, "Never mind, you will remember to read the right chopri next time." The moral of the story is that social activists who want to take on the police should read the IPC and CrPC properly and not the Constitution!

The police, right from the lowly constable to the highest officer, see no difference between criminals and people protesting against injustices. If anything, they are better disposed towards criminals from whom they can extort money. The first elite Indian Police Service (IPS) officer that I ever met, a Superintendent of Police (SP), told me after the first few introductory sentences that he would have me locked up in prison if I did not stop my anti-government activities. This, when it had become abundantly clear that the police lockup or the jail did not hold any terror for me. Subsequently, many other SPs have used the same language with me. Some have locked me up under preventive sections only to have to release me unconditionally as mentioned earlier. One SP even went to the extent of regretting that I was able to do what I was doing because unlike in neighbouring Pakistan, we had a democratic constitution in this country, which allowed me to go to the higher courts against the illegal actions of the police. Yet another SP told me that the National and State Human Rights Commissions were a nuisance because their continuous monitoring of custodial deaths had hamstrung the investigation into crimes as the police had to be wary of using third-degree methods to the hilt! The piece-de-resistance was one SP, who brazenly told me that he did not think anything of the Constitution, because given the illiteracy and poverty of the people, they could not go to the higher courts, and so effectively it was the police that ran the country by using the IPC and the CrPC! He went on to say in the same vein as all the other SPs before him that he would screw me. This was after the Mehendikhera firing and its aftermath, which had conclusively established that nothing that the state or its minions could do, short of killing me, was going to stop me in my tracks.

The jail conditions are nothing to right home about. Whenever I have gone to jail, the inmates have said that my entry into the jail premises resulted in the improvement of the quality and quantity of food served. But this was not the case the first time I went to jail as an accused in a murder case in Maharashtra. I was holed up along with seventeen other accused in the police lockup in Shahada, which was the nerve centre of the Shramik Sangathan. Our arrival created a severe lack of space, and we were cramped up with the other inmates in what can best be described as a black hole. The worst part of the whole stay of about a fortnight, before most of us got bailed out, were mosquitoes. They would buzz twenty-four hours and bite us like crazy. One of my co-accused would joke and say that the mosquitoes came singing "kun kun chhe ta, kun kun chhe ta" - *who all are here, who all are here*. The answer to that question of course was "we who are not all there"! After all, it is sheer madness to fight the police with the dice so heavily loaded in their favour. While in the lockup, I contracted malaria for the first time; thereafter I got it again and again over the next four years or so, which forced me to forsake my utopian life in Alirajpur and shift to Indore to cure myself.

This particular case is a typical example of the way the police goes about systematically trying to break mass movements. The KMCS had totally stopped the extra earnings that the police used to get from the many cases that would come to them earlier. Even such trivial things as a dog having bitten another dog would end up for resolution at the police thana with the inevitable extortion of money. The main source of income for the police was from disputes regarding the love affairs of men and women. To the extent that women who became pregnant due to pre-marital or extra-marital sex and wanted to get an abortion had to take the permission of the police and pay them a fine to do so! Like in the case of all other reactionary oppressions, patriarchal oppression too was ultimately maintained by the police. On one occasion, after such a case had reached the thana, the aggrieved party who was from a village that had not yet become part of the KMCS came to Khemla for help as the police were demanding an exorbitant sum. In his typical style, Khemla went to the police station, admonished the police and came away warning them to desist from such extortionate practices. The police decided to arrest the girl's father and forced him to make the girl give a statement that it was Khemla who had seduced her and made her pregnant. We got to know of this, and in the nick of time, before the police could get to them, we brought the pregnant girl and her father to the SDM in Alirajpur to get their true statements recorded. Khemla almost drowned himself when he jumped into a stream in spate to swim across and get to the village of the girl by taking a shortcut to pre-empt the police. Like me, the last thing that Khemla wanted was to be saddled with a false rape case against him!

The police then decided to instigate one of its dalals, whose income had also been affected because of the KMCS, to try and break the organisation. This dalal was a murderous man and he began going around beating up the members of the KMCS. The dalal and his cohorts attacked a meeting being conducted by the KMCS; this resulted in a fight after which the dalal and his henchmen ran away and were followed by the villagers. The meeting was being held on the banks of the Narmada river. So the dalal and his cohorts swam across the river on to the other side, and the chasing KMCS members followed suit. In the ensuing battle with bows and arrows, the dalal's brother was killed. This led to the murder charge against the members of the KMCS in which I, too, was implicated for having allegedly said that I had brought orders from Delhi to kill the dalal and had conspired to hold the meeting that led to the death of the dalal's brother. Khemla somehow escaped the charge of rape, but I got indicted for murder. All that is required to register a false case are a statement or two from some people saying that they have seen the accused person saying or doing something that is culpable under some law. There may not be any circumstantial or physical evidence to substantiate these false statements, but that is a matter to be decided during the trial.

Following the Mehendikhera incident, the police once again cooked up a false case against us to cover up its own illegality in having fired on and killed defenceless adivasis. Apart from such standard sections of the IPC as attempt to murder and armed unlawful assembly for the first time, we were also implicated under the serious charge of waging an armed war against the state. When the case finally came up for trial, we invoked the relevant section of the CrPC to have the case discharged because there was no prima facie evidence to support the charges made, especially the charge of waging war against the state. A lot of pressure was brought to bear on the poor judge not to discharge us. Ultimately, he dismissed the application for discharge and framed charges against us, and we had to go in appeal to the High Court.

My longest stay in jail and also my most enjoyable resulted from this case. I spent two and a half months in prison before getting bailed out. When I went in, I was initially on a hunger strike, and had I persisted with it, I might have got released earlier. However, I desperately needed some rest at the time—both physical and mental as various kinds of pressures had made me tired. Since there was no possibility of my going on to bear death, I also felt that my going on hunger strike just for securing my release would be the same kind of half-hearted individualistic Gandhian action that I was ideologically against. The whole idea behind the work that we had done in Katkut and Dewas was that the people should carry on the struggle by themselves. I thought that with the state having come down like a ton of bricks, the people should have a full taste of this pounding so that they had a clear idea of the kind of strength and stamina required for fighting the state.

Jail is an ideal place for someone who wants to spend time in deep thought. For undertrial or preventively detained prisoners, there are no worries as the food is supplied on time, and all one has to do is sit and twiddle one's fingers if one does not busy oneself with study and thought. Nehru read and wrote on Indian history while in jail in the early 1940s and firmed up his modern temple building plans. While in jail at about the same time as Nehru, Antonio Gramsci, the Italian Communist, on the other hand, churned out an inspiring and innovative analysis of capitalist state oppression and insights into the reasons for its dominance that remain relevant to this day. So I began by reviewing my years of activism and that is how the idea of writing this book first took a nebulous shape in my mind. I decided to use the time in reading and asked my well wishers outside to supply me with some books. That's how I unexpectedly received the Hindu scripture, Madbhagwata Purana, written by the sage Vyas. The book was given to me by the jailer who happened to be a devout man. This tour-de-force in ancient Hindu mysticism advocates renunciation of worldy desires for the pursuit of transcendental truths, ideas that had held little appeal for me until then, but could not have come at a better time. After taking daily dips in the Madbhagwata, I became less sensitive to the setbacks to the adivasis' struggles and began enjoying my sojourn in prison to the full.

This was also the first time that I got an opportunity to talk at length to criminals. There were adivasi thieves and robbers in the jail with me. These people had been implicated in a number of cases. It is the practice of the police that once they catch a thief, they torture him and make him confess to having done several other thefts for which they had hitherto had no clues. At one go, these thieves become hardened criminals, and even after their release they are pestered by the police whenever some place is robbed in their vicinity. These poor adivasis asked me if there was a solution to this. I told them that the best solution was that once they were acquitted—as they invariably would be, given the police's poor quality of investigation—they should institute criminal defamation proceedings against the police. My general advice on various things related to the law and rights turned out to be so interesting that soon I was holding regular informal sessions for the jail inmates on the legal methods of fighting the state.

News of this soon leaked out to the police. The police had charged me with having conspired to wage an armed war against the state. Obviously, they did not have an iota of evidence to support this charge. They had recorded some fabricated statements by witnesses, but these were vague, to say the least. So this news of my holding informal legal classes was sweet music to their ears. One day the jailer who was sympathetic to me, called me and told me that there was a complaint that I was instigating the adivasis inside to stage a revolt and seize the weapons in the jail and stage a break out. Thereafter, I had reportedly planned to take the weapons and the adivasis and begin a full-fledged war against the state. I told him that he could ask the adivasis if I had said or planned anything so crazy. Soon after this, I was removed from this jail to another one. After that, the Subdivisional Magistrate and the Superintendent of Police went to the jail and began beating up the poor adivasis severely to try and force them to give statements to the effect that I had planned a jailbreak and a subsequent war against the state with them. They refused to do so despite this harassment and later told me about it when I met them again outside the jail.

This reminds me of an anecdote about Mao ze Dong related by the American Marxist historian William Hinton. Once when Mao was camping in the house of an old villager, he and his comrades were listening to a radio they had with them. The old villager, who had never seen a radio before, wonderingly said that this must be the voice of God coming from the heavens. At this, everyone began laughing. But Mao immediately scolded his comrades and then spent a painstaking half an hour explaining to the old man how the radio worked and that it was not conveying the voice of God. Later, this particular village fell into the hands of the Kuomintang and they tortured this old man to get some information about the whereabouts of Mao. The old man refused to divulge any information, despite the torture. In the same way, the poor adivasis I had talked to in jail were hungry for knowledge and a little sympathetic treatment. They valued the few hours I spent with them so much that they refused to bow down to the demands of the police to give false statements against me despite being beaten up.

The intention of the police is not to contain crime, but to profit from it. Typically, those that are not hardened criminals already pay thousands of rupees in bribes just to spare themselves the beatings from the policemen, who use the fear of these beatings to extract confessions. The police keeps itself informed about the various kinds of underhand goings on through their informers, yet nothing much is done to root out this crime except for some occasional cases. Flimsy charge sheets are prepared with statements from professional witnesses. Their palms greased, the police are only too happy to look the other way on most occasions. The French author Anatole France once sarcastically wrote - "The law, in its majestic equality, forbids the rich as well as the poor to sleep under bridges, to beg in the streets, and to steal bread." The rich can always violate the law with impunity, and it is only the poor who are caught by the long hand of the law and packed into jails. All in all, I have found my sojourns in Indian jails to be among the best experiences of my life. And like all exclusive clubs, entry into these hallowed portals is only by invitation!

Not surprisingly, the police are sulking about the monitoring of custodial violence by the Human Rights Commissions, which has made the use of third-degree methods for eliciting information a risky proposition these days. Things, however, continue to be bad despite the greatly increased surveillance of human rights and the absolute number of custodial deaths has gone on increasing. This has forced the Supreme Court to keep pending the original petition filed as far back as 1987 against arbitrary detention and torture and monitor the police continually. The problem is that political parties support the use of the arbitrary powers by the police to settle scores with their opponents and to crush any radical people-oriented mass mobilisation movement, and so there seems to be no light at the end of this tunnel.

The police have never touched me physically. Not even when I went to jail for the first time under the serious charge of conspiring to murder. In the Mehendikhera incident, the moment the police took me into custody I began pestering them to make out an arrest memo against me as had been ordered by the Supreme Court. They dithered around for all of twenty-four hours, deciding on what to do while I continually put pressure on them to prepare the arrest memo. They finally did so on the dot when the time limit of twenty-four hours for the preparation of an arrest memo was about to elapse. Since the arrest memo was not prepared they could not inform anyone as to where I was, and under what sections I had been arrested. So people outside had to be fobbed off with vague replies, which led to their fearing the worst. Amnesty International sent out red alerts saying that my life was in danger and mails and faxes began pouring in to the Government of Madhya Pradesh. As a consequence of this international pressure, nothing happened to me. But all the other first few detainees in the case were badly beaten up, and as usual, the judicial magistrates did not take cognisance of the complaints being made to them about this illegal chastisement.

One of our comrades, Basruddin, was apprehended under section 151 of CrPC and similarly beaten up. It took the wind out of his sails so much so that the once die-hard activist resigned himself to passivity. After the Mehendikhera incident, he was kept in jail for two and a half months, which is illegal because this section is a preventive one and an accused under it should be automatically released after fifteen days at the most. It was only after I got out of jail and threatened to take the SDM to the High Court that he relented and set him free, though the jail staff was sorry to see him go off because Basru was a former water quality analyser turned Ayurvedic practitioner, and while in jail, had everyone from the jailer down to the warders eating out of his hands to resolve some of their chronic ailments, including the oldest one of impotency!

The most bizarre of all was the tale of one old man, who would come to the jail on the first week of every month to spend a fortnight before going out again. This man was regularly charged under the provisions of the law for control of public gambling. The old man was part of a betting or "satta" operation centred in Mumbai, but with a chain all over the country. The police and political parties all shared pieces of this operation's pie. Occasionally, the police have to arrest a few people to maintain a façade. This old man was paid a daily wage by the boss of his group to spend fifteen days in jail as part of the deal he had with the police! One of the most lucrative earnings for the police is in the form of "haftas" from illegal liquor selling and gambling, the two most vicious businesses that have kept the poor firmly tied to their poverty. Both these socially and economically harmful activities go on under the benign eyes of the police. The moment there is a popular mobilisation against these activities, the police begin flexing their muscles and those foolhardy enough to initiate the protest find themselves firmly lodged in jail as Subhadra and the women of Katkut did.

Most of the poor and deprived all over the world have to, in order to survive, resort to crime, illegal migration, illegal occupations, living in illegal habitations, drowning their sorrows in drug abuse or taking part in mass agitations for social and economic justice. This brings them continually into confrontation with the police and leads to their constituting an overwhelming majority in the jails. The mass jail bharo programme advocated by Dr. Lohia is a potent strategy for fighting the state, but this requires that the masses and activists learn to make the most of their sojourns in jail, instead of treating them as avoidable aberrations. The quintessential American Dreamer, the "King of Rock and Roll", Elvis Presley, advocated the adoption of precisely this positive attitude towards stints in jail when he sang in Jailhouse Rock -

> Shifty Henry said to Bugs, "For Heaven's sake,
> No one's lookin', now's our chance to make a break."
> Bugsy turned to Shifty and he said, "Nix nix,
> I wanna stick around a while and get my kicks."

23 The Elusive Holy Grail of Justice

When Subhadra was produced before the magistrate in the false case lodged against her for sitting on a dharna before the police station, the magistrate reprimanded her by saying that she should not indulge in "netagiri." Subhadra, not one to take such pejorative language lightly, told the magistrate that he had no right to make such a comment and should restrict himself to what was mentioned in the case papers. "Netagiri" is the word used to taunt those who dare to speak up for the disadvantaged. While the upper classes have "netas", those who try and fight for the disadvantaged can only aspire to be "netas" and are doomed to do netagiri and invite the state's backlash. In the debate that ensued, Subhadra questioned the legitimacy of the IPC itself, since it was a colonial law, which should have been struck down because it violated the Constitution in many respects. The upshot of all this was that Subhadra, along with the other women was refused bail, despite the case against her being a bailable one. Instead, they were sent to jail, though it is another matter that it was their intention to go to jail anyway as part of a jail bharo campaign. Subhadra complained against this arbitrariness of the magistrate to the District Judge and the High Court, but the result was that the magistrate became even angrier and slapped a fine on her.

Subhadra subsequently went on hunger strike in jail demanding that she be released unconditionally on a personal bond as she was not a criminal but a political activist. This forced the police higher ups to agree to withdraw the case after a review, and she was immediately released. However, later the Inspector General and the Superintendent of Police who had acceded to this demand got transferred, and as usual the police reneged and did not withdraw the case. The animosity of the initial magistrate and the apathy of the one after him meant that eight years elapsed before the case finally came to an end. Some witnesses were examined, but the case dragged on as others were yet to show up. Being a false one, the case should have been dismissed at the charge stage itself. Due to preoccupation with other work, we failed to prepare an application at the charge stage for discharge. A decade was spent by the courts to acquit Subhadra and teach her not to engage in "netagiri".

In the Anjanwara incident, as many as four false cases involving such serious sections as attempt to murder were filed, and some thirty odd people and activists were implicated in them. The police beat up most of the accused in custody and then paraded them on the streets of Alirajpur in handcuffs before producing them before the magistrate. When I pointed out to the magistrate that I had been produced in handcuffs before him despite several Supreme Court rulings that undertrial accused who are in custody are not to be handcuffed, he said that in the special circumstances prevailing in Alirajpur, the Supreme Court's ruling did not apply, and the police had the discretion to handcuff anybody they considered to be dangerous. Nevertheless, I insisted that it be put down in writing that I had been produced before him in handcuffs. He did so, and this was to prove his nemesis later on.

After the Mehendikhera incident, my bail application was not moved at all in the first month after my arrest, given the false charge of my being a Naxalite. During this time, widely publicised enquiries by many independent commissions had established that the administration had resorted to illegal destruction of the villages of the Sangathan, killed four of its members in arbitrary police firing and then cooked up a false case against us. Yet, the district judge refused to grant bail when an application was made, despite the flimsy hearsay evidence on which I had been arraigned. Pressure was brought to bear on him by the administration to refuse me bail and it worked.

The civil service administrators in India are also executive magistrates who sit in judgment both on law and order issues and others like the settlement of land records, where they have vast discretionary powers and can easily give an adverse judgment, which then has to be challenged at a higher level, necessitating much trouble and expense. They can make life hell for a lawyer who rubs them the wrong way. After the Anjanwada incident, the District Collector threatened our lawyer in Alirajpur with serious consequences if he moved bail applications for us. Medha Patkar had to plead in court on our behalf in the immediate aftermath of the crackdown and arrests, and lawyers had to be brought in from outside Madhya Pradesh to move our bail applications later. This

District Collector even had the sign board on our office in Alirajpur torn down by the police ruling that it was a "defacement of public space!"

Most lawyers are no better. They have a vested interest in the cases that drag on for years and provide them continuous earnings. Most lawyers try to prolong the cases and get as much money out of the accused as possible.

The prolonging of cases also gives the clerical staff in the courts the chance to earn some extra money. It is common practice for these people to take small bribes from the accused to give them their court dates. Not obliging them would mean getting court dates at very short intervals. This takes place under the eyes of the magistrates and judges. Once I asked one of these clerks whether they gave a cut of their earnings to the magistrates. He said that they did not do so in a direct manner. The way in which the exchange happened resembled this: the magistrate would say to the clerk one day that he had gone to the market and found that a certain shop had a very good brand of cooking oil on sale. He would ask if the clerk would not purchase a fifteen-litre can of the cooking oil and bring it to his home. The clerk had no option but to oblige! This is, of course, only the tip of the iceberg. The magistrates and judges regularly take hefty bribes to decide cases in favour of one party or another. This has become so much of a menace that recently the Madhya Pradesh High Court had to terminate the services of many magistrates and judges on finding that the complaints of corruption against them were true.

The only saving grace in this sordid story is that the higher courts, and especially the Supreme Court, currently functions with much more appreciation of the crucial watchdog role of the judiciary in a liberal democracy committed to social, economic and political justice. So some relief can be gained from the arbitrary and illegal actions of the executive as well as its failure to implement beneficial legislation. However, this was not the case in the years immediately after independence when the higher judiciary used its power of judicial review to block progressive legislations being enacted by Parliament and the state legislatures, especially those relating to land reform.

Over the years this has changed for the better, as judicial activism in support of the rights of the oppressed resulted in favourable judgments in a plethora of cases in support of human, economic, social, political and environmental rights being filed in the form of public interest litigations or class actions on behalf of the poor who were being exploited or otherwise harassed by the administration or vested interests. The provisions of the Constitution thus began to be interpreted in a way that was much more favourable to the poor. Thus, it was no longer necessary for aggrieved persons to move the higher courts by themselves and third parties in the form of NGOs and Human Rights Organisations could do so on their behalf.

Doubts have recently begun to be expressed regarding the commitment of the Supreme Court to social justice and the efficacy of public interest litigation for securing the rights of the poor after some adverse judgments in a few cases, following the liberalisation of the economy in the 1990s and most notably its decision to wash its hands off the thorny issue of proper rehabilitation and resettlement raised by the NBA. Nevertheless, on the whole, the positive intervention by the higher courts has provided great support to the beleaguered mass environmental movements in general and to those in Madhya Pradesh and Chhattisgarh in particular. It can be said without hesitation that without this support of the higher courts, these mass movements would have long folded up, and people like I would either have been permanently behind bars or forced into inaction by the illegalities of the executive and the insensitivity of the lower judiciary.

In the Anjanbara incident, the Supreme Court Bench led by the Chief Justice came down hard on the Madhya Pradesh government for such a blatant violation of human rights and irresponsiveness from the government in the face of repeated orders by the court against custodial torture and handcuffing. This put the Government of Madhya Pradesh and the respondents on the run, as it were. The court ordered hand delivery of notices to those who had been absent. This led to a hilarious denouement, when the KMCS members went to deliver these notices to the policemen concerned, who fled at the sight of the notice bearers! One head constable fled from the police station to his house, and when he was followed there, he escaped via the backdoor and made haste to hide himself in some other house. The adivasis had the time of their life seeing the police run away from them in this manner. The Government of Madhya Pradesh had to suspend one of the policemen and all the major officials involved. The District

Collector and the Superintendent of Police were transferred. The apex court ordered an investigation by the Central Bureau of Investigation (CBI) into the allegations made by the KMCS.

The CBI confirmed the allegations of torture and handcuffing that we had made and also revealed how the police had tampered with the daily logs and the case diaries to hide their culpability. The court directed the CBI to register cases against all the guilty officers and it also pulled up the magistrate, who had told me that the Supreme Court ruling on handcuffing did not hold in the special circumstances prevailing in Jhabua. When this magistrate went to the hearing, he was singled out for a special tongue-lashing for having not known the law despite being a member of the judiciary and the judges expressed displeasure at "the sordid picture and sorrowful plight of public spirited men who desire to prevent exploitation of poor Adivasis" and stated, "It cannot be denied that there have been acts by the police, which should concern everyone who values human rights. It cannot be said that the day of the silent poor is over. There is anger and bitterness among those who are poverty stricken. One should have regard to these aspects in enforcing law."

For the accused in the Mehendikhera firing case, the saga of their appeal to the High Court proved to be a theatre of the absurd. The prosecution would continuously demand time and avoid a final hearing. Their game plan was to delay the consideration of the case so that the lower court judge would proceed with the trial and then they could plead that since the trial had already started, the petition for discharge was un-maintainable. The High Court judges too kept on changing and none would give the petitioners a stay on the proceedings of the lower court. The proceedings in the lower court were kept at a standstill by various means, and the appeal was pursued in the High Court, resulting in an order quashing the farcical charge of waging war against the state, but keeping the other charges intact after five months. The problem for the High Court was that the prosecution, meaning the police, had appended the statements of as many as 106 witnesses in support of their charges. Now the High Court could not be expected to go through all those statements to ascertain our claim that these did not prima facie support all the charges made out against us. Thus, by quantity if not quality, the police try to get their investigations pass muster enough to entangle the accused in never-ending litigation.

Subsequently, this was heard in the lower court, and after some fifty odd witnesses having been examined, it was clear that the case is totally fabricated and so the judge decided to dispense with more of such useless evidence and finish the case. The case after dragging on for six years finally came to an end with our inevitable acquittal.

The judgments of the Supreme Court in the Bhopal Gas Tragedy and the NBA case have already been mentioned. The NBA continued to depend heavily on the Supreme Court to get some purchase against the highhandedness of the executive, even after the latter finally disposed of the case, allowing the construction of the SSP dam to continue. This is because the Supreme Court made it clear that the construction of the dam would proceed only in stages subject to the proper rehabilitation of the oustees. In the face of lack of progress on rehabilitation, the NBA continued to file objections, thus further delaying the project. This strategy was later adopted for the Indira Sagar and Omkareshwar dams, too. While the Narmada Hydro-Development Corporation and the Government of Madhya Pradesh rode rough shod over the protests of the people and forcibly evacuated the town of Harsud in 2004 without providing proper compensation and rehabilitation, the Corporation's efforts to do the same with the rest of the villages in the submergence zone have been stayed by the Madhya Pradesh High Court, and the Corporation has been prevented from closing the gates of the dam until the affected people are compensated and resettled. In a recent judgment in the Omkareshwar dam case the High Court has also gone to the extent of ordering that the state should pay the NBA legal costs for needlessly forcing it to come to the High Court for relief.

Even though the Supreme Court has now sneaked out of the SSP case and pulled the rug from under the NBA's feet, there can be no gainsaying the fact that from 1995, when the Supreme Court stayed the construction of the dam till 2006, when it finally distanced itself from the NBA's radical line, its pronouncements did provide a fairly stable dance floor on which the NBA could choreograph its anti-dam jig. One of the comments about the Mughal Empire in India that preceded the British rule is that one should not bemoan that it finally fell, but should wonder that it survived for such a long period spanning two centuries. Similarly, one should not complain about the Supreme Court having finally betrayed the oustees of the SSP as it was bound to do sooner or later, but should be thankful that it, too, chanted the slogan of " bandh nahi banega, koi nahi hatega" in chorus with the NBA for as long as a decade.

The most important judgement in favour of the adivasis has been the upholding of the Fifth Schedule in the Samatha case. The provisions of the Fifth Schedule of the Constitution state that land, including government land, in scheduled areas cannot be transferred to non-adivasis. Apart from this, there are other statutes preventing transfer of adivasi land to non-adivasis. However, despite these provisions, land in scheduled areas in Andhra Pradesh had been transferred to private companies and public corporations for the purpose of mining through leases. Samatha, an NGO in Vishakhapatnam district, challenged these leases as being unconstitutional in the High Court. The court rejected the Samatha contention that the private companies were juristically non-tribal 'person's and allowed the leases to continue. Samatha then appealed to the Supreme Court against this order.

The Supreme Court upheld the Samatha argument that private mining industries were also non-tribal 'person's and hence all mining leases in tribal lands in scheduled areas to private industries are null and void. Although the case was filed on behalf of a few remote tribal villages in Andhra Pradesh, the Court's judgement is a boon to the millions of adivasis in the nine states of India, which have Fifth Schedule areas. While the government could, in the public interest, still launch mining operations on its own, it was expressly forbidden from leasing land to private parties. Instead, the Court suggested that cooperatives of the adivasis be formed and the leases be given to them along with appropriate training. The Court also directed the Government to formulate an overall policy for development of adivasi areas so that the mining operations benefited the adivasis instead of devastating them. The Court even prescribed that twenty percent of the profits from these operations be set aside for this purpose. The Court further ruled that the permission of the adivasi gram sabhas would have to be taken before a mining project could be implemented. The Government filed a review petition against this judgment, which was rejected by the Supreme Court. The Government even thought about amending the Constitution to get round this judgment, instead of heeding the advice that it should help in forming cooperatives of the adivasis for exploiting the natural resources in their areas and formulate a pro-adivasi development plan. Such are the odds stacked against the adivasis in this country.

Similarly, in the area of human rights, the Supreme Court has continually intervened to monitor and control the persistent aberration; the torture of those in custody, whether in police lockups or in jails. In a recent case it has noted with concern that "... death in police custody is perhaps one of the worst kinds of crime in a civilised society governed by the rule of law and poses a serious threat to an orderly civilised society." The Supreme Court goes on to note, "Rarely in cases of police torture or custodial death, direct ocular evidence is available of the complicity of the police personnel, who alone can only explain the circumstances in which a person in their custody had died. Bound as they are by the ties of brotherhood, it is not unknown that police personnel prefer to remain silent and more often than not even pervert the truth to save their colleagues."

Giving a major new direction to jurisprudence, the Supreme Court expressed concern on custodial torture, remarking, "tortures in police custody, which of late are on the increase, receive encouragement by this type of an unrealistic approach at times of the courts as well because it reinforces the belief in the mind of the police that no harm would come to them if one prisoner dies in the lockup because there would hardly be any evidence available to the prosecution to implicate them in torture." The court cited approvingly the 113th report of the Law Commission that recommended amendments to the Evidence Act 1872 so as to rule that in the prosecution of a police officer for an alleged offence of having caused bodily injuries to a person while in police custody, if there is evidence that the injury was caused during the period when the person was in custody, the court may presume that it was caused by the police officer having custody of the person during that period, unless the police officer can prove to the contrary. The Supreme Court recommended appropriate changes in the law, not only to curb custodial crimes, but also to ensure that such crimes do not go unpunished, though the government has not yet listened to this sage advice to reign in the police.

Possibly the most important and effective intervention of the Supreme Court has been its effort to ensure the right to food for the vast majority of the poor in India under the larger rubric of the right to a dignified livelihood. The Supreme Court has come down hard on the union and state governments in the course of hearing a petition filed by the Rajasthan unit of the PUCL regarding the anomaly of widespread hunger and malnutrition, despite the existence of massive buffer food stocks with the Food Corporation of India. Commenting on the fact that it was more expensive to store these stocks of food grains than distribute them among the poor and needy, it has coaxed the state governments to prepare lists of people living below the poverty line and has impressed upon the Union Government the need to ensure proper implementation of the various schemes it already has for providing food at cheaper prices or through relief works to such people. The Supreme Court has appointed Commissioners to monitor and report on the way in which its orders were being implemented. This case, too, like the D. K. Basu case on custodial torture has been kept pending so that the Supreme Court can continue to monitor the working of the government. Refusing to entertain the argument of financial incapacity of the government, the Supreme Court has held that hunger spreads not because the state lacks the funds to act, but because it chooses to use its money elsewhere in "perverse expenditure logic."

Although the higher courts do provide some relief from the waywardness of the politicians and bureaucrats, approaching these forums is an expensive proposition. In most of the more famous cases like the Bhopal gas tragedy, the NBA, Samatha or PUCL Rajasthan, top-notch lawyers have appeared pro bono. However, apart from the Anjanbara case, we have always had to hire lawyers by paying through our nose. Even when deciding in favour of the poor petitioners, rarely do the higher courts order as to costs. The petitioner is left to file a case for damages in the lower courts, which have little sympathy for their cause.

Once Subhadra and I, along with our nine-month-old son, were in Barwah to attend a court hearing. We went to the house of an old Socialist activist so that Subhadra could nurse our son before we went to the court. There we met a member of the Bharatiya Janata Party. That person had already heard of our exploits, but this was the first time we were meeting. He said that he himself had once taken part in a roadblock agitation and had been implicated in a case. That case had dragged on for eighteen years before finally ending a few weeks back. He had never again participated in any agitation for fear of more such cases. He said that he was impressed to see Subhadra and me making the rounds of courts with our infant son. He could not think of bearing such harassment to struggle against the state! This, coming from the member of a mainstream political party, shows how effective the colonial repressive laws and the conservative judicial culture of the lower magistracy are in stifling popular dissent and how elusive indeed is the Holy Grail of justice for the vast majority of the poor citizens of this country.

24 The Interest on the Kohinoor Diamond

When Subhadra and I came to Indore in penniless straits and were forced to beg for help from our friends and family, we were looked down upon as worthless panhandlers instead of public spirited citizens trying to make democracy more meaningful for the less privileged citizens of this country. Begging, of course, is an exalted Indian pastime with mystic greats like the Buddha, Mahavira and an illustrious line of Hindu saints having survived on it. The grand idea that the mystics propagated was that the supreme spirit behind the world can be known only through inward meditation. This has fascinated people throughout history. All the Indian religious sages have advised the people to give up their desires and meditate on their inner selves as a way to end their miseries. But common people, while being fascinated by this idealistic mysticism in theory, have, in practice, turned to a form of grosser religion, that has grown up around the mysticism of the saints, for solace from their every day problems.

On one occasion, I was taken aback when an adivasi woman met me at a shop in Katkut and said that she was going to our Mandir or temple. Neither the shopkeeper nor I could make out what she was saying until she explained that she was going to our office-cum-residence! When the shopkeeper asked her whether she was going to take some dakshina or offering to the temple and its Goddess, the woman said that Subhadra was the bread giver for all the adivasis of the area so there was no need to take anything to her temple. We had taken great pains to build up a democratic mass organisation, but animism, which reinforces the belief in supernatural powers, is so deep rooted in the psyche of the common people in this country that there is no escaping from it. We had been converted into Gods too and particularly benevolent ones at that because we did not demand any dakshina from our devotees! We had learnt the hard lesson from our experiences earlier that one can't rely on the masses to provide for one's sustenance and so had made our own arrangements. But the mediators between the Gods and the masses these days, the many saints and evangelists, do not have such worries. They are not only able to garner much more mass support than political organisations but also money from the people at large only too willing to buy salvation rather than fight for it.

The reality is that when it comes to fighting the Leviathan of the state, bent on further beggaring its poorest citizens, begging does not provide much financial succour. Globalisation and the consumerism that it has spawned have so impoverished the poor and their sympathisers that not much is available for the support of radical action anymore. Consequently, the university town of Oxford in Britain, which used to pride itself on being their traditional home, now finds that the whole world has become littered with utopian lost causes without so much as a penny being paid to it for the replication of its unique geographical indication!

The initial modern anarchist response to the penury imposed on the masses from the 18th century onwards by the centralisation of political powers in the state and its control by industrialists who had centralised economic power within society was to deny the existence of the state altogether and hope that this ostrich-like attitude would reduce the costs of mobilisation against it! The French anarchist Pierre Proudhon went to the extent of labelling all private property as robbery. But like in the case of the anarchist political challenge to the state, in the case of its funding, too, ground realities have forced anarchists to compromise on their principles, and they have gone in for institutional funding to sustain their activities. No less a figure than Gandhi had to do this by relying on the nascent Indian capitalist class to fund both his political and social work. In the post independence era, the Gandhian ashrams have had to rely heavily on the government for their funds, in addition to contributions from industrialists and businessmen. The net result has been that these institutions have gradually become appendages of the state system without any dynamism of their own and mostly cut off from the realities of rural life.

Dhirendra Mazumdar, the first chairman of the Sarva Seva Sangh, grappled with this problem of bureaucratisation and marginalisation of the Gandhian institutions with little success throughout his incumbency. He finally resigned from his post in 1960 on reaching the age of sixty to try and blaze a different trail, deciding to work towards a non-violent mass movement from below.

He went and dropped anchor in a remote village in Bihar, which had a highly skewed land distribution in favour of the upper castes and a surfeit of landless lower castes. People initially agreed to work with Dhirendrabhai, and both the rich and the poor pooled in their resources to support his communitarian efforts. This noble experiment was to be short lived though, since the villagers had hoped that he would be able to bring in vast development funds to the village by leveraging his status as chairman emeritus of the Sarv Seva Sangh. While Dhirendrabhai wanted to persist with the project despite the odds, his young companions who had given up their jobs in various Gandhian institutions to work with him found it difficult to continue in such circumstances and had to leave, thus putting paid to the experiment. Later, Dhirendrabhai tried the same experiment in another remote village in eastern Uttar Pradesh and met the same fate. The lesson he learnt the hard way was that there was tremendous corruption in the redistribution of the land donated as part of the Bhoodan campaign in which the sarvodayis, who were members of the Bhoodan committees at the various levels, had colluded with the powerful landed castes to prevent any real redistribution to the lower caste landless peasants.

A large number of jobs available in the government sector immediately after independence, during the years of expansion of the state, led to a continuous drain of lower caste youth from the villages to the cities. Very few opted for voluntary or low-paid social service. The idealistic urban youth who provided the leadership to Gandhian institutions also drifted away as these institutions got bureaucratised, and only those for whom Gandhism became a majboori or last resort remained, like in the case of Radheshyam Bohre - whose sole work and headache in Machla, when we arrived there, was to prevent the people of the village who were at one time active participants of the programmes of the Gramodyog Vidyalaya, from encroaching on its land and pilfering its materials. He used to spend most of his time chasing the village boys and girls who came to steal the mangoes, custard apples, bananas, lime, drumsticks, bamboo and sandalwood that used to mature at various times of the year. Finally, when Mahendrabhai passed away in 2003, Bohre resigned from this thankless job and is back to enjoying farming on his own piece of land in Khategaon once again.

This highlights yet another Catch-22 that bedevils anarchists in particular and radical social change in general. A mass movement for radical social change can be initiated and sustained only on the strength of a continually increasing committed and knowledgeable grassroots cadre of youth. But youth will be drawn in sufficient numbers to a movement and their living and operating expenses borne by the masses only if it is a vibrant one. While addressing this question, Dhirendrabhai came to the conclusion that the monopoly of the state in the provision of social and developmental services through a corrupt and insensitive bureaucracy had killed the people's initiative to improve their situation by pooling their own resources. He found that the Gandhian institutions too had become a surrogate for the state in their style of working, and the people regarded them as another government department. This was in the early 1960s when the stranglehold of the state over its citizens had not become as widespread as it is today. Moreover, since he worked within Vinoba Bhave's Gandhian paradigm that stressed on cooperation rather than confrontation as the panacea for the mitigation of disparities between classes and castes, he did not have to contend with the phenomenon of state oppression that a confrontationist approach invariably involves.

During the Sampoorna Kranti movement in 1975, Jayaprakash Narayan brought these contradictions of post-independence Gandhism out in the open, causing a split in the Gandhian fold. Narayan emphatically stressed that the Gandhians must once again engage in mass civil disobedience against an oppressive and unjust state as opposed to collaboration and cooperation with it. The government decided to hit back by instituting enquiries against Narayan and the Gandhian institutions that supported the movement despite taking government funds to run their programmes. After the lifting of the emergency, most of the youth leaders who had been mobilised by the movement opted for participating in mainstream electoral politics instead of pursuing the considerably more challenging anarchist agenda of Narayan who himself was bedridden and eventually passed away in 1978.

The years after that were marked by a paradigm shift in the thinking of the international funding agencies. NGOs in developing countries were heavily funded to bring about "participatory development" in an attempt to ensure greater participation of the people in development without addressing the structural inequalities in society and the economy. India too was drawn into this new wave and there was a mushrooming of NGOs of all kinds engaged in service delivery, rural development, mass mobilisation and policy and legal advocacy.

In this new dispensation, the Indian state encouraged mass mobilisation by NGOs through such programmes as the National Literacy Mission, National Watershed Mission and the like, and the formation of the Council for Advancement of People's Action and Rural Technology (CAPART). Thus, under cover of the rhetoric of participatory development, it became possible for the first time to garner funds for mass mobilisation from the government and foreign funding sources. Rajaji, faced with the eternal problem of getting youthful cadres and funding them when he wanted to expand his grassroots mass mobilisation work in Chhattisgarh, fell back on both these sources. That is how Subhadra, who would otherwise have had to spend her time making bidis for a living, became a social activist. Similarly, I too along with Khemraj and Amit could give shape to our mass mobilisation work among the Bhils in its initial shaky stages as a part of the SWRC and could also benefit from its varied funding sources as well as its clout with bureaucrats and the Central Government. The NBA too started out with NGO support in its early stages and has continually been supported overtly or covertly by various national and international NGOs and has used an admirable mix of policy, media and legal advocacy and rural development work to complement the mass mobilisation work on the ground.

However, there are serious drawbacks to the involvement of NGOs in movements for radical social change. On the one hand, when the mass mobilisation work begins to threaten the state or local power structure in any substantial way, the funding tends to dry up or not measure up to the heightened demands resulting from the imposition of false criminal cases as we found to our cost in our relationship with the SWRC. Rajaji and the Ekta Parishad too have had to rein in their activities so as to avoid any direct confrontation with the state, which might lead to the imposition of false cases and a cessation of funding. On the other hand, the funding can corrupt the activists and make them give up cutting edge mass work for some support work like running micro-finance groups or doing policy, media, human rights or legal advocacy that can only partially alleviate the problems of the masses. Examples of this latter makeover, a desired outcome as far as the fund giver's objectives go, are too legion to require enumeration. Numerous hot debates are going on over the Internet; workshops and jan sunwais are being held off and on and online petitions are being filed left, right and centre. But there are very few actual mass movements on the ground.

The immense amount of funds coming into the NGO sector has thus turned out to be a bane rather than a boon as far as mass social action is concerned. Activists who are prepared to live on a pittance among the masses and organise them to achieve this are even rarer to come by. This is the principal reason for the waning of mass movements for social change over the last decade or so, coinciding with the new phase of globalisation of the world economy.

In 1996, Subhadra's sister-in-law, Narmada once came over from Jepra to Machla for a few months to get treated for a chronic illness she was suffering that required surgery. At the time, Jacob was carrying out a project to conserve and promote the indigenous cereals, pulses and oilseeds of the Malwa and Nimar regions and had about five acres of experimental farming plots in the ashrams at Machla and Kasturbagram under cultivation. He had employed two youth to help him with his work and was paying them each fifteen hundred rupees a month as salary. Narmada who was used to working for twenty rupees a day as a farm labourer in Jepra to supplement the meagre harvests from her own farm was puzzled that Jacob could afford to pay so much to his workers despite cultivating low value and low yielding crops. Try as she might, Subhadra could not make Narmada understand then that Jacob was running an NGO that was being liberally funded by an agency, and so he was not constrained by the generally weak bottom-line of subsistence agriculture in India. Now, a decade later the same Narmada is working as a grassroots worker vaccinating children in and around Jepra for an NGO and getting paid three thousand rupees for the same. She phoned us from Jepra after landing this job and proudly told Subhadra that like her she, too, was now part of the NGO sector!

Things become even more desperate when a mass movement grows to the level where it faces state repression like in our case after the Mehendikhera crackdown, which had smashed the backbone of the Sangathan and reduced its efficacy. Leading adivasi activists like Chhotelal had tens of cases against them and spent most of their time attending the court dates of these cases. A few funding agencies such as SRUTI will at the margin fund mass mobilisation work, but will never agree to fund the expenses of the cases that invariably get foisted on the people and the activists when the mobilisation assumes threatening proportions. The contrast between mass mobilisation against inappropriate and unjust state policies and service delivery, rural development or advocacy work becomes starkly visible in such circumstances, even to the people at the grassroots. Not many among activists and the people are going to take such risks when comparatively much easier pickings are available in service delivery, rural development, advocacy or consultancy, or in just providing training. Many from among the cadre that we had so painstakingly trained have either taken up jobs with NGOs, become members of mainstream political parties acting as agents for them or have become inactive.

Little accountability either for funds received or work done in the case of NGOs has rendered them a handy via media for the government and corporations for working in the social sector. While it allows the former to dodge parliamentary scrutiny, for the latter it acts as a cheap recompense to society for the tremendous social and environmental costs that the corporations are externalising on it and nature in their quest for more profit. Thus, instead of paying taxes and bearing the true costs of modern industrial development, the big corporations are apportioning a miniscule proportion of their profits to NGOs and basking in false glory by naming this as Corporate Social Responsibility. A lot of NGOs have been set up by the government and the corporates, and these have begun to dominate the sector, given the immense resources they command. Not surprisingly, these days the leading social workers and change agents in the country are politicians of mainstream political parties, bureaucrats, corporate honchos and godmen! The media focuses only on the newsmakers, and a poor grassroots worker, toiling to bring about a change in the social order and her mass movement are never newsmakers. So Bill Gates flexing his financial muscle for AIDS prevention or Azim Premji doing the same for primary education get all the bytes in the media. One would not be too far off the mark in saying that the NGO sector, as it stands today, is a Punch and Judy Show being staged to divert people away from the serious and taxing work of overturning the prevailing exploitative, destructive and over-centralised system of development and governance through widespread mass action.

Some classification of the NGO sector is thus necessary if any sense has to be made of it. First of all, there are PGOs or pro-government organisations, which work with and as a complement to the government to provide services and development and also to formulate policies. Then there are the SGOs or surrogate government organisations, set up by the government or corporates and headed by mainstream politicians, bureaucrats—both serving and retired, and corporate executives or business magnates that have been set up to control the NGO sector and see that it effectively co-opts all serious opposition to the prevailing forms of government and development. Finally, there are the AGOs or anti-government organisations, which are uncompromising in their opposition to the prevailing modes of governance and development. These are mostly of a neo-Gandhian bent that have taken off from where Jayaprakash Narayan had left his task unfinished and have added on an environmental dimension to it. The AGOs are very few in number, and in Madhya Pradesh and Chhattisgarh, they can be counted on one's fingers. The PGOs are the largest in number and have spread across the length and breadth of the country, penetrating into the remotest corners, doing work that should ideally be done by the community on their own or by the government. The SGOs are numerically in between the former two categories but they are the most powerful because they have the greatest command over resources and easy access to the established centres of economic and political power and the media.

A plea is advanced on behalf of the PGOs that they are, in general, less corrupt and more efficient than the government departments. However, given the abysmal quality of performance of the government, this is not saying very much. Only a few PGOs of repute are actually doing good work and some even creatively mix service delivery, advocacy, activism and fundraising to do exceptional work in favour of the poor and oppressed. However, the sector as a whole still represents a miniscule proportion of the services in the two crucial social spheres of education and health, which are dominated by the formal and informal private sector in this country. The government too remains a major player in both these sectors, despite the roll back of its services post liberalisation. There is very little chance of the government's functioning in these two sectors improving through PGO participation or consultation.

These two categories, the agencies that fund them and the intellectuals who eulogise them, have perfected the tactic first developed in the western world to counter the revolutionary upsurge of the late 1960s, which has been succinctly summarised by the Marxist historian, E. P. Thompson, as being based on the consideration that "Everything which disturbs the harmonious coexistence of groups performing different social roles... is an unjustified disturbance symptom" and that a disgruntled group should be "conditioned to accept its social role, and the state should find out how its grievances may best be handled and channelled." So much so, that even the much-touted World Social Forum (WSF) of mass movements and NGOs, against the deleterious effects of globalisation has been co-opted to a great extent by the funding agencies and their protégés. Ostensibly, the WSF is organised to bring together movements and NGOs from around the world to coordinate the efforts to make "another world possible" from the one being promoted by the MNCs and institutions like the World Bank, International Monetary Fund, the World Trade Organisation, and other funding agencies. However, in reality, the idea of holding it grew out of a need felt by the proponents of globalisation to provide a forum for the safe venting of the protests from the below. Moves were made to get some leading NGOs in France and Brazil to organise the event and rope in people who were opposing globalisation. Thus, a considerable portion of the tremendous costs of staging the show and transporting people from all over the world to attend it are, in fact, borne by funding agencies like the Ford Foundation. Thus, the really uncompromising opponents of globalisation who demand a total dismantling of the present system of modern industrial development are excluded from it.

Naturally, the AGOs are wary of the PGOs and SGOs and never overtly take funds from the government, corporates or funding agencies so as to preserve the independence of their actions. However, the exigencies of conducting a mass movement in highly adverse conditions and the inability of the poor to pay for the huge costs of struggle invariably force the AGOs to covertly source funds and other kinds of help from the other two categories and from funding agencies—both Indian and foreign. In Madhya Pradesh at present, only the Kisan Adivasi Sangathan in

Hoshangabad can claim to be totally free of outside funding, as they have the resources of some of their members who have gained from the successful functioning of the cooperative fishing society that is being run by them in the reservoir of the Tawa dam, set up following an agitation conducted by the Sangathan. Similarly, the Chhattisgarh Mukti Morcha in its heydays, before it became moribund, financed itself solely through the contributions of its members who had gained much by way of their sustained agitations. But since it could not expand its base to make it more widespread and firm by including the workers in Bhilai in its fold, the Chhattisgarh Mukti Morcha gradually lost out in the battle to forge an alternative to the dominant paradigm when the mines in Dalli Rajhara in which its members worked gradually wound up. Similarly, the fishing cooperative of the Kisan Adivasi Sangathan is constantly under threat of being taken over by the government, which eventuality will deprive it of its source of funds for mass mobilisation work and plunge it into crisis.

Ideally there should be a large number of AGOs of various disadvantaged communities and especially their women, with numerous and active dues paying members, operating on principles of thrift, cooperation and equality that challenge the status quo of ruling class domination through mass civil disobedience. This will ensure that grassroots democracy functions properly and pressure is created on the rest of the players in the NGO sector itself, as well as on corporates, political parties and governments in larger society for the adoption of socially and economically just and environmentally sustainable development and governance policies. However, this anarchist dream is much more difficult to actualise since very few young people opt for the rigours of working in an AGO, and only a few of us are still left rolling the stone of mass mobilisation up the hill of state insensitivity and oppression.

Ever since we came to Indore, Subhadra and I have been out on our own. Left to plough a lonely furrow, we had perforce to do without the ideological luxury of being prim about the sources of the external funds that we had to garner for our mass organisational work. As long as they did not influence the direction of our grassroots work, we did not bother about their character. Operating as we do in a very limited area and with a practical understanding that there is not much chance of our work escalating to a scale where it can bring about far reaching changes in the socio-economic arrangements that prevail, we can afford to take this cavalier attitude towards funding sources as the funds required are not very large. This attitude has allowed us to work freely in the field without much hindrance while funding this through research work, which is sometimes of dubious provenance. Thus, I have done research consultancy work for the same World Bank, the opposition to whose policies had once landed me in jail! Foundations and agencies in the West that believe in maintaining the status quo rather than upsetting it radically have been, and continue to be, the sources of funds for our research work, while similar agencies in India that know our true colours are not prepared to adorn their canvases with our mugs.

The state had the intention of completely wiping out the mass organisation in Dewas in the course of the Mehendikhera crackdown, but failed to do so primarily because we had a respectable financial buffer with which to fight it. Try as it might to prove that this buffer was illegal, it failed because it had been built up legitimately through completely legal fellowships and research assignments and was well accounted for and professionally audited. If we had baulked at taking these funds we, too, would have had to run away, leaving the poor adivasis to fend for themselves as best as they could. Instead, we are still rolling the stone and that very act itself has some braking effect on the arbitrariness of the state, if nothing more. In the end, it does not really matter whether one is taking foreign or Indian funds because all external funds have some strings attached and have the tendency to restrict the capacity to genuinely mobilise the masses. It depends on the persons taking these funds as to how far they can put them to good use, given these restrictions. We can only say that we have tried our best to retain our effectiveness as activists. Since in the present milieu taking foreign funds either directly or indirectly has become a necessity that cannot be avoided, the best way to get over one's qualms about accepting them is to treat them as the interest being paid on the famous Kohinoor diamond, which was taken away by the British from India and is now embedded in the British Crown!

25 Fighting for the Indian Revolution

On September 3, 2005, a van carrying twenty-seven armed policemen returning from a sortie into the deep jungles of Bastar was blown up in a landmine blast, which killed twenty-four of the policemen. The blast was so powerful that the supposedly anti-landmine vehicle, which was carrying them, was thrown thirty-five feet up in the air and landed a good ninety feet away. This was a retaliatory action by the Naxalites or Indian Maoists against a combined armed and civil offensive launched a few months earlier by the Government of Chhattisgarh to finish them off, in which fifty odd cadres and some of their sympathisers had been killed in combing operations. This established, literally with a bang, the Naxalites' ability to carry on their armed struggle despite the heavy repressive and co-optive tactics adopted against them by the state. This act was preceded by the killing of a senior Congress legislator in Andhra Pradesh on August 15 and followed by a successful daring raid on the jail in Jehanabad town in Bihar on November 3 to free some of their comrades incarcerated there, interspersed with raids and bombings on state institutions and the police in the states of Karnataka, Orissa, Tamil Nadu and Jharkhand.

This fascinating admixture of pre and post modernism with modernism in a typically post-modern "micro-narrative" of the tenacious armed struggle being waged by the Naxalites to overwhelm the state apparatus and bring about a New Democratic Revolution through the armed mobilisation of the peasant masses has significantly challenged the attempt of the Indian ruling classes to foist a counterfeit meta-narrative of socio-economic progress, based on corrupt electoral politics and centralised industrial development on the Indian masses. In fact, the current second phase of the Naxalite movement has gained much more support among the masses and been much more of a headache for the Indian state than the resistance put up by the mass environmental movements, which have emerged in the same period since the late 1970s.

Despite the early ferocity of the Naxalite uprisings, there was not much of a positive impact of the movement towards bringing about land reforms. The deep-rooted feudal control of the landlords over the peasants continued unabated. This was especially true of the states of Bihar and Jharkhand, which had earlier seen the Bhoodan movement being reduced to a mockery. The subsequent Sampoorna Kranti Andolan in the mid 1970s, which had considerable peasant support, was also crushed. This failure on the part of the Congress governments at the centre and in the states to pay serious attention to the problems of the peasantry in most parts of the country provided a fertile ground in the states of Bihar, Jharkhand and Andhra Pradesh, which had witnessed some armed mobilisations in the initial phase, for a rekindling of the Naxal rebellion from 1980 onwards. In the meantime, all through the 1970s, the movement had remained alive in the form of many splintered groups scattered all over the country. One such group, the CPI(ML) Liberation, began mobilising the peasants openly in Bihar and Jharkhand and also participating successfully in electoral politics. Two other groups in Bihar and Jharkhand, the CPI(ML) Party Unity and the Maoist Communist Centre, opted to renew the armed struggle. Similarly, the CPI(ML) People's War Group and some other marginal groups, too, began the armed struggle in Andhra Pradesh.

This time round, the movement began among dalit and adivasi peasants with a clear-cut understanding that it would be subjected to heavy repression by the state. So right from the beginning, armed squads were built and provided with sophisticated weapons. These squads were extremely mobile and mostly stayed in the dense jungles only to carry out armed actions and then retreat into their safety and anonymity once again. Simultaneously, open mass organisations were built up among peasants, workers, students, intellectuals and artistes, which worked towards raising the level of political consciousness of the masses and solving their immediate socio-economic problems arising out of social and economic oppression. These mass organisations also provided the cadre for the armed squads and the underground party. Moreover, awareness of the fact that the state forces could easily ring in an isolated armed movement like they had done earlier in Naxalbari and Srikakulam, led the movement to spread its wings early on into the contiguous states. So now it has a vast area of influence, extending from Tamil Nadu and

Kerala in the south through Karnataka, Andhra Pradesh, Maharashtra, Chhattisgarh, Madhya Pradesh, Orissa and Jharkhand to Uttar Pradesh, West Bengal and Bihar in the north. It is interesting to note that in West Bengal, the movement has struck roots among the impoverished adivasis. The adivasi regions of Bengal have been neglected by the CPI(M), which is dominated by the Bengalis. This has resulted in a lot of discontent in the state, something the Naxalites have capitalised on.

The armed Tamil separatist movement in Sri Lanka and the armed Maoist movement in Nepal, too, provide the Naxalites with considerable moral and military support. When the going gets too hot in one place, the squads shift their action to some other place where things are relatively easier. This keeps the movement going. Consequently, even though coordinated police action in Andhra Pradesh has put a lid on Naxalite activity, this has resulted in all the cadre and armed squads migrating to neighbouring states of Maharashtra, Chhattisgarh and Orissa to intensify their operations. This mobility has become so crucial to their survival and effectiveness that in 2004, all the major armed factions of the Naxalites resolved their ideological differences and came together to form the CPI (Maoist). There is also a Coordination Committee of Maoist Parties and Organisations of South Asia that includes the strongest of these, the Communist Party of Nepal (Maoist), which is in effective control of most of rural Nepal. Now with the sidelining of the royalty, it has gained an open presence even in capital Kathmandu.

This ability to sustain an armed struggle against the state has earned the Naxalites enough credibility among the poverty-stricken youth, mainly from among dalits and adivasis and also from other sections of the masses to inspire them to sacrifice all for overthrowing a patently unjust politico-economic dispensation. The commitment to the overthrow of the bourgeois Indian state, though they themselves term it as being semi-feudal and semi-colonial, through the successful conduct of an armed New Democratic Revolution is total in the movement. So much so, that despite the killing of hundreds of its cadres in extra-judicial "encounters" after arrest and the jailing of thousands of its cadres and supporters, it continues to wax strong. Strong enough indeed to force the Indian state to plan a coordinated higher scale armed intervention against the movement spread across all the states in which it has an influence. Like a blinkered horse, the Indian state, dominated as it is by feudal elements and colonially minded bureaucrats, is still refusing to address in any serious way the basic socio-economic injustices that have given rise to the movement in the first place. But there are limits to the violence that the state can resort to. While the state has been able to deploy the regular army to suppress to some extent the armed separatist movements in the peripheral areas in the Northeast, Jammu and Kashmir and Punjab, it cannot do the same so easily in the very heart of the country without affecting its combat readiness for meeting external threats, which are of a far more menacing nature. There is also the problem of human rights violations that the army will commit on the general populace, alienating them from whichever political party decides to launch full-scale military operations against the Naxalites over such a large swathe of the country.

However, this cycle of violence and counter violence has meant that the people in the areas of influence of the Naxalites have been caught in the crossfire between them and the state's forces. The exigencies of a civil war like situation have led to both sides targeting those people whom they consider informers and sympathisers of the enemy. The scope for democratic mass action has, as a result, been severely curtailed. At present, all the open mass organisations of the Naxalites are officially banned with their leading activists in jail. Moreover, to keep alive the false Maoist meta-narrative of the character of the Indian state as a semi-feudal and semi-colonial entity in the face of the considerably stronger, but equally false meta-narrative of modern market-centred development, the Naxalites have had to oppose modern development and the further penetration of the market in the areas of their influence, thereby keeping them in a backward condition. All this has effectively put a brake on the spread of the Naxalite struggle beyond the really remote rural areas of the country and also led to disaffection among the masses and activists in these areas in some cases, with a tiredness setting in due to the endless wait for the elusive revolution.

For instance in south Bastar, which has now become the separate district of Dantewada, a spontaneous protest sparked off among the adivasis against the Naxalites, and the people got organised under the banner of an organisation named Salwa Judum, meaning quite ominously *purification hunt* in the Gondi language, to oppose the way in which Naxalite activities had led to an increase in the isolation and backwardness of their areas. The state immediately pitched in, adopted this movement, armed the adivasis, dressed its policemen in plain clothes and made them its activists. Within no time, a low-intensity conflict in the jungles of Bastar has been converted into a full-scale civil war, with the state evacuating the villages in the interior to the roadsides under the pretext of providing the adivasis with protection. In reality, the administration has only left the field open for armed combing and killing operations against the Naxalites and for depriving them of local sustenance. The state has even brought in Naga adivasi armed police, trained in counter-insurgency operations from the northeast to add to the miseries of the local people. However, this has not deterred the Naxalites as they have so perfected their guerrilla strategies that they still continue to operate, albeit with higher losses. In a daring attack on an explosives dump of the NMDC in Kirandul, the Naxalites killed eight personnel of the CISF and wounded nine others on February 10, 2006. They also looted a huge cache of weapons, ammunition and explosives. In 2007, they have blown up electric transmission towers and killed more than fifty armed personnel of a government combing party in a well-planned ambush.

Nevertheless, despite the boast that they have now spread their organisation to a hundred and forty districts across twelve states, the Naxalites' actual influence over the politics and consciousness of the vast masses of people in India is marginal. In fact, their sole "liberated zone" in the southern part of Dantewara district is now under siege by paramilitary forces. The Naxalites had cleared this area of government servants completely and established their own "Janathana Sarkar" or people's government. But now a training school in jungle warfare has been established for the policemen, and this liberated zone is gradually being recaptured by the Indian state. The state forces have evacuated most of the villages from inside the jungles into relief camps along the roadside to deprive the Naxalites of their people and sustenance. In desperation, the Naxalites have begun attacking the soft targets of the adivasis in these camps—whom the state has forced to join the Salwa Judum—and are wantonly killing them. Thus, at present there seems to be little possibility of the ideological and military dominance of the Naxalites rising to the level where they can engineer a desertion by the regular armed forces of the Indian state to their side, which is a necessary pre-condition for bringing about a successful revolution. The net result is that the poor adivasis, the major residents of these areas, are destined to keep suffering as neither the Indian revolution nor the total supremacy of the Indian state in the areas of Naxalite influence are anywhere in sight.

This second phase of Naxalite mobilisation has come at a time when the colonisation of the minds of the masses all over the world, resulting from the television propelled cultural imperialism of the West has pushed the meta-narrative of capitalist industrial development and its triplets of consumerism and militarism onto the centre stage of the post-modern world. So unfortunately, in the 21st century, the repositories of various kinds of post modernist "difference" such as the Naxalites and the anarcho-environmentalists are doomed to acting themselves out as peripheral micro-narratives. Nothing can be more evocative of this than the phenomenal box-office success of the Hindi film Lagaan released in 2001. In the film, the persistent problem of the extortionate levying of lagaan or land tax from peasants during the British colonial rule in India, even in times of severe economic stress arising from crop failure, is the cause of dispute between the British and the peasants in a fictitious location. However, whereas in reality such conflicts gave rise to many bloody mutinies during the British rule, in the film, absurdly, the peasants are shown to score a bloodless victory and secure a moratorium on the payment of lagaan by winning a thrilling cricket match against the British. The film was later nominated to the short-list of five for the Oscar award in the Best Foreign Film category. The enticing prospect of an Indian film actually winning the Oscar sparked off a nationalistic hysteria among the Indian media, which only cooled down when the voters of the American Motion Picture Academy chose a Bosnian film instead, perhaps with the thought that it was more expedient to make up for the much more recent bloody deeds of their own imperialist forces in erstwhile Yugoslavia than that of the British a century earlier in India.

It is not too difficult to imagine that given this level of readiness among the masses to suspend their disbelief, the chances of the Naxalites bringing about a revolution in India are remote at best. Mao had said that power flows from the barrel of a gun, but in today's milieu, it flows more readily from the electron gun of a television set! Through their terrorist armed actions, the Naxalites have only succeeded in reducing the space for democratic mass action, not only for their own mass organisations, but also as we have seen, for anarcho-environmentalist ones, which, too, are regarded by the police to be close to the Naxalites and are thus subjected to extra-legal harassment. The Chhattisgarh government has legislated a new draconian Act to limit the civil liberties of those found to be supporting the Naxalites, which has recently been misused to incarcerate the noted human rights activist Dr. Binayak Sen.

The American anarchist Thoreau once wrote, "If a man does not keep pace with his companions, perhaps it is because he hears a different drummer. Let him step to the music which he hears, however measured or far away." This was a plaintive cry against the homogenising effects of modern industrialisation. Things have now become considerably more problematic for maintaining economic, social and cultural diversity in the post-modern era. The possibility of launching a concerted challenge to the hegemony of capitalist industrial development has diminished considerably. That is why the widespread limitation of a space for democratic dissent that the peripheral violence of the Naxalites is a matter of concern. It reduces the number of drummers who are beating a different beat. Of even greater concern is the fact that the Naxalite cadres belong to the marginalised dalits and adivasis, and these organic intellectuals who could have made a significant contribution to the fight for a better world are all dying an untimely death in the wild goose chase after the Indian revolution. Lesser and lesser are the numbers of people that are opting out from the destructive march of the meta-narrative of modern industrial development.

Thoreau is as lonely as ever.

26 Time for a Sabbatical

One day in the summer of 1998, Subhadra and I went to meet the Divisional Commissioner in Indore regarding the police's false propaganda that the two of us were Naxalites. The police in Barwah had sent out enquiries regarding our antecedents to Kolkata and Bastar. This proved to be the last straw and had a profound impact on Subhadra. She had first drifted into social work a decade back and then gradually into political activism in search of a living. It wasn't her conscious choice to fight for the rights of the poor and dispossessed. She had had no idea about the real character of the state and its bureaucracy, even at the highest level. She had naively assumed that the state was indeed well disposed towards the poor, and it was only the people at the lower level who were bad and corrupt. But especially over the past three years or so in Katkut, she had learnt the hard fact that the state itself was biased in favour of the rich and powerful. She decided she had had enough of beating her head against an unyielding wall and withdrew totally from activism for some time to concentrate on catching up with her studies instead.

She turned towards reading books on social and political theory on her own for a deeper understanding. However, the education she had received in school was inadequate for her to comprehend these books. So in 1997 she decided to resume formal studies by pursuing a bachelor's degree in Political Science. While searching for a college, she came upon a brochure of the Indira Gandhi National Open University (IGNOU), which offered distance-learning courses. The brochure said that the courses were tailor-made for those who might have missed out on higher education after high school. She enrolled for the Bachelor's Degree Programme of the university. However, on receiving the course material she found that like all advertisement brochures, IGNOU's too had overstated the ease of the course to snare unsuspecting people into its fold. She found that to pass the exams she would have to put in much more time than was possible while continuing with her work. This further caused her to take a sabbatical from political activism to start studying in earnest.

The main reason behind Subhadra being unprepared for higher studies of a tough standard was the poor quality of the basic education she had received in school. This is a common refrain in most rural areas. The sordid fact is that education in India traditionally has been the privilege of a few upper caste people. The Aitareya Brahmana of the Rig Veda has a story of an upper caste brahmin sage who had two wives—one a brahmin and the other a dalit. He had a son each from his two wives. In Vedic times, the sages used to teach their disciples, including their sons, by chanting Vedic verses during yagnas or fire sacrifices to the Gods. Both the wives sent their sons to their father for their lessons when he was in the midst of one such yagna. The sage fondly took his brahmin son onto his lap and began teaching him the verses, but totally ignored his other son who was half dalit. The dalit son came away crying and complained to his mother that his father had ignored him, and so he would not be able to study. The mother was depressed at first, but said later that she was a shudra or the daughter of mother earth and so would ask her mother for a way out of this impasse. Vasundhara, the Earth Goddess, told her not to worry and said that she would herself teach her grandson. Thus, this son of a shudra, who was taught by the Earth Goddess became a very learned sage.

This dalit sage then took his revenge. Sanskrit is a language in which words have many meanings; there can be different interpretations of a sequence of words. A particular verse can have many meanings, ranging from the nonsensical to the highly philosophical. In order to understand the true philosophical import of the verses in the Samhita portion of the Vedas one has to know which meanings of words and which syntax of sentences to pick. This key has been given in the Brahmana portion of the Vedas. The dalit sage composed the Brahmana for the Rig Veda and named it after himself. The name he chose was Aitareya or son of an itar or dalit person. So the most sacred of the brahminical Hindu texts can only be understood with the help of the key written by a dalit.

The parallel between the ancient dalit sage Aitareya and his modern counterpart Babasaheb Ambedkar is too striking to be missed. Not only did both of them acquire immense learning through personal perseverance in the face of difficulties, but similar to Aitareya's enlightening contribution to the understanding of the philosophical import of the Vedic verses, Babasaheb, as Chairperson of the Constituent Assembly, was the guiding light behind the libertarian and affirmative portions of the Constitution of India, which are its only redeeming features. Just as the high spiritual philosophy of the Vedas has been drowned out in the crass materialistic rituals of the actual Hindu religious practice of the priests, so also the emancipating and egalitarian liberal and socialistic principles of our Constitution have been smothered under the colonial anti-people policies of the priests of the temples of modern India—mainstream politicians and bureaucrats. Nowhere is this more evident than in the sphere of education.

The British very cleverly reinforced the divisive and oppressive character of the Brahminical social order so as to minimise the chances of widespread revolt by the masses against their rule. The upper castes, who largely collaborated with the British, took advantage of the restriction of modern education facilities to extend their sway over Indian society and monopolise the English medium education system introduced by them.

Gandhi, wanting to make a break with this legacy, had talked of "Nai Talim" or a new education system to train youngsters in their own language and idiom and in matters more suited to reviving the rural economy devastated by the British colonialists. Like much else of Gandhi, however, independent India jettisoned this, too, and continued with the half-baked British pattern of school education for the expanding government education system in rural areas. To this day, uninspiring and unsuitable syllabi, written in an alien language, are taught by poorly qualified teachers and learned by rote by masses of rural children. This prevents a proper development of their cognitive and analytical skills. A common joke in Madhya Pradesh is that the State Education Board Examinations are so named because in these, the teachers write down the answers to the question paper on the black board for students to copy from! Despite this, a majority of the students are unable to pass the exams since most of them are incapable of even copying. .

This faulty system did work for sometime in the initial two decades after independence as its products were absorbed into the expanding state system of production, marketing and services, which began filling up the massive gap left by two centuries of colonial rule. But from about the time that Subhadra passed out of school, the demand and supply mismatch, which had remained favourable to the students for nearly two centuries, turned unfavourable. Globalisation and technological development rendered the huge number of poorly trained products of the school education system redundant. A need was felt for a much less number of highly qualified personnel in specialised disciplines. The government school system, which was never properly equipped in pedagogical and human resources, found itself even more of an obsolescent remnant from an earlier era. At a time when a huge infusion of funds and ideas was required for the revamping of the education structure, the state and central governments was lacking in both. Thus, the state education system—right from the primary to the highest levels—has very few quality institutions. So a political battle is now on between various sections of the society to try and corner as much of this as possible.

In Madhya Pradesh, the government decided to divest its responsibility for school education to the Panchayats with minimal salaries for teachers and almost no funds for infrastructure. It then publicised this as a revolution in the provision of education to hitherto underprivileged sections like the adivasis and dalits in remote rural areas under the rubric of the "Education Guarantee Scheme" (EGS) aided by the World Bank, though on the ground little more than rudimentary schools were set up. Consequently, in urban areas of Madhya Pradesh, the government school system has been almost totally superseded by private schools. Even in rural areas, this is slowly becoming the norm.

A headmaster of a village government school in Jhabua district once told me that he had instructions to pass at least fifty percent of his students; else his annual increment would be withheld. Similarly, during the census of 2001, the government teachers who did the enumeration work were given orders to put down as many people as possible as literate, regardless of their actual reading and writing abilities. This has resulted in the phenomenal increase in literacy in the state from 44 percent in 1991 to 64 percent in 2001! This is the kind of spurious data on the basis of which planning and research takes place in this country and little wonder that they fail to address the burning issues that affect the poor and marginalised.

Realising that relevant education of good quality was a sine-qua-non for building up a sustainable mass movement, the KMCS set up primary schools in remote villages in Alirajpur tehsil as early as 1987. Reading, writing and arithmetic were taught in the Devnagari script, but using the Bhili language. Initially, there were no textbooks. Instead, the teachers and the students used to conduct surveys of various kinds of their immediate surroundings and then analyse the results. The data and understanding gained from this were used to create textbooks for language, arithmetic, science, geography and history in Bhili. The teachers and the students together participated in the creation of the learning material. Later, a primer for learning in Hindi was developed in the same way. Learning by doing was the watchword.

Later, when in the mid 1990s it became clear that political struggles were up against a wall that stifled creativity; many activists began seeking newer avenues to work in. Amit and Jayashree wanted to continue working among the Bhils, but with two toddlers to look after, they could not continue living the topsy-turvy life of political activists. They thought of concentrating on the systematic development of education materials and an alternative pedagogy in accordance with the ideology of village-centred adivasi self-rule for the establishment of a socially equitable and environmentally sustainable society. The members of the Adivasi Mukti Sangathan supported the setting up of a training centre-cum-school called the Adharshila School in village Sakar near Sendhwa in Barwani district on a five acre piece of minimally productive agricultural land.

The experience of the KMCS of having run schools earlier had shown that to effectively teach adivasi children of illiterate parents they need to be drilled even after regular schooling hours. Since this was not possible with day scholars, it was decided to run a residential school. Parents were asked to pay in cash and kind for the education of their children so as to make the everyday running of the school financially self-sustaining. This, in turn, meant that the school would have to make the children proficient enough to perform well in the board examinations at the class five level to accord with the expectations of the parents, most of whom were willing to pay for an education that could get their children jobs later on. Thus, the syllabus and teaching had to take care of both the needs of inculcating a critical attitude towards modern development in the children as well as providing them with the skills to make it good in the modern sector. Obviously, this is a tall order and requires a lot of hard and committed innovative work on the part of the teachers. Funds were collected from various external sources including SRUTI for the costs of curriculum development, teaching aids and part of the teachers' salaries.

The school started from scratch without textbooks. The language used was Bareli, a dialect of Bhili. Once again, the KCMS's method of conducting surveys and writing down the rich oral literature of the Bhili creation myths was used to acquaint the children with the basics of language and arithmetic and in the process, create primers. One such survey, which was both entertaining and educative, was conducted to find out how, if at all, the teachers were teaching in the government schools and then comparing the results with the procedures being followed in the Adharshila School. The local environment provided the material for scientific learning through observation and analysis, and local history as related by the elders was recorded to prepare history lessons. In addition to their studies, the children have to put in two hours of labour every day on the five-acre farm of the school so as to ensure that they do not lose touch with their peasant farmer roots. Possibly for the first time, academic learning has become fun for Bhil children in a systematically run school environment.

The biggest problem confronting the teachers is that of reconciling the contradictory goals of developing and teaching a curriculum that critiques modern development and simultaneously prepares the children to take the board examinations of the government school system. Commensurate with the high levels of technological development, the learning load of students in the mainstream schools has been increased phenomenally. Even children of families that have received education for many generations find the syllabus tough and have to put in long hours after school and take special coaching to be able to perform well in examinations. Under the circumstances it is unrealistic to expect first or second generation literates, coming from a pre-modern culture, to digest the heavy syllabus. Just acquiring language, mathematical and analytical skills are not sufficient to ensure good results in examinations. Cramming of massive information and an uncritical acceptance of modernist assumptions on which the school system is based blunt the critical faculties of the child and reduces the possibilities of a generalised revolt against the system.

Most of the students leave after passing the class eight board examinations to join a mainstream school for further studies, instead of continuing in the Adharshila School.

Amit and Jayashree, in fact, have to contend with multiple problems such as sourcing of funds, recruiting, training and retaining teachers, developing curricula, envisioning inspiring and enjoyable extra-curricular activities and managing the day-to-day operation of the school. While doing this, they also have to look after their two young children who live with them and study in the Adharshila School along with the adivasi children. Most importantly, they have stuck to the basic principle that the school should be run on the strength of the fees paid by the students and voluntary contributions made by individuals who agree with the style of schooling being provided, rather than by procuring large funds from institutional sources and thereby following their diktats. Over the past ten years, a barren piece of hilltop land has become a green arbour and a fountain of knowledge for a people who have never had the privilege of good education. It may be just a drop in the ocean, but one that nevertheless sparkles with hope for the future. I have unending respect for Amit and Jayashree as they struggle on to improve the quality of education available to adivasi children in a remote village like Sakar, which does not even have regular electricity supply.

In the early 1970s, the NGO Kishore Bharati had begun experimenting on the same lines as the Nuffield Program for popularising science education among school children that had been tried out in Britain by introducing activity and discovery based learning, tailored to a child's physical, social and cultural environment. The only difference in Kishore Bharati's case was that they were carrying out this experiment in a rural area. Later, this became a full-fledged programme named the Hoshangabad Science Teaching Programme (HSTP), involving the central and state governments and various educational institutions. Following a review of its operations, a decision was taken to extend it beyond Hoshangabad district and some of the people involved in it set up the NGO Eklavya in 1982 to oversee this expansion. Later, 1986 onwards, this innovation was extended to social science teaching, both at the middle and primary levels. A novel aspect of this experiment was that it tried to work within the government school system and reform it, rather than set up a parallel system outside of it.

However, Eklavya's achievements have been limited as it has been confronted by the ingrained cynicism of teachers and the bureaucracy, despite the incentives given by the government and despite the development of alternative texts and teaching methods of high quality, which have gained worldwide recognition and conducted umpteen teacher trainings. Eklavya has thus failed to develop a sustainable school educational system with enough support from the parents who can effectively demand that this new mode of teaching must continue and spread.

In a bizarre development, the HSTP was scrapped by the Government of Madhya Pradesh in 2002, mainly at the behest of a local BJP MLA. It is the tragic fate of this country that even after more than half a century of independence, politicians and the bureaucrats still feed on the manger of the state. So its second class citizens, who cannot afford to pay for quality education, have to remain satisfied with what has come to be called "second track schooling facilities" of dubious quality provided by the government.

Meanwhile, Subhadra found herself at sea in the deep waters of the IGNOU course material. The language is arcane since the course material is translated from English into a very Sanskritised version of Hindi and uses terms not found in standard Hindi dictionaries. Thus, making sense of the IGNOU course material is almost as difficult an exercise as deciphering the true meanings of the Vedas. I had to assist her in a big way, not only in understanding the meaning of the texts, but also in doing the assignments, which too had to be written in the same high-quality Sanskritised Hindi. The crunch came during the examinations. The papers were set in a way that thoroughly tested whether the student had read and assimilated the course material properly. A study of past question papers revealed that there is no pattern discernible in the questions asked. It is very difficult to predict the possible questions and prepare accordingly as is the custom in most universities in this country.

The inevitable result of all this was that in the initial stages, Subhadra mostly passed her examinations by the skin of her teeth. At times, she couldn't secure the minimum passing marks. The only saving grace is that a student could take as many as eight years at that time to pass the three-year course and so failed papers could be reappeared for or a lesser number of papers could be taken per semester. Just when Subhadra had begun to get the hang of things after about two years, she conceived accidentally. Subhadra said that since she had decided not to work in the field for sometime she would like to go through the pregnancy and thus free herself from the accusation that she faced continually from women in the villages that she was infertile! "Baanjh kya jaane prasav ka dard" meaning *what does an infertile woman know about the pains of childbirth,* is a common taunt used in rural settings. So Subhadra decided to pick up this knowledge and set her pursuit of academic knowledge in abeyance for two years until our son Ishaan was born and weaned into walking around on his own.

Following this, she resumed her studies and passed her papers without much trouble, save for the English paper. In tune with the rest of the subjects, in this too, the question paper was extremely tough. There were difficult questions on grammar, which I can only label as sadistic as they tested even my knowledge of English. Finally, there were essays and dialogues to be written on any subject under the sun. Since the questions were totally unpredictable, they could be answered successfully only by a student who had a very good command of the English language. So even after a year of practice it was quite clear to us that Subhadra's passing the paper would depend totally on chance. I did a review of the question papers of a decade and prepared four sets of essays and dialogues on topics that I thought were most likely to appear and had Subhadra mug them up. Given the toughness of the other questions and the low number of marks she would get in them, the only way she could pass her paper was that one of the topics for which she had prepared appeared on the examination question paper.

Subhadra was naturally nervous before the examination and constantly asked me if she would pass or not. On seeing her distress and searching around for something to comfort her with, I suddenly had a brainwave. One of the topics I had prepared was one that was asked most often in some form or other: "Write about the person who has influenced you the most." I had prepared an essay on Dr Bhimrao Ambedkar for this topic. One of the salutations that members of the Bahujan Samaj Party frequently use is "Jai Bhim," *Long live Bhim,* acknowledging the contribution of Ambedkar to the cause of the dalits. So I told Subhadra to forget everything else and just go on repeating Jai Bhim to herself until she got the question paper and hope that a topic would come on which she could spew out an essay she had prepared. Not having much choice, this is what she began to do, and lo and behold, when she opened the question paper and went straight to the essay portion, she found a variation of a topic, which allowed her to write on Babasaheb Ambedkar! She passed the examination by a whisker on the strength of this essay and finally became a graduate, seven years after she had first enrolled.

Her struggle to pass the IGNOU exams prompted me to write to IGNOU for statistics regarding the pass percentages disaggregated by caste category in the B.A. course over the past decade. I got no reply despite the intervention of some journalist friends in Delhi and even after writing to the Principal Secretary, Higher Education.

When I filed an application with the Public Information Officer of IGNOU under the Right to Information Act, a subordinate of this officer replied and tried to fob me off with a vague excuse. I sent a strong letter to the Vice Chancellor who is the Designated Appellate Authority for IGNOU under the RTI Act, pointing out that the Public Information Officer was liable for penal action for having wilfully obstructed the furnishing of the information that I had demanded. This had some effect, and I was sent the data for the years 1996 to 2002. There were a lot of problems with the veracity and logical consistency of this data, and so I appealed to the Central Information Commission to help me get the correct data. This appeal too was not very fruitful as the Information Commissioner told me to go to IGNOU and see their records myself so as to verify the data. I did not have the time for this. However, whatever data was given to me was alarming.

The fact that students enrolled in a particular year do not all pass or finally get struck off the rolls for non-completion of the course in the stipulated time means that the data for enrolled, passed and failed students for a particular year are not for the same students. But by 2002, fourteen years had elapsed since the first batch passed out in 1988, and yet the data for 2002 reflected more or less a similar pattern as the data for the previous years, from 1996 onwards. The data provided a fair indication of the substandard performance of IGNOU with regard to the B.A. degree course it offers. In 2002, a total of 35,844 students had enrolled, of whom 63.4 % were females and 36.6% were males. The Scheduled Castes constituted only 6.2 % whereas their percentage in the population as a whole is 15%. Their female to male ratio was about the same as that for the total students enrolled. The Scheduled Tribes constituted 5.9 % whereas their proportion in the population as a whole is 7%. Their female to male ratio was again about the same as the total. The number of students who passed was a miniscule 1490, which, if compared to the number enrolling, is just 4.2 %. This percentage has secularly come down from 15.9 % in 1996. This is because while the numbers enrolling have gone up by 257 %, the numbers passing out have decreased by 32.2 % over this period of seven years. The number of students who have failed to complete the course in the stipulated time and so been struck off the rolls have increased in the same period by 204 % to 21178 in 2002. This resulted in the ratio of students struck off the rolls to those freshly enrolled going down from 74.3 % to 59.1 % in the same period. This means that given the continually decreasing numbers of students passing out, there must be a big backlog of students who have to be struck off the rolls. Possibly they have been so struck off in the years subsequent to 2002, and so the disturbing data for those years have been withheld from me!

The most striking feature of the results is that of the considerably fewer number of female students passing as compared to male students, between 1996 and 2002, the number of successful female students was approximately 30%, even though the percentage of those enrolled hovered around 65% between the same years. This means that there are a lot of women like Subhadra with a poor schooling background who are unable to take admission in colleges that require regular attendance who are enrolling in IGNOU with the fond hope of getting a B.A. degree. However, the toughness of the course, the examination papers and their evaluation, coupled with inadequate coaching are putting paid to their dreams leading to these women not being able to pass the tests.

No wonder then that these standard statistics regarding pass percentages, that are easily made available by most universities, are such a closely guarded secret in IGNOU and not readily disclosed to anyone! What is most appalling is that an institution that projects itself as the best distance learning university in the world does not have the honesty to review the continually deteriorating performance of its most basic B.A. degree programme.

When this is the level of mendacity practiced by a premiere educational institution of higher learning set- up aimed at helping the disadvantaged, what hope is there for the adivasis and dalits and especially their women, in spite of affirmative action legislated in their favour? Babasaheb Ambedkar must not just be turning, but doing a few revolutions in his grave!

Jai Bhim.

27 The Aging and feuding Young Turks

The mass environmental movements in Madhya Pradesh and Chhattisgarh that began in the final two decades of the 20th century have been able to leave their mark on national and global politics because of the presence of a host of middle class activists who have backed up the better known charismatic leaders. They are now becoming a vanishing breed because the increasing privatization of the social work sector has meant that social activism too has become a mainstream well paid career option. The great thing about some of these colleagues of ours is the maverick and happy-go-lucky style of their functioning, which has provided a lot of colour to the struggles we have participated in.

A Lohiate socialist and the son of the veteran Gandhian Kashinath Trivedi, Anilbhai, earned his law degree when incarcerated during the emergency. After a brief stint in electoral politics, he has devoted most of his energies in brilliantly using the law in favour of the poor. As a candidate for the Janata Dal, he has fought and lost quite a few elections, but his faith in using the legislature to bring about reform remains steadfast, as does his belief in legal activism. He has been instrumental in providing relief to adivasis affected by the lack of rights given to them under the Madhya Pradesh Land Revenue Code because they have been living in forest villages governed by the Forest Department. Since the latter could at any time abrogate the rights of the adivasis to cultivate and reside in these forest villages, this effectively meant that the adivasis became its bonded labourers. In one instance in the village of Chainpura near Katkut, the adivasis were not being allowed to collect even the dung of their cattle from the forests. Anilbhai challenged this in the Indore High Court through the first ever writ petition filed against the arbitrariness of the Forest Department on behalf of adivasis in Madhya Pradesh.

The great thing about Anilbhai is that he remains unruffled even in the worst of circumstances and continues to propagate his cause. For many years, Anilbhai used to commute to the court by public transport until the increasing pressure of his legal work forced him to opt for a gearless scooter. No wonder that he commands tremendous respect among all and sundry in Indore. What could be a better testament to his integrity than the fact that once when the journalists of Indore, owing allegiance to rival political parties, fell out among themselves over the conduct of the elections to their representative association, they appointed Anilbhai as the supervisor to ensure that the elections were conducted impartially. This was in spite of the fact that he was an active member of a political party himself.

Taking on the state is a complex matter and traditional modes of social, political and legal activism need to be supplemented with innovative strategies to get media attention and mobilise funds. Satinath Sarangi or Sathyu as he is popularly known is a past master in this. The hidden force of the struggle of the Bhopal Gas affected people and the secret behind its longevity, he teamed up in 1994 with a leading creative designer in advertising and novelist in the United Kingdom, Indra Sinha, to launch full-page advertisements in the Guardian and Independent newspapers, just before the anniversary of the Bhopal gas disaster, detailing the continuing suffering of the gas leak survivors and the apathy of governments and the MNCs towards their plight. They spent eight thousand pounds on the advertisements and raised fifty thousand pounds in no-strings-attached donations from thousands of individuals. More importantly, they brought the important issues relating to this disaster alive in public memory and created a massive worldwide network of people in support of the Bhopal gas movement. Such was the impact of this advertisement that the flagging class action suit in the United States against first Union Carbide Corporation and then its later owners Dow Chemicals came to life once again, as major law firms agreed to fight the case pro bono. This advertisement campaign has now become an annual feature and is the main instrument for garnering financial and other support for the movement from common people without any conditions attached except those ethical ones followed by the users of the funds themselves. Sathyu has also cobbled together a host of organisations in India in support of the mass struggles of the Bhopal gas victims and has actively pursued the various legal cases in progress, including the crucial one in the Supreme Court that has brought so much relief to the victims.

Sathyu had begun his political career by participating in radical left politics as a student of engineering in the Banaras Hindu University. Factional squabbles within his group disillusioned him, and he opted for a job with a government research facility in Bhopal in 1983. That was when he came in touch with the people in Kishore Bharati and gave up his research job to join them in Hoshangabad. He was in the first batch of people from Kishore Bharati who rushed to Bhopal in the wake of the gas leak and has stayed put there ever since. He refused to slow down even after the Zahreeli Gas Kand Morcha split up in 1986. He formed a separate organisation, the Bhopal Group for Information and Action, to carry on with individual actions in addition to mass struggles for not only the Bhopal gas victims, but also in support of other movements.

On one occasion, when the BJP government of Chief Minister Sunderlal Patwa was wielding the stick ferociously on the NBA in 1990 and most of us were in jail, Sathyu and another activist undertook an unprecedented action. The two of them chained and locked themselves to two pillars in the secretariat building in Bhopal, where the offices of the Ministers are located and gave the keys to an accomplice who slipped away. The pillars they had chosen were strategically located in the lobby from where all the ministers, including the Chief Minister had to pass. They then started shouting slogans denouncing the government. Immediately, a crowd collected and so did the police. There was a massive commotion and this persisted for a whole hour and a half as the police ran all over trying to find a mechanic to break the chains and take the two slogan-shouting activists to jail.

Sathyu has continually adopted such outlandish tactics to make an impact. On one occasion, he launched a campaign against Dow Chemicals in Mumbai. He had activists paste stickers in local trains and buses in the city, advertising that people could contact certain phone numbers for answers to problems related to infertility, impotency, unrequited love, jobs, foreign travel and the like. The numbers that were given were those of the Dow office in Mumbai. The Dow office began to be flooded with phone calls from distraught couples, jilted lovers and sundry other such people who were disgruntled with life. Eventually, Dow had to change all its phone numbers! The Jharoo Maro campaign launched to force Dow Chemicals to clean up the environmental mess in the factory at Bhopal was also his brainwave. It was tactically a brilliant move, since getting Dow to clean up the mess would be equivalent to getting them to acknowledge that they had the responsibility for paying enhanced compensation to the affected people of Bhopal who were still suffering from the effects of the gas leak. That is why Dow is trying its best to avoid doing this. Sathyu has also used the weapon of the hunger strike, and by limiting his demands to what the state can agree to under pressure, has been successful in getting concessions. But his efforts to nail Dow to take the responsibility for clean-up and provide greater compensation, he has not yet been successful. After all, he too is labouring under the Sisyphean curse!

Besides being a firebrand agent provocateur, he is also a capable manager of an effective social service organisation. To remedy the abysmal level of treatment provided to the survivors of the gas leak, he set up the Sambhavna Clinic and Trust in 1995 with the proceeds of the first advertisement campaign in 1994, which also conducts research into the causes and effects of the gas leak generated ailments. Over a decade of operation, funded by what is now called the Bhopal Medical Appeal, this clinic has evolved into a world-class facility providing much needed relief to the gas victims. An eclectic combination of therapeutic methodologies spanning across various disciplines like ayurveda, unani, yoga, and the dominant allopathy are used in this clinic. The medical research output that has been generated from this work has been published in leading research journals. The Sambhavna Trust has won many prestigious awards for its humanitarian work among a people left stranded by the state and MNCs, the most prominent being the Margaret Mead Award in 2002. Despite having achieved so much, Sathyu is a self-effacing man who lives frugally, works democratically and gives credit for the work done to his many colleagues, the most eminent among them being the indomitable Champa Devi and Rashida Bee. He has remained true to his basic dictum that "Political action must involve fun and laughter!"

Like Anilbhai and Sathyu, another such committed activist is Sunil Gupta who hails from the obscure town of Rampura in Mandsaur district of Madhya Pradesh. His family was displaced from its original village, which had been submerged in the reservoir created by the construction of the Gandhi Sagar dam on the river Chambal. His father is an economist who used to teach in government colleges and is an acolyte of Ram Manohar Lohia. Sunilbhai picked up the basics of Lohiaite Socialism from his father and wended his way to the Jawaharlal Nehru University (JNU) for his post graduation in the late 1970s. JNU was the hotbed of radical left politics at that time, with both the faculty and the students distinctly red in colour. Sunilbhai took an active part in student politics in the student wing of a faction of Socialists, but soon gave up academics to move to the defunct and so vacant Lohia Academy in Kesla village in Hoshangabad district to start mass organisational work in the mid 1980s.

Sunil began organising the Gond and Korku adivasis, who were on the verge of starvation, having lost forest access rights as well as their homes after being displaced numerous times because of the construction of the Tawa River dam and a ballistics missile range to demand that the government initiate relief works in the area. A mass organisation named Kisan Adivasi Sangathan (KAS) was formed, and agitations involving rallies and sit-ins and long marches to the administrative headquarters began. This was countered with police repression by the state; Sunil and his comrades were beaten up and put into jail. They were handcuffed while being taken to the court from the jail to attend their dates. They challenged this illegality in the Supreme Court, which passed strictures against the administration in what has gone down as a landmark judgment regarding the right of under-trial prisoners not to be handcuffed. This repression, combined with some sops given to the people, had the typical result of weaning them away from the KAS, and for a while, it lost some ground.

Things came to a boil once again in 1994, when the fishing rights in the Tawa dam reservoir were auctioned off to a private contractor in Bhopal, and a proposal was put forward by the Forest Department to evict the adivasis residing within the Bori Wildlife Sanctuary to make way for the preservation of tigers. The government, through its Fisheries Department, had controlled the fishing ever since the Tawa dam had been built. The department had brought in people from outside to do the fishing. This had left the adivasis literally high and dry. However, the adivasis had learnt to fish and in the absence of any other viable livelihoods used to poach fish from the reservoir and sell them by bribing the department staff. But the contractor from Bhopal would have none of this, and he descended with his musclemen and began beating up the adivasis when they were caught poaching. The Forest Department staff too began harassing the adivasis so as to force them to leave the forest. This became a major issue, and once again, the KAS, under the leadership of Sunilbhai, began agitating for the rights of the adivasis through rallies and sit-ins and finally a roadblock agitation. This was brutally suppressed and the agitators thrown into jail. However, the agitation finally paid off as the government took a decision to revoke the eviction orders on the adivasis in the Bori Wildlife Sanctuary and it agreed to give the right to fishing in the reservoir to a cooperative of the adivasi fishermen.

This cooperative has proved to be a resounding success. Not only have the earnings of the members increased substantially, but the fishing environment of the reservoir, too, has been improved. This has resulted in a higher and more sustainable output. Since this enhanced output is more than can be sold locally, the adivasis have become adept at transporting the fish in refrigerated trucks to far off locations like Kolkata and Mumbai and are earning greater profits. The government is also earning much more from royalties now than it had done ever before. Being members of the cooperative, all the adivasis have a vested interest in ensuring that the reservoir is well taken care of and stocked and that fishing is stopped during the monsoon months when spawning takes place. The bonus from the profits is distributed during these months so as to balance the loss of income. The social fencing by the adivasis is so effective that even the illegal poaching of tigers and timber has declined. On one occasion, some adivasis from a distant village wanted to poach turtles from the reservoir for some ceremony. They were not allowed to do so. They were asked that even if the KAS did allow them to take the turtles, how would they cart them through the Bori Wildlife Sanctuary to their village, which was outside it? The answer was that the forest guards were far easier to convince than the KAS members!

The immense success of the cooperative in increasing the earnings of their members has meant that they now contribute from their wages to the KAS and so fund its political activities, which are an insurance against any possibility of the government rescinding the fishing rights. Sunilbhai is the national secretary of the Samajvadi Jan Parishad, which is a national level party of Socialists. He is also the convenor of the Jan Sangharsh Morcha, which is a federation of mass organisations in Madhya Pradesh. Thus, the KAS now takes part in people's action right from the local to the national level. Sunilbhai is very active in his efforts to build up national and state level movements of people that espouse a more humane and nature friendly model of development. A combination of mass agitations and lobbying has ensured that the cooperative has had its fishing license renewed. Once again, the spectre of not only the withdrawal of fishing rights, but large scale displacement arising from the expansion of the area of the Satpura National Park in the Pachmarhi region of the district by the inclusion of the Bori Wildlife Sanctuary as well as the reservoir of the Tawa dam in it looms large. The sequestration of ecological niches as carbon sinks and bio-diversity reserves to compensate for the environmental profligacy of the elite has become a new cause for the displacement of adivasis from their habitats throughout the country. And once again, like the rest of us, Sunilbhai too has to relive the Sisyphean curse.

Yet another follower of Lohia who has added considerable verve to the movements for alternatives in Madhya Pradesh is Dr. Sunilam. He has been organising the farmers in the Betul district neighbouring Sunilbhai's area of work for more than two decades now. He shot into fame in 1998 when the police fired on and killed nineteen farmer members of the Kisan Sangharsh Samiti who were demonstrating before the Tehsil building in Multai demanding compensation for crops damaged due to heavy hailstorms. Thousands of farmers had been demonstrating for more than a month under Sunilam's leadership, but the government and administration, as is so typical in this country, chose to look the other way for fear that giving in to their demands might encourage other farmers elsewhere to voice similar demands. The government only responded with guns blazing when finally the farmers got impatient and conveniently put the blame on Sunilam for having incited the farmers. However, Sunilam's uniqueness transcends this grassroots mobilisation of farmers, which others too have done quite well and sometimes with better results than him.

Sunilam is the only one among the middle class activists of the environmental movements in Madhya Pradesh and Chhattisgarh who has translated mass mobilisation around grassroots issues into electoral success. Despite being heavily handicapped with nearly fifty false criminal cases following the Multai massacre, Sunilam successfully contested the 1999 elections as an independent candidate from Multai to the Madhya Pradesh legislative assembly. Not only that, he even retained the seat in the 2004 elections. He has thus been able to raise the many issues dear to all the mass environmental movements in the legislative assembly and put the government in the dock. One significant contribution of his has been his expose of the government's cover up of the persistent starvation deaths among tribals that were taking place in Madhya Pradesh in 2005. The great orator that he is, he has single-handedly raised the level of the debate on environmental issues in the house. His main thrust obviously has been on the issue of the adoption and implementation of an agricultural policy that is both environment and farmer friendly, as opposed to the current green revolution strategy that has proved to be a disaster. He has been so vociferous and trenchant in his lonely mission that the legislature Speaker has suspended him from the house quite a few times. Typically, he has refused to leave voluntarily on such occasions and so has had to be dragged away by the wardens! However, there is a limit to such lonely battles, and so he has now become a member of the Samajwadi political party and has busied himself in building up its base in Madhya Pradesh, along with the other law makers of that party. Not everyone fancies a Sisyphean lifestyle!

It's not as if only the male activists have shown spunk and grit because there is one woman who has matched them in every way and even surpassed them in some. That is Chittaroopa Palit, known to all and sundry as Silvy. Amit and I were the only two middle class activists left holding the fort of the KMCS in Alirajpur after the exit of Khemraj, when one day in 1988, Silvy came down to our office in Attha to interview us regarding our political perceptions so as to be able to judge whether we were worthy enough for her to join us or not! Silvy had completed her diploma in rural management from the Institute of Rural Management in Anand in Gujarat and had put in two years of compulsory apprenticeship in various NGOs before she decided that she wanted to be a political activist instead. She was visiting various mass organisations in Madhya Pradesh evaluating them. She took out a sheet with questions and began grilling us with them. I remember only one after all these years because it annoyed me much at the time. She asked us whether we did not think that by fighting for the provision of land rights to the adivasis within the reserved forest area we were following a reformist line of action as against the ideal course of building up a broader movement for the repeal of the Indian Forest Act itself. Anyway, we passed the test because she eventually came to work with us.

Subhadra says that all men are pigs and the self-righteous ones like me even more so, and it is the misfortune of women that they have to bear with them. Much before I came to know Subhadra, however, it was Silvy from whom I got my first formal lessons in feminism. Amit and I are fairly decent chaps as far as men go and have rejected the cruder forms of male dominance, which manifest themselves through a clear division of labour, especially in terms of domestic work. But we had not then given any deep thought to the way in which patriarchy still constrained women in society. Silvy's advent into the KMCS was like a feminist tornado in an all-male teacup. Despite being handicapped by not being able to traverse the hilly terrain as well as we used to, she nevertheless made up for this with her combativeness and began organising the women and taking us to task for not having done much in this sphere. Unfortunately, this initial enthusiasm for women's mobilisation around the issue of patriarchy soon took a backseat because Silvy decided to concentrate all her energies on the struggle against the Sardar Sarovar dam in which she immersed herself for a long time. When that struggle waned in the field, the passion to save the river Narmada made her move upstream to try and prevent various other dams being built on the river itself and on its tributaries.

Silvy has a bubbly personality, and she brought a welcome whiff of light banter into the austere and ascetic life that I used to lead in Alirajpur. She would go away to Vadodara, Mumbai and Delhi and come back full of colourful gossip about who was dating whom and about someone who had been jilted by some other person. She herself was married at that time, but being a follower of the school of feminists which held that women could be bisexual if they so wished, she once said to me that she would not baulk at a parallel relationship with a woman if the opportunity came by. I could not keep myself then from commenting cryptically "God save the other woman!" This was one joke that did not go down at all well with her to the extent that she shooed me out of her house in Alirajpur with a broom. I used to hear a lot about the sexual escapades of the Bhils during the course of my travels through the villages and also by participating in their panchayats to settle the disputes that inevitably arose, but these all seemed far removed from my own personal life, which was a firmly celibate one! So the memory of the many evenings spent listening to Silvy's jokes and gossip while we sat, cooked and ate our evening meals in the jumping shadows of the lantern lit kitchen in Attha is something that I will always treasure.

By 1993 I had begun having misgivings with the way in which the NBA was going about its work. Most members of the KMCS were not inclined to devoting all their energies solely to the struggle against the dam as Silvy and Medha would have liked. Hot headed as we both are, this led to some furious debates and our eventual estrangement. I left the area to depart for Indore, and we lost contact for a number of years, only to patch up somewhat after the Mehendikhera incident. However, the camaraderie and banter that used to mark the earlier phase of our friendship and was a very valuable part of those golden years spent in Alirajpur are no longer a part of the equation.

If the struggle in Bhopal has remained alive and kicking after all these years because of Sathyu, the struggle for the Narmada in Madhya Pradesh continues to act as a brake on the arbitrariness of the state in no small measure due to the all-round tenacity of Silvy. Whether it is in organising at the grassroots; lobbying at the higher levels right up to international fora; writing analytical papers, popular articles and press notes; or in mobilising funds, she has proved herself to be a veritable reincarnation of the ten-armed Goddess Durga, who in Hindu mythology brought salvation to the Gods by killing the evil demon, Mahishasur. Although Silvy hasn't been as successful, and the Mahishasur of the state continues to oppress the children of God and nature in the Narmada valley, she has nevertheless kept the hope alive of a final deliverance from destructive development and repressive governance. Just before the 2005 monsoons, the people to be affected by imminent submergence due to the closing of the gates of the Indira Sagar dam were in dire straits. The state adopted the time-tested policy of flushing out the people by flooding them, thus depriving them of rehabilitation and reducing the attendant costs.

The only course left was to move the High Court in Jabalpur against this blatant violation of the NWDT Award and the recent Supreme Court judgment supporting it in the case filed by the NBA with regard to the rehabilitation of the Sardar Sarovar oustees. Lawyers from Delhi came down and the petition was filed in the High Court. In the absence of any local lawyers willing to take up the case, Silvy, who had earlier drafted the petition along with lawyers in Delhi, decided to plead the case herself. Undeterred by the sarcastic comments of the senior lawyers in Jabalpur, Silvy prepared her plea and began arguing on the appointed day. The judges heard her for thirteen days and finally ordered that the gates of the dam should remain open until proper rehabilitation had been provided. This was later repeated in the case of the Omkareshwar dam also which today stands completed but its gates cannot be closed because rehabilitation is not complete.

One persistent problem among radicals involved in mass political movements, right from the time of the French Revolution is that of internecine squabbling. The communists, socialists and environmentalists in India too have squabbled similarly. The activists of the mass environmental movements in Madhya Pradesh have not been able to buck this trend either.

The two decades of trudging through the dusty activist trails of Madhya Pradesh have been a sad lesson for me in this regard. There are a host of talented, brave-hearted and committed activists, both men and women, who have consistently fought the state over this long period, many of whom have not been mentioned here because of the limitations of space, or my lack of a deep acquaintance with their work. Apart from me, there are three other IIT alumni, Shripad Dharmadhikari, Himanshu Thakkar and Alok Agrawal who have provided creative midfield support to the striking prowess of Medha in the game to save the Narmada. Nevertheless, the mass environmental movements in Madhya Pradesh and Chhattisgarh have not been able to fulfil their promise because at the end of the day, we have not wanted to collaborate in any serious way to build up a common front that can challenge the state significantly. Ideological and programmatic differences have taken a backseat as the trading of personal charges, questioning the integrity and commitment of one-time comrades in arms have come to the fore, a phenomenon that has been characterised by Trotsky as striking not at a political opponent's ideas, but at his skull. Fortunately or unfortunately, none of us, with our small outfits, have come close to winning state power and so have not been able to murder each other!

So much and yet so little—that sums up the contribution of the one time Young Turks who have added so much colour to the political spectrum in sleepy and backward Madhya Pradesh and Chhattisgarh over the past three decades or so. Today, these diehard activists have all passed into middle age and are mostly ploughing lonely furrows in the absence of a second generation of equal mettle that would carry on the battle. Matters have been compounded by the fact that today's middle-class youth prefer rolling bowls at pins in swank bowling centres to rolling stones up hills even more than they used to a decade or two earlier.

28 The Treasure of Terra Madre

The yawning gap between the traditional adivasi worldview and that of modern humans is most succinctly brought out by a quaint story set in Mexico. There was an indigenous tribal there who used to weave eye-catching baskets out of a weed dyed in organically prepared colours. On seeing these baskets an American businessman immediately saw a market for them back home in New York as containers for chocolates. Since the baskets were selling at a cent a piece, he expected to make a commercial kill and asked the tribal to weave him ten thousand baskets at a discounted price. After some thought, the tribal answered that he would sell the baskets at a hundred dollars a piece. When the startled American asked why he was quoting such a high price, the tribal replied that to make ten thousand baskets in such a short time, he would permanently exhaust the sources of the weeds and dyes and thus lose his livelihood. So to make up for this permanent loss, he would have to charge a higher price.

The response of modern humans to this sound environmental logic of the adivasis has been to forcibly dispossess them of the natural wealth they have so wisely husbanded. These natural resources are then used recklessly in modern industrial development, disregarding the future consequences. Over the past four centuries or so, the two crucial factors responsible for sustaining this modern developmental surge have been the supply of cheap food in adequate quantity for the vastly increased population and natural resources for the ever-increasing needs of industry and trade. The most important natural resources were fossil fuels, which provided the energy to run the machines that tremendously improved the productivity of human labour. Crude oil and natural gas have now become the most important of natural resources, as they are not only the main providers of energy, but are also the raw materials for a variety of other products like plastics, fibres, chemical fertilisers, pesticides and drugs that have become indispensable to the modern industrial economy. Thus, the whole of the 20th century has seen many wars fought basically for the control of crude oil reserves.

The Second World War saw the USA amassing huge surpluses from the sale of food and arms and ammunitions to its European allies, which, along with the axis powers, were devastated totally at the end of the war. The military-industrial-agricultural complex that emerged in the USA during the war was in danger of collapsing in the post-war era unless the shattered economies of Europe and Japan were boosted again. So a massive transfer of resources through outright grants was made by the USA to its allies and to the defeated axis powers to rebuild the world capitalist economy. Trade and not imperial preference was to be the new watchword of capitalist development. A number of countries, including India were gradually given freedom, and they were sold the spiel that they were on a lower stage of growth than the developed nations of the capitalist world, and all they had to do was open up their economies and follow the path of market-led and high consumption driven development being prescribed by the developed capitalist nations. The "unholy trinity" of The World Bank, International Monetary Fund (IMF), and the General Agreement on Tariffs and Trade, which was later to become the World Trade Organisation (WTO) in 1994, were set up to oversee this reworked capitalist world system and ensure that the exploitation of human and natural resources continued unabated.

Initially, immediately after the war, the USA was faced with the problem of reorienting the production of its massive war-oriented industry and agriculture. This was done on the one hand by making civilian cars, trucks, planes and cargo ships instead of armoured vehicles and on the other, by transforming the explosive manufacturing units into fertiliser and pesticide producing units. Obviously so many cars, planes and ships and so much fertiliser and pesticide could not be consumed by the Americans alone. So the high-flying consumerist lifestyle of cars and private jets and heavy eating of processed meat and cereals was spread all over the world, and a market created for these products. Cattle can eat much more cereals than human beings, and so the people of the developed world were encouraged to eat the former, and the people of the poorer countries, along with their cattle, were fed the excess cereals resulting from increased use of fertilisers and pesticides. A significant development was the worldwide adoption of soybean at the behest of the Americans who pushed its exports and cultivation through cheap aid to developing countries so as to provide cheap feed for beef production and also cheap edible oil for processing this food into ready-to-eat marketable forms. Thus, an artificially highly productive and environmentally unsustainable agricultural system was established worldwide. This was backed by massive state subsidies. A golden era of capitalist development, booming on the production and sale of the "world car" and the "world steer" by multi national corporations (MNC), ensued in the 1950s and 1960s.

The party came to an end in the 1970s, with a double whammy being delivered by nature. Firstly, biologist Rachel Carson sounded the first warning cry in 1962 about the way in which chemicals and especially pesticides were causing immense environmental and health hazards. This sparked off the modern environmental movement and seriously questioned the excessive gorging of the world steer. The tremendous groundswell of protests that followed saw environmental pollution resulting from modern development emerging as a burning issue by the early 1970s. The first United Nations Conference on Environment was held in Stockholm in 1972. Secondly, the finiteness of the natural resources that were being so wantonly consumed was driven home as the Arab crude oil producing countries increased oil prices by four times in 1974, thus pushing the capitalist world economy into a deep recession by undermining the very basis of the world car.

Ever since then, human beings have been confronted by what is termed as a prisoner's dilemma. In the classical form it goes like this: two suspects are arrested by the police who have insufficient evidence for a conviction. Having separated both prisoners, the police visit each of them to offer the same deal: if one testifies for the prosecution against the other and the other remains silent, the betrayer goes free and the silent accomplice receives the full 10-year sentence. If each betrays the other, each will receive a two-year sentence. If both stay silent, the police cannot get the prisoners sentenced because of lack of sufficient evidence, but they do not reveal this to the prisoners. Each prisoner must make the choice of whether to betray the other or to remain silent. However, neither prisoner knows for sure what choice the other prisoner will make. Nor do they realise that if they both kept mum, they would scot free. So the question this dilemma poses is: how should the prisoners act? Since one prisoner does not know what the other is going to do, and the prisoner who remains silent would be made to bear the whole prison term if the other prisoner squeals, the tendency is for both prisoners to betray and so get sentenced.

In the case of modern humans, faced with the choice between environmental sustainability and modern development, if all people cooperate and keep their consumption within safe limits, and redistribute the immense wealth that has already been created, instead of blindly going on accumulating further wealth, both nature and human beings will survive. If, however, some people limit their consumption while others go on satisfying their greed then those taking the saner environmentalist path will end up as the losers as they will be pauperised even more by the rapacious practices being followed by the greedy ones. The best example of this are the adivasis who have been continuously dispossessed of their lands for the purpose of modern development. Since the MNCs and the world's rich people are refusing to follow a saner environmental path and pushing the world towards an inevitable environmental disaster that will kill everyone anyway, the tendency is for all people rich and poor, even the once environmentally wise adivasis, to consume as much as they can lay their hands on, leading to ever increasing and irreparable environmental damage.

All this has had a devastating effect on the Indian agriculture and the millions of people who are dependent on it for their livelihoods. The vast majority of farmers in India cultivate small plots of land on terrain that is unsuitable for flood irrigation and have traditionally been driven by the desire to produce for subsistence rather than for profit. Over thousands of years, they have developed a system of agriculture that makes the most of the locally available resources, in terms of seeds, organic fertilisers, soil moisture and natural pest management. This led Sir Albert Howard, the pioneer of modern organic farming who did most of his work in Indore, to remark some sixty years ago, "What is happening today in the small fields of India ... took place many centuries ago. The agricultural practices of the orient have passed the supreme test, they are as permanent as those of the primeval forest, of the prairie, or of the ocean." The clever use of rotation of a wide variety of crops ensured that despite floods and droughts, some part of the harvest was always saved. Famines occurred not because of the failure of agriculture, but because of socio-economic factors such as excessive levies imposed by kings and colonial rulers or due to usury and hoarding by sahukars. Since ancient times, the levying of excessive taxes and usury has been a severe constraining factor on the development of agriculture all over the world. In India, this strain became even more intense as the sahukar doubled up as the tax-collector, resulting in one Bhili proverb that goes like this, "I love the sahukar so much that I have given him a fat belly."

What was needed after independence in India was to remove the obstacles in the path of development of traditional agriculture and strengthen it with further research, extensive land reforms, cheap institutionalised credit and market support. Studies have shown that the indigenous agricultural practices of India, which have been honed by farmers over the centuries, are as productive as the high yielding hybrid seeds and artificial input based green revolution agriculture. But this was not to be because the Americans had, since the 1930s, devised a new model of industrial agriculture in which hybrid seeds, fertilisers, pesticides, big dam irrigation and machines were used to ramp up agricultural production with huge state subsidies, which eventually went to the corporations that not only supplied these inputs, but also owned most of the farms and traded in the outputs. So farm gate prices remained low, leaving the actual small farmers who had always struggled against usury like elsewhere in the world no alternative but to gradually sell out and become unemployed, leading to their pathetic destitution.

At the behest of the research foundations set up by American MNCs and with financial support provided by the World Bank and the money from the exports of American wheat to India, which were recycled for this purpose, the American agricultural pattern was promoted as green revolution agriculture in the late 1960s. Foreign hybrid varieties of wheat and rice were introduced in a few pockets in the country, leaving the other areas literally high and dry. The Americans forced the Indian government to sideline Indian agricultural scientists who had developed indigenous strains and had opposed this introduction of foreign hybrids. This form of agriculture has now become problematical throughout the world (because of reasons to be discussed a little later) and can be sustained only through the provision of massive state subsidies to the MNCs that produce its inputs and trade in its outputs. In this way, the comparative advantage that the third world countries have in the agricultural sector is not only neutralised, but the excess production thus achieved is dumped in those countries, devastating their agriculture. The current Doha round of trade negotiations of the WTO has revealed as never before, the hollowness and hypocrisy of the WTO's claims of promoting "free trade." The negotiations are deadlocked at the moment because the developed countries are refusing to reduce these subsidies.

The main problem with artificial input agriculture is that there is a natural limit to the artificial inputs that the soil can take; so the amount of fertilisers, pesticides and water to be applied keeps increasing, while the yields keep declining. At times, the crop fails altogether. Consequently, the economic costs continue to increase while the realisation of the value of agricultural products in the market does not keep pace. This inevitably leads to farmers falling into the clutches of the sahukars and spiralling debt. The crisis has now assumed serious proportions, with thousands upon thousands of farmers committing suicide, selling their lands, houses and even kidneys. Things have come to such a sorry pass that in a survey conducted by the National Sample Survey Organisation of the Government of India in 2003, forty percent of the respondent farmers expressed the desire to give up farming and take up other professions.

The American MNCs' maniacal obsession with promoting more and more beef eating worldwide as the panacea for the ills of the inevitable market slumps that hound capitalism, has now manifested itself in the development of genetically engineered Bovine Growth Hormones to push up beef production. This has driven even the cows mad! The continuing loss of natural bio-diversity, the concentration of genes of landraces in the hands of MNCs and patenting of life forms by them have together led to a precarious scenario, wherein the future of the planet has been permanently mortgaged to the MNCs' greed for profits. While the Americans have become obese from this over consumption of beef and are suffering from a number of physical and mental disorders as a result, the Bhil adivasis in Madhya Pradesh have become proportionately under-nourished so as to be able to provide for this overeating of the former. With the reduction in the acreage under coarser cereals and pulses, which have been replaced by soybean and the greater monetisation of the rural economy, the marginal adivasi farmers have had to buy their food from the market instead of getting it cheaply from their farms. This has reduced their nutritional levels well below healthy standards.

This deep tragedy of the ever-present hunger of the poor has been cynically parodied in a farce that is being enacted in Madhya Pradesh under the auspices of the cigarette manufacturer, Indian Tobacco Company (ITC). Faced with severe and increasing restrictions on the sale of cigarettes, the company has diversified into the processed food and hospitality businesses. As a support to these ventures, it has an International Business Division, which trades in agricultural unprocessed and processed products, including soybean feed and soy oil, in the international markets. To cut down on the costs of procuring soybeans through middlemen, it launched a direct purchasing initiative called "e-choupal" or electronic agricultural markets in Madhya Pradesh. It set up Internet kiosks in villages where the farmers could get to know the price being offered for their soybean crop on a particular day by ITC. This price was more than what the farmers would get from the traders, but considerably less than what the ITC would have had to pay to these traders to procure soybean from them. The catch was that the farmers would have to book their sale at that price with the agent running the kiosk and then transport their produce to the collecting centre, which was far away and get their payment there. This meant that only large farmers could avail of this opportunity, as the transportation cost would be prohibitive for small farmers. So effectively what has happened is that the small farmers have continued to sell to the local traders at lower prices and the latter have then sold to the ITC! The big traders in the cities who used to supply to ITC earlier have lost out and so have raised Cain about this system.

Thus the e-choupal has benefited ITC the most with windfall profits. The big farmers too have benefited somewhat as have the chemical and food sector MNCs who have now been able to integrate a peripheral agricultural region into the international capitalist economy. The small farmer adivasis have been left in a bigger lurch than before, as the acreage under soybean has kept soaring, making them more and more dependent on the market for their food. The black comedy is that this fraud, being perpetrated in the name of benefiting small farmers, has been hailed by the management guru C K Prahlad as a great new rural development initiative that will solve their problems. This is a typical example of Corporations spending miniscule amounts in ostensibly developmental initiatives that actually increase their access to remoter and remoter areas and so multiply their profits. In 2005, the e-choupal initiative was awarded a prize of USD 100,000 by the Development Gateway Foundation in the USA for having supposedly used information technology to enhance the incomes of poor farmers. Since in reality the incomes of poor farmers has not increased, the prize must actually have been given to ITC for ensuring the supply of soymeal and uninterrupted gorging of roasted beef by the Americans!

The biggest problem arising from the adoption of green revolution agriculture, however, has been that of the increasing scarcity of water. Most of the water needed for irrigation in India is being provided by groundwater extraction. This has led to a situation of water mining, wherein water collected in deep confined aquifers over hundreds of thousands of years were used up in the space of a decade. Large parts of the country have been facing a ground water drought since the 1990s . Ever since, there has been a steady decrease in ground water not only for irrigation, but also for drinking. The cost of groundwater extraction is continually going up. Big dams, however, are environmentally and socially the most harmful component of the green revolution package and have come in for serious criticism in recent years. In developed countries, dam construction has been totally halted, with a number of dams having even been broken to limit environmental damage.

Across the world, there is a burgeoning movement in ecological farming combined with local area watershed development that has come up as a reaction to the deleterious effects of modern agriculture. This movement is theoretically underpinned by the green ideology of development in harmony with nature and at its own leisurely pace. Many localised efforts have thrown up viable solutions to the intransigent problems created by unsustainable agricultural production and inequity in the distribution of benefits and costs of water resource development. In the western Madhya Pradesh region, too, there have been successful localised experiments in this sphere. A blueprint for the development of sustainable dry-land agriculture, backed by local area watershed development involving poor people in project formulation and implementation has been drawn up. There are no takers for the blueprint, though.

Faced with the reality of the destitution of billions of people and not willing to jettison the centralised industrial development paradigm, the World Bank has embarked on yet another fraudulent game of wishing away the extent of this poverty. It arbitrarily defined a poverty line consumption expenditure, equivalent to the value of US$ 1 per family, per day, in 1986 and thereafter has been carrying out some dubious statistical estimation of the number of people below it from time to time to show that over the decade of the 1990s, the absolute number of people below this poverty line has decreased. The Indian Government isn't behind in this game either. Dubious assumptions and calculations have been resorted to by the Planning Commission so as to show a decline in the poverty head count over the period of economic liberalisation in the 1990s. This theatre of the absurd has reached a stage where the results of the actual household survey, carried out for the purpose of the distribution of Below Poverty Line Ration Cards to those eligible for cheaper food grains from the Public Food Distribution System in accordance with the orders of the Supreme Court, has been doctored so as to make the actual poverty head count tally with the figure estimated by the Planning Commission!

All this statistical jugglery was not able to hide the stark reality of increasing poverty due to the failure of structural adjustment policies adopted by developing countries, in consonance with the World Bank's diktats in the 1980s, which became evident by the end of that decade. This led the World Bank to review these policies and search for ways in which "growth with equity" could be ensured and poverty "attacked." One major failure that was pinpointed was the inability of financial institutions like banks and credit cooperative societies to address the credit needs of those living in poverty. This led to the search for alternative modes of credit delivery. The initial success of some NGO initiatives in providing easy access to credit to the poor in Bangladesh and Indonesia and a consequent reduction in their economic vulnerability was picked up and modified by the World Bank and formalised into a model to be replicated worldwide. The micro-finance boom of the 1990s was thus kicked off.

The experience of the operation of micro-finance the world over has shown that with proper intermediation by NGOs, this paradigm does improve the access of previously deprived poor populations to institutionalised credit with the reduction of transaction costs and so reduces their economic vulnerability. However, if the costs of this crucial intermediation by NGOs in the formation and operation of SHGs, which is currently being met by outright grants or by the supply of subsidised credit from funding agencies, are factored in, then the economics of micro-finance begins to wobble. Without grant support, the long-term viability of micro-finance is in doubt and with it micro-finance stands in danger of being overwhelmed by self-defeating bureaucratisation through its institutionalisation. The SHG members have little control over the actions of the NGOs and their sponsors. Without proper regulation, there have already been cases of funds saved by the poor from their meagre earnings being misappropriated by unscrupulous NGOs and non-banking financial companies who have resorted to disguised usury.

The net result of this massive propaganda and funding by the World Bank and the central and state governments of green revolution agriculture has been that the ordinary farmers in this country are unable to pursue more sustainable agricultural alternatives since switching from the one type to another takes time and money. After securing control of her share of her ancestral land in Jepra in 1999, Subhadra decided to revive the cultivation of the tasty, nutritious and scented indigenous Dubraj rice on it. After the first harvest came in, I packed two sacks of the rice and took them with me to Indore. When I got down from the bus in Raipur and lugged these sacks on to a cycle rickshaw to take them to the railway station, the rickshaw puller said to me "Babuji, you have Dubraj rice in these sacks." I was surprised because the sacks had been double packed and there was no outward sign that they contained rice. So I asked the rickshaw puller how he found out, and he replied that he had smelled the scent of the rice. My city-bred nose had missed what this rickshaw-puller could sense. He went on to lament that he too had once grown Dubraj rice on his land, but had been forced to sell out because of debt, and now he was pulling a rickshaw for a living. Not many people grew Dubraj anymore, he said, because it required a lot of tending and its yield was low. He wondered how I had laid my hands on this rice. Little did he know that I was married to a person made of more earthy stuff! Unfortunately, in later years, Subhadra could not go to Jepra regularly to supervise the cultivation of her land, and her brother promptly switched to a hybrid variety, which was easier to cultivate and sell. This is what the market has done to agriculture and India's rural society.

Going back to a sustainable agricultural paradigm will provide the rural poor with ample livelihood opportunities for wholesome living, while at the same time reorienting development to fulfilling the needs of the majority. This will, in turn, ensure a much more peaceful world than the present one and obviate the heavy and wasteful expenditures being incurred worldwide on military and police. Expecting this to happen, however, is as distant a dream as that of actually finding a Mexican tribal like the one mentioned in the beginning of this chapter. The author of the story, Berick Traven, was a mysterious German revolutionary anarchist and novelist who, since the 1920s onwards, led a reclusive life in the Chiapas jungles of Mexico which, in the 1990s, were to witness the uprising of the Zapatista National Liberation Army. He is best known for his allegorical novel "The Treasure of the Sierra Madre", which was later made into an Oscar winning film in 1948 by the American director John Huston. The film has been acclaimed as the best portrayal ever of what greed can do to human beings. The story shows three down and out Americans in Mexico going to the Sierra Madre Mountain to search for gold and strike it rich. The drama begins as one of the prospectors, Dobbs, becomes greedy and wants to take more gold than the others. This makes the other two greedy as well, and they all begin distrusting each other in a typical playing out of the prisoner's dilemma. Dobbs runs away with all the gold dust after shooting and wounding one of his fellows, while the other is out for some work. But he meets Mexican bandits on the way who kill him for his pants, boots and guns, but throw away the gold dust, mistaking it for sand. These bandits are later apprehended by the police and shot to death. A dust storm rises and disperses the gold dust all over the earth from where it had been extracted. All the treasure accumulated is lost, and the greedy men die violent deaths.

Like Dobbs and his mates, the modern tycoons have been accumulating the treasure of mother earth, Terra Madre, over the past three centuries at an increasingly hectic pace and have been killing common people in the millions to do so, either directly, through war or indirectly, through lack of employment and food. Unlike the dumb witted Dobbs who met his nemesis for being too greedy and not wanting to share anything with his partners and lost both his gold and his life, the modern tycoons have been cleverer by half and have thrown a few crumbs here and there, notably by funding NGOs. So they continue to thrive by co-opting opposition. However, the ominous portents are not very encouraging regarding the indiscriminate mining of natural resources and the pollution of the biosphere, which has now begun to threaten the two basic requirements of capitalist industrial development—the adequate and assured supply of cheap food and industrial raw materials. Since nature cannot be co-opted by bribing, there is every chance of the environmental backlash that has begun in agriculture, spreading to other spheres of the economy, leading to a situation wherein the future of the human race itself is in jeopardy as Terra Madre begins to reclaim all the treasure that has been looted from her.

29 The Lost Art of Political Daydreaming

"Do not go upon what has been acquired by repeated hearing; nor upon tradition; nor upon rumour; nor upon what is in a scripture; nor upon surmise; nor upon an axiom; nor upon specious reasoning; nor upon a bias towards a notion that has been pondered over; nor upon another's seeming ability; nor upon the consideration, 'The monk is our teacher.' When you yourselves know, 'These things are good; these things are not blamable; these things are praised by the wise; undertaken and observed, these things lead to benefit and happiness,' enter on and abide in them.

- attributed to The Buddha

"At that subtle moment when man glances backward over this life, Sisyphus returning toward his rock, in that slight pivoting he contemplates that series of unrelated actions which becomes his fate, created by him, combined under his memory's eye and soon sealed by his death. Thus convinced of the wholly human origin of all that is human, a blind man eager to see, who knows that the night has no end, he is still on the go. The rock is still rolling. I leave Sisyphus at the foot of the mountain! One always finds one's burden again. But Sisyphus teaches the higher fidelity that negates the gods and raises rocks. He too concludes that all is well. This universe henceforth without a master seems to him neither sterile nor futile. Each atom of that stone, each mineral flake of that night-filled mountain, in itself forms a world. The struggle itself toward the heights is enough to fill a man's heart. One must imagine Sisyphus happy".

- Albert Camus

I was moved in my youth by the romantic dreamer Rubhasov—one of the most tragic characters of 20th-century fiction and the central character in Arthur

Koestler's novel "Darkness at Noon"—to begin dreaming of doing something to improve matters for the poor and down trodden and eventually find my way to Jhabua.

This tendency to daydream on the part of philosophers and political radicals is nothing but a subtler manifestation of the animism that has been a part of the human psyche since man began to ponder over nature and is manifested in religion in the form of myths, in philosophy in the form of utopian ideas and in science in the form of the teleological assumption of there being some overarching purpose behind natural processes. But there have also been another group of dreamers, the naturalists, who have held the key to human freedom over the millennia by denying the existence of Gods or any overarching purpose or design in nature. Both these kinds of dreamers have fought exhilarating intellectual battles in the arena of political thought and action through the ages and enriched human existence.

As the concept of private property and then the need for the state to regulate these relations matured, God was brought in to legitimize the new repressive institutions of the state, marriage and patriarchy, and organised religion made its debut. The initial radical reactions to this false legitimisation through organised religion were from within the animist tradition and were included in the religious texts as an idealistic alternative as in this famous quote from the Bible - "they shall beat their swords into ploughshares, and their spears into pruning hooks; nation shall not lift up sword against nation, neither shall they learn war any more." Later still, this idealism manifested itself in mystic spiritualism, as in that of the Vedas and in idealistic philosophy, as in that of Plato and Confucius. Socrates, the great Greek philosopher, broke with the animistic tradition and plumped for naturalism instead, developing the dialectical method of enquiry in the process. Another student of Socrates, Antisthenes, not only carried forward this critical tradition, but considerably enhanced it and handed it down to Diogenes of Sinope who gave it a definitive philosophical form. Diogenes inveighed against both Gods and received wisdom, but more importantly, he stressed that human beings should lead a life of hard labour in harmony with nature and should refrain from accumulating property. Diogenes can be said to be the first conscious atheistic environmental anarchist.

The Charvaks, a long line of anonymous materialistic philosophers, mounted the challenge to animism in India from the time of the Vedas. They denied the existence of God and the doctrine of rebirth and afterlife and insisted that instead of wasting time in prayers, people should busy themselves with living simply in harmony with nature. A much more significant challenge to animism and Brahminism was launched later by the Buddha, about a century before Socrates. He said that all the miseries of humans arose from their desires. The desires of innumerable people from time immemorial had given rise to an intricate web of cause and effect, creating the world as people saw it. There is no God who controls the destiny of human beings; instead they should rein in their desires and live a life of moderation if they want to end their sufferings.

Buddha places the onus for one's destiny squarely on the individual. Unlike Diogenes and Epicurus, however, the Buddha was a mystic. He did not believe in the existence of a supreme spirit, but said that the only way to know the absolute truth and thereby be completely liberated from desires and achieve a state of "Nirvana" was through inward meditation on nothingness. He also built up a democratic order of "Bhikkhus" or meditative mendicants who would give up all their desires in the search for absolute truth. He was so democratic that even though initially he was averse to having women in his order because of the problems it might cause for the practice of celibacy, eventually he bowed down to the pressure of his fellow Bhikkhus and allowed women in too. His criterion for acceptance of true knowledge, quoted at the start of this chapter, remains unsurpassed even today. After the Buddha's death, however, atheism slowly receded among his followers and mysticism took an upper hand, with the Buddha himself being converted into a God. All kinds of myths were built up around him, and Buddhism became an organised religion.

Another great naturalist and a contemporary of the Buddha, the Chinese Lao Tzu came up with the idea that the basic natural principle of Tao should be allowed to operate freely without the imposition of human desires on it. Like the Buddha, Lao Tzu was a mystic, and his Tao is a mystic principle. I love one particularly cogent anarchistic quote of his:

Why are people starving?
Because the rulers eat up the money in taxes.
Therefore the people are starving.

Why are the people rebellious?
Because the rulers interfere too much.
Therefore they are rebellious.

Why do people think so little of death?
Because the rulers demand too much of life.
Therefore the people take life lightly.

The early idealistic animism and atheistic naturalism of ancient times were soon buried under the grosser forms of organised religion throughout the world, which tended to support the greed of human beings and the oppressive state structure developed to protect the property accumulated as a consequence of this greed. In Europe, the teaching of Jesus Christ, which was unabashedly against the accumulation of property and for compassion towards fellow human beings, was itself subverted once the institutionalised Church set up in his name became the official religion of the rulers. Radical thinking was ruthlessly suppressed to prevent any possibility of revolt against the prevailing order.

The major casualty of religious obscurantism was science. Science based on rational interpretation of observed reality had made good progress in the time of the Greeks. Aristotle, the philosopher of philosophers, although he, too, believed in a God as the initial cause of the universe, nevertheless put Greek science on a firm basis by systematising the scientific method of experimentation and logical interpretation for getting at the truth. The Church, however, put the scientific content of his thought on the backburner and instead upheld the mystical strain for many centuries. The extent of the brake that the belief in God put on scientific inquiry can be gauged from the fact that in the third century BCE, the Greek mathematician and astronomer, Aristarchus, had postulated from a study of the movement of the stars and the moon that the earth moved around the sun and not vice-versa, but this was discarded by his contemporaries because of the Platonic belief supported later by Aristotle that the earth, where the Gods were housed, had to be fixed at the centre of the universe. Later, some people tried to follow up this earth-moving postulate, but were suppressed by the Church until almost two millennia later Copernicus, despite being a cleric of the Church, once again revived it and kicked off the modern scientific revolution with his mathematical proof to confirm his findings.

Thereafter, science progressed inexorably, if hesitantly at first, as its practitioners began conducting experiments and deducing inferences from them that clearly contradicted the theistic views of the Church. The Italian scientist Galileo was hauled up by the Church for supporting the helio-centric theory of Copernicus and was forced to retract at the peril of death. His contemporary, Descartes, provided what has come to be called the Cartesian Framework of modern philosophical and scientific thinking by stressing that everything in the universe could be doubted until proved to be true through observation and analysis. The first truth thus arrived at by him was the fact that he himself existed because he doubted - cogito ergo sum. Thereafter, by logical analysis of the external world, perceived through the senses, all other truths could be determined. This duality between the observer and the observed and the observation and analysis by the former of the latter is the basis for knowing all objective truth to this day.

This posed the crucial problem for Descartes of proving the existence of God, as otherwise he would have been seen as going against the Church and thus risking its wrath. To avert this, he advanced the argument that he is able to perceive "clear and evident truths" because God exists, who being a perfect being would not deceive him, and who had also given him the capacity to discern the true from the untrue. But this then created the problem that in order to argue that the existence of God is also a clear and evident truth, Descartes requires God to exist beforehand in order to guarantee the certainty of what to him is a clear and evident truth. In other words, Descartes assumes a priori the existence of God without any proof so as to be able to say later through a logical sleight of hand that God exists. So Descartes failed to provide any independent objective proof of the existence of God. This logical fallacy is known as the Cartesian Circle for the circularity of argument involved in assuming beforehand what is to be proved. It arose because of Descartes' attempt to do the impossible—objectively prove the existence of God!

After this, throughout the entire 18th century, the intellectual firmament was dominated by the brilliant socio-political satire of the towering French rationalist Voltaire. Early on in his adult life, the irreverent Voltaire fell foul of the Regent of France. Reportedly the former said to him, "I will wager that I can show you something that you have never seen before." When Voltaire asked what it was the Regent replied "The inside of the Bastille prison!" Voltaire not only battled throughout his life against the animism of the Church, but he was also a feisty votary of the freedom of speech and expression, which is the most basic requirement of democratic governance. This is encapsulated in his pithy saying "I do not agree with a word you say, but I will defend to the death your right to say it."

However, Rousseau, by introducing the concept of the General Will in political philosophy, started a new and subtler kind of animism that replaced God with a deterministic intelligent design, which directed the destinies of men. He argued that all the problems of governance would be solved if the people entered into a Social Contract to reduce the physical freedom that they would have enjoyed in a state of nature without any social formation, in exchange for the advantages of living in a society and cooperating with each other. This society would then have a General Will that would function for the good of society, rather than only for that of the individual and so overcome the individual recalcitrant who might want to upset the system. At about the same time, Adam Smith introduced the similar concept of the invisible hand in economics, and the German philosopher Kant brought in the concept of an absolute and supreme inner moral law that operated for the ultimate good of humanity. This trend continued with Hegel's conception of an Absolute Idea and the progress of humanity through a dialectical process of negation and synthesis towards perfection, Marx's conception of the inevitability of the movement of history through a similar dialectical process in the material world, to a communist society free of exploitation and finally the current widely held belief that science and technology can by themselves, through the discovery of natural laws based on empirical observation, solve the problems arising out of the cupidity of human beings. There is a circularity of reasoning involved in all these propositions because they assume a priori without any objective proof the existence of a deterministic law or principle that then ensures through logical sleight of hand the inevitability of utopian end results.

Thus, a new set of comforting myths have developed from the subtler animistic propositions mentioned above: the liberal one that the centralised liberal democratic state and parliamentary democracy constitute the best form of government; the Marxist one that such a state is in reality the executive committee of the bourgeoisie, which will unerringly be overthrown by a revolution and be replaced with a state that is a dictatorship of the proletariat, which in turn will eventually wither away with the formation of a communist society; the universal modernist one that centralised industrial development is the only path of economic progress for human beings; and the capitalist one that the market is the best and most efficient institution for the allocation of resources and incomes. While the old myth around Gods had given rise to the powerful institution of the Church, which ruthlessly trampled on individual freedoms, so also these new teleological myths have given rise to the institutions of the State, which as we have seen, are much more powerful in comparison to the individual and civil society.

The French sociologist Foucault has perceptively noted the modern state, regardless of its political ideology, has become a gargantuan power machine that "automatises and disindividualises power. Power has its principle not so much in a person as in a certain concerted distribution of bodies, surfaces, lights, gazes; in an arrangement whose internal mechanisms produce the relation in which individuals are caught up." So there is not much of a difference between the pre-revolutionary and the post-revolutionary states in Russia and between the colonial and post-colonial states in India as far as suppressing the protests of the masses is concerned. In the present day world, there are even more powerful institutions than nation states in the form of the unholy trinity of the IMF, World Bank and WTO and the MNCs. This powerlessness of modern human beings has been vividly and disturbingly portrayed in the tragi-comic allegorical novels and short stories of Franz Kafka who wrote in the crucial first two decades of the 20th century when anarchist, Marxist and libertarian dreams of liberation were buried in the quagmire of capitalist greed.

Unlike the orthodox Marxists, however, Rosa Luxemberg held the somewhat anarchistic and supremely naturalist view that mass organization should not be a product of an animistic belief in the historical imperative of revolution, but rather be a conscious product of the struggles of the working classes: "The modern proletarian class doesn't carry out its struggle according to a plan set out in some book or theory; the modern workers' struggle is a part of history, a part of social progress, and in the middle of history, in the middle of progress, in the middle of the fight, we learn how we must fight...That's exactly what is laudable about it, that's exactly why this colossal piece of culture, within the modern workers' movement, is epoch-defining: that the great masses of the working people first forge from their own consciousness, from their own belief, and even from their own understanding the weapons of their own liberation."

The second longest serving myth after that of the existence of God is that men are superior to women. So deep rooted is this myth that even Mary Wollstonecraft, who began the modern movement for the liberation of women from patriarchal oppression, could not free herself from it entirely. She considered men to be the ideal towards which women needed to aspire. This myth was finally challenged in its entirety by the French philosopher Simone de Beauvoir in the immediate post World War II era. She argued that women had been historically considered to be deviant and inferior by men and that to break this myth, women had to discover their own unique strengths and pursue them instead of imitating men. Women must create their own identity from scratch without reference to men and their oppressive social structures. The great surge of radical feminism in the post World War II era initially drew its inspiration from the ideas of De Beauvoir. Thus, the current stress on the importance of women's work and sexuality by feminists and the militant positing of women's separate identities, free from oppressive patriarchal structures, owes a lot to the path breaking intellectual rebellion of De Beauvoir.

Simone De Beauvoir was part of a tradition of thinking that had from the beginning opposed the absoluteness of the Cartesian framework of observer-observed duality and the objective rationality built up from it. Philosophers in this tradition struggled with the problem of trying to find the meaning of human existence without reference to the outside world. Jean Paul Sartre, belonging to the same existentialist school, averred that human beings existed without any pre-determined purpose and had to define the meaning of their existence and construct their own identity. So human beings are totally free and fully responsible for the choices they make and the values and norms they create. Later, he became associated with Marxism, and this led to his estrangement from his one time friend, the other great exponent of this tradition, Albert Camus.

In the aftermath of World War II, the Holocaust of the Jews and the inhuman excesses of the Stalinist dictatorship in the Soviet Union, Camus pondered over the futility of an "absurd" life and came to the conclusion that the naturalist myth breaker, whom he called the absurd hero, would have to carry on an endless struggle against the power of the mythmakers in pursuit of human freedom. To this end, he reinterpreted the Hellenic myth of Sisyphus as quoted at the beginning of the chapter.

Being an anarchist, Camus conceived of this struggle only in individual terms. But to be really effective, the modern Sisyphus' struggle cannot just be an individual one, but must involve the masses in large numbers. This is the central problem of anarchism—the near impossibility of organising the masses to fight the tyranny of centralised institutions without setting up massive counter institutions of their own, based on some animistic ideology or other. The only course left for activists is to endlessly roll the stone up the hill, organising and strengthening civil society as much as possible to resist the onslaught of destructive centralising institutions on the rights of citizens and on nature. Thus, there was a need in the post World War II era for some other means in which the masses could be mobilised than those being used by leftist and liberal parties. These parties follow their own teleological myths with consequent problems for individual freedom. What was needed was a new mode of struggle that could involve the masses without the dangers of centralisation and myth making.

The crucial break came in 1961, when a group of lawyers, journalists, writers and others in London, formed Appeal for Amnesty, 1961, against the sentencing of two Portuguese college students to twenty years in prison for having raised their glasses in a toast to "freedom" in a bar. This finally led to the formation of the Amnesty International and the modern human rights movement was born. No new principles were set forth, but the crucial difference from previous anti-statist action was the explicit rejection of political ideology and partisanship and the demand that governments everywhere, regardless of ideology, adhere to certain basic principles of human rights in their treatment of their citizens. This appealed to a large group of people not interested in joining a political movement and not bothered about the creation of a utopian society, but nevertheless concerned about the way in which modern states were encroaching on the rights of individuals.

This was followed in the 1960s by Martin Luther King's Civil Rights Movement in the USA and later still by the movement against the Vietnam War and the rebellion of the youth in Europe, which gained momentum with philosophers like Herbert Marcuse and Sartre providing intellectual leadership to these revolts. In India, we had the Sampoorna Kranti Andolan, led by Jayaprakash Narayan in 1975.

This mode of action has subsequently inspired numerous small groups to organise themselves around various kinds of rights issues, and today, all over the world there is a vibrant civil society. Even though these small organisations cannot match the power of the states or MNCs, they have been able to make their presence felt in many ways. That the grassroots movements in Madhya Pradesh and Chhattisgarh have survived and are still making an impact, however marginal, despite heavy state repression, is testimony to the efficacy of this mode of action.

These diverse protest movements are not able to substantially subvert the present world system of destructive development because of the shrewd machinations of the villain of the piece—the World Bank! The World Bank has led the international foundations set up by various MNCs in co-opting grassroots action through NGOs as mentioned earlier. For example, they have diluted the concept of "social capital" to defuse the radical political challenge that non-party grassroots movements pose to modern industrial development. The concept, mooted by the French left-leaning sociologist Pierre Bourdieu, was originally employed to underline the potential of smaller social groupings like the family to counter economic and political capital of the upper classes. But the American political scientist Robert Putnam winked away the radical interpretation of the term. Instead, he suggested that cross-class social formations such as sports clubs and birdwatchers associations were an ideal means of fostering economic and political cooperation between people across classes! The World Bank has seized on this theory of depoliticised social action and made it the basis of its thrust for apolitical people's participation in development through self-help groups, water user associations, forest management committees and what have you—all mediated through various well funded NGOs. A combination of consumerism, broadcast through television and professional NGOism, spread through funding agencies has meant that the youth these days do not dream of radical social change anymore. Political daydreaming is increasingly becoming a lost art. "To attack poverty watch birds" is the new slogan!

At the time when Camus was reinterpreting the myth of Sisyphus, Babasaheb Ambedkar was busying himself with reworking the teachings of the Buddha. Ambedkar heeded the advice of the Buddha about not blindly trusting received wisdom and instead testing it out in real life. Realising that the dalits at large would not be able to discard their animism so easily, he offered them the alternative of a heavily reinterpreted Buddhism, shorn of its mysticism. Such was the impact of this conversion that Subhadra's parents and many others in Dargahan converted to this Ambedkarite Buddhism, even though they were situated hundreds of kilometers away from Nagpur. Subhadra remembers that there were never any idols or prayers in their house.

Given the likes of institutions such as the World Bank, the task of recovering lost tongues is always fraught with a danger that is termed by Bengalis as the cool wind from the river Ganges blowing on one's back. Whenever a mass movement reaches its peak, there are a lot of people lending their active support to it. However, as state repression gradually intensifies, most of the supporters melt away, preferring to watch birds instead. So the cool wind from the Ganges, which had earlier been kept at bay by their once numerous supporters, begins to uncomfortably caress the backs of the activist leaders and deters them from fighting on!

That is why the shining example of the practical naturalist Ambedkar should act like a beacon for all those who still dream of freeing the human race from the destructive myth of modern industrial development. This "Mook Nayak" or *heroic leader of the dumb*, right up to the day of his death, single-mindedly pursued the goal of recovering the lost tongue for the dalits, regardless of the support he had. As for him, our battle cry should be, "The battle to me is a matter of joy, for ours is not a battle for wealth or power, it is a battle for freedom."

Freedom from the age-old tyranny of animistic myths.

30 Glossary

All vernacular words and acronyms have been explained in the text. Nevertheless a few of these that appear throughout the book have been explained here once again.

Adivasi	The tribal or indigenous people of India the word literally means original inhabitants possibly due to the theory that the dominant Hindus are the descendants of the Aryans who are supposed to have come in from Central Asia in the second millennium BCE
Andolan	A protest movement for securing rights or demands.
CPI	Communist Party of India.
CPI (M)	Communist Party of India (Marxist).
CPI (ML)	Communist Party of India (Marxist Leninist)
CPI (Maoist)	Communist Party of India (Maoist)
CrPC	This statute describes the procedure to be adopted for apprehending and prosecuting criminals and also for controlling activities that are against society.
Dalal	A pejorative term for those tribals who act as informal agents of the administration.
Dalit	The previously untouchable lower castes of traditional Hindu society who now refer to themselves by this term which means oppressed.
FIR	First Information Report. This is the report that is written by the Police when a complaint is lodged with them regarding some problem.

Gayan	Traditional Bhil tribal bard who knows the tribal epics by heart and sings them during the festivals.
Gram Sabha	The general body of the village which on paper has supreme power regarding matters of the village under the Panchayati Raj or local government system that prevails in India.
IAS	The Indian Administrative Service which is the centralised cadre of civil service officers of the Government of India
IFA	Indian Forest Act (1927), the main law that governs the management of forests in India.
Indal	A major festival of the Bhil tribals in which a single family feasts the whole community thereby ensuring harmony with nature and with fellow human beings.
IPC	The Indian Penal Code which is the main statute defining criminal offences in India.
IPS	The Indian Police Service which is the centralised cadre of police officers of the Government of India.
Jowar/Kansari	The cereal sorghum which is the staple food of Bhil tribals and is consequently venerated by them as a powerful life giving Goddess.
Khadi	Handspun and hand woven cloth introduced by Gandhi as an antidote to mill made cloth which forms the centrepiece of his concept of an autonomous rural economy.

KMCS	Khedut Mazdoor Chetna Sangath, a mass organisation of the Bhil Tribals.
Kharif	The monsoon crop that is sown in June and harvested in October.
LAA	The Land Acquistion Act 1894 that is the law regarding the displacement of people due to projects undertaken by the Government in public interest.
Mahua	A tree that yields a flower that is fermented to produce liquor and a seed that is crushed to produce cooking oil and so it is prized by the Bhil tribals.
MLA	Member of Legislative Assembly who are the elected lawmakers at the state level.
MP	Member of Parliament who are the elected lawmakers at the national level.
Naxalites	The popular name for the revolutionary group of Maoists who believe in conducting an armed struggle to establish a people's state.
NBA	Narmada Bachao Andolan which is the umbrella mass organisation for the struggle against the damming of the Narmada river.
NWDT	The Narmada Water Disputes Tribunal which was constituted by the Government of India to resolve the differences over the sharing of the waters of the Narmada between the states of Rajasthan, Gujarat, Madhya Pradesh and Maharashtra.
Panchayat	The elected executive body of the village level government.

PUCL — People's Union of Civil Liberties which is a human rights organisation.

Rabi — The winter crop that is sown in November and harvested in March.

Sahukar — Moneylender come trader who dominates the rural political economy.

Sangathan — A mass organisation of the people.

Sarvodaya — Literally meaning the development of all, this is the Gandhian prescription of decentralised and people oriented autonomous village development.

Satyagraha — Gandhi's mode of peaceful resistance literally meaning truthful pleading which involves disobeying unjust laws and trying to win over the hearts of the oppressors by peacefully bearing their excesses.

SC — Scheduled Caste or those castes that have been recognised in a special schedule within the Indian Constitution as having been socially oppressed and so being eligible for affirmative action in the form of reservations in government educational opportunities, jobs and elected bodies.

ST — Scheduled Tribes or those tribes that have been recognised in a special schedule within the Indian Constitution as having been socially neglected in the development process and so being eligible for affirmative reservations like the SCs.

SRUTI — Society for Rural Urban and Tribal Initiative, an NGO that supports mass organisational work through financial and other support.

SSP   The Sardar Sarovar Project on the river
                         Narmada at Navagam in Gujarat.

SWRC   Social Work and Research Centre, an NGO
                         in Rajasthan.

Tehsil   An administrative unit of the government
                         just below the district level.